THE BROKEN WHOLE

SUNY series in Theology and Continental Thought

Douglas L. Donkel, editor

THE BROKEN WHOLE

Philosophical Steps Toward a Theology of Global Solidarity

Thomas E. Reynolds

State University of New York Press

Published by
State University of New York

Printed in the United States of America

For information, contact State University of New York Press, Albany, NY
www.sunypress.edu

Production by Judy Block
Marketing by Michael Campochiaro

Library of Congress Cataloging-in-Publication Data

Reynolds, Thomas E.
The broken whole : philosophical steps toward a theology of global solidarity / Thomas E. Reynolds.
p. cm. — (SUNY series in theological and continental thought)
Includes bibliographical references (p.) and index.
ISBN 978-0-7914-6611-7 (hardcover : alk. paper)
ISBN 978-0-7914-6612-4 (pbk. : alk. paper)
1. Religious pluralism. 2. Philosophical theology. 3. Globalization—Religious aspects. I. Title. II. Series.

BL85.R49 2005
201'.5—dc22

2005003766

10 9 8 7 6 5 4 3 2 1

Contents

Acknowledgments

The following pages represent several years of thought on a topic that has become of increasing importance in an ever-complex world of global interaction. The luxury of such thought, however, is possible only because of the support I have received from others in numerous ways.

I owe a profound debt to St. Norbert College, the place of my present teaching employment. If not for the college's show of confidence in me, I would still be a professional musician (a career that sustained my family during my graduate work), not only missing out on the joys of teaching, but lacking the time and means to complete this present work. I am indebted especially to my colleagues in Religious Studies and Philosophy—in particular, to Donald Abel, Thomas Bolin, Bridget Burke Ravizza, Julie Claassens, Darin Davis, David Duquette, Howard Ebert, Scott Geis, John Holder, Paul Johnson, Michael Lukens, and Paul Wadell—whose kindness and inspiration have helped sustain my efforts over the past four years. In this context, the most profound thanks goes to John Neary, my close friend and colleague from the English Department at St. Norbert, for his constant support and fruitful editorial commentary as preliminary forms of the manuscript took shape. It is not an overstatement to say that the argument represented in these pages owes itself to the many hours of stimulating conversation I have had the fortune of sharing with John.

The text as it appears now has gone through several preparatory stages. I am deeply grateful for the friendship, advice, and patience of Peter Hodgson and Edward Farley. Their careful readings and generous support helped to make the project "work" originally as my dissertation at Vanderbilt University, and for this I am grateful beyond measure. My appreciation also goes to Eugene TeSelle, Paula Arai and John Lachs, who offered their time and valuable suggestions as dissertation committee members.

As the manuscript developed beyond the dissertation stage, several readers provided helpful commentary. I am appreciative of the anonymous readers from State University of New York Press for their insightful criticisms and suggestions, both in terms of content and style. Thanks also go to Julie Claassens, Paul Johnson, Brian Robinette and Robert Vosloo, who read selected chapters and made recommendations that have no doubt improved the text. Finally, I am indebted to Eric Dobberton for his prudent counsel regarding more than a few stylistic changes. Of course, any faults that may remain in the text are due to my own shortsightedness.

In a different way, I owe my family perhaps the greatest thanks. Through the years I have come to recognize that family, for all its fallibility, is the fertile ground out of which our deepest assurances and hopes blossom. My parents have always encouraged me despite my own misgivings about my abilities. My two brothers and sister, along with their spouses and children, have shown their love and support in ways too numerous to count. My two wonderful children, Chris and Evan, have offered me the gift of parenthood, a gift I fear I neglected far too often in the process of writing this book, but which they have graciously overlooked time and again. And finally, my partner and spouse, Mary, has given me more than I could ever ask for: patience, love, friendship, and more. Through it all, thank you Mary. This book is for you.

Introduction

THE PROBLEM AND ITS CONTEXT: LOCATING THE BROKEN WHOLE

Perhaps one of the most salient features of our time, indelibly marking its ethos, is the flourishing of a dynamic cultural diversity. Stunning advances in communication technologies and rapid means of transportation now make it possible for the widest variety of peoples to have direct access to each other, cultivating an increasingly global network of political and economic interdependency. Even as new possibilities emerge, however, certain perils present themselves. Varied perspectives engage one another with unprecedented frequency and vigor, and because of this a daunting sense of the heterogeneity of human life impresses itself upon our everyday awareness. Like trees in a dense forest, multiple ethnic, social, political, and religious perspectives surround us in ways that make it quite easy to lose our bearing. This is only intensified by the frequent militancy with which cultures and religions protect or revitalize themselves against pressures placed upon them by undue contact with the "foreign" and threatening.[1] The tragic events of September 11, 2001 and the resulting "War on Terror" are powerful and painful examples of our new global reality in its most alarming shape.

Yet it is more than the mere acknowledgment of genuine cultural differences or the precarious fact of their larger scale, and sometimes violent, interaction that has fostered the contemporary experience of heterogeneity. Our predicament is defined by the peculiar way in which the difference of the culturally other is recognized and accounted for. In the West, widespread exposure to diverse worldviews and lifestyles has been refracted through the paradigmatic lens of the "historical consciousness," which has gradually grown to dominate Euramerican intellectual self-awareness since the advent of secularism. By emphasizing the historicity of human life—that is, the contextual and interpretive nature of all expressions of meaning and value—the historical consciousness has cultivated a keen sense of sociocultural relativism. This forces the issue of diversity in a more radical way by underscoring the irreducible *particularity* and *perspectivity* of human standpoints. And precisely this allows us to characterize the differentiation of the many in our contemporary situation as a robust *plurality*, constituting a teeming multiplicity of disparate sociohistorical centers of meaning and value—a pluriverse. Hence, in our situation of globalization, modern historical consciousness has developed into a postmodern kind of *pluralistic consciousness*. The experience of the concrete "other"—its foreign quality and difference from the "same"—has become the hallmark of present-day diversity.

The effects of this emergent pluralistic consciousness have created a double-sided ambiguity, one being broadly cultural and practical in nature, the other focused more upon cognitive and theoretical concerns. Both, however, are intrinsically related. First, genuine diversity has contributed significantly toward dismantling the hegenomy of the so-called Judeo-Christian vision of the world that once saturated Euramerican culture, furthering the process that secularism had begun a century earlier. Erupting with volcanic intensity, a carnivalesque profusion of dissonant voices now seems to preclude the possibility of any monolithic, overarching ideological synthesis of values and practices, creating a fundamental cultural instability. The particular differences of the many prevail over any sense of their homogeneity or sameness. These differences resist being assimilated into some artificial consensus or imperial unity, their distinctness reduced to some common (and imposed) cultural denominator. Given this, an ambiguity results—one that arguably has been stretched to the point of crisis—concerning whether there can be any form of intercultural solidarity or alliance at all, the kind of collective coherence that would seem to be essential to a nonviolent and fruitful existence together. The issue is whether and on what basis an interactive solidarity may be forged, one that encourages mutual respect and appreciation while facilitating cooperative problem-solving efforts with enough momentum to yield results when confronting challenges of shared import (be they social, economic, political, or environmental). Are there discernible cultural-historical grounds upon which the many can draw together in their differences, or are differences utterly irreducible and incommensurate, enclosed within their own respective set of circumstances, needs, and agendas?

Second, related to and closely following the logic of its more practical compatriot, a cognitive problem is created. The presence of diversity within a sociohistorical relativism undermines the normative posturing of any special set of claims. Meaning and truth are seen as interpretive constructions grafted onto the fabric of existence from within specific frameworks and their own "traditions" of discourse. And no tradition is innocent. There is, therefore, no privileged access to some pristine foundation, standard, or set of criteria external to the horizonal play of cultural traditions. Cognitive claims cannot be grounded independent of their respective fields of relative reference. And this prevents any kind of universal, transcultural validity. The goal of critical distance and impartial or unprejudiced objectivity (characteristic of Enlightenment rationality) seems impossible; there is only a plurality of interpretive positions. A post-Enlightenment intellectual ambiguity is created, spawning a crisis focused on the problem of finding hermeneutical criteria to adjudicate competing voices, each of which proffers its own claim to meaning and truth. Are differences incommensurate, each realm of discourse irrevocably caught up within the movement of its own tradition or language game? Or is there a way to break out of such monadic self-referentiality and to discover shared criteria of meaning and truth? If the latter question can be answered affirmatively, it is evident that such criteria must be found within the cross-currents of plurality itself.

Accordingly, genuine plurality is not only a sociohistorical *fact* conditioning the way in which the world is seen and experienced, but also a cognitive and practical *challenge* to be taken up and critically reckoned with. Plurality intensifies the sense that we live in a decentered universe—a pluriverse—where no center holds weight. Gone is the notion of an *axis mundi* saturated with meaning and vitality, to which human beings belong, around which human life revolves, and from which human life takes its place in the greater scheme of things. A relentless iconoclasm has erased the remnants of such cosmological thinking; indeed, the cosmos appears silent, overcome by the anarchic noise of the multitude.[2] And the result is a gravityless plurality that threatens to disperse all into monadic solipsisms.

As an integrated and unified totality, the whole has been irreparably broken. This is comparable to what those influenced by Emmanuel Levinas have called a "disruption of the same." It signals a displacement of universal categories of being, which feign the inclusion of all differences—all singular others—in order to ground, stabilize, or substantiate reality. Everything now seems swept off balance; there is no equilibrium. The first major question for us then is whether this broken whole signifies (1) an opening with the capacity to sustain the weight and value of differences or (2) an empty vacuum that annuls all but fractured sparks of the will-to-power. Is there space in such a broken whole for mutual responsibility as a praxis of solidarity, for a form of dwelling capable of being shared by all human beings in their particularity, a space in which differences might converge relationally in the shape of mutuality, justice, and love? Put directly: can plurality yield a productive pluralism? I wager so.

My thesis is this: precisely as ruptured and broken, a nonclosure, the "whole" is an opening toward new possibilities of dwelling together on a potentially global scale. Why? Because local acts of communicative solidarity, fragile and vulnerable as they may be, anticipate a translocal horizon of interrelatedness. Within the inescapable fact of human dialogue lies the boundary-transgressive inscription of an open whole, not a new totality of the same, but a pluriverse of differences in relation that is shot through with the promise of value. Ironically, the purgative experience of the broken whole—and its relentless iconoclasm—makes it possible to discern the trace of something otherwise, something outside the totality of metaphysical horizons. An uncircumscribable surplus is embedded in the very praxis of dwelling together, a "leftover" that neither can be exhausted nor contained. Here, as metaphysical idols are disrupted, the infinite possibility of new possibilities comes to pass, exposing us to a beyond, a transcendence, in the midst of heterogeneity, not despite it. But such transcendence is not a knowledge or content; rather it ensues in a relational performance. And it is precisely here where religious themes arise.

Indeed, it is my contention that this kind of "exposure to a beyond" has intrinsic religious value. While it is true that, as Peter Berger acknowledges, "modernity has plunged religion into a very specific crisis, characterized by secularity, to be sure, but characterized more importantly by pluralism,"[3] it is also the case that religious traditions contain resources to address such a crisis. It can be argued that religion, if for no other reason than its ubiquity and power in motivating human behaviors across the widest of spectrums, must be an essential component in mobilizing justice and peace amidst a world of strife and conflict.[4] I wish to push further, however, suggesting that religious traditions, in their varied shapes, have something of consequence to say about the nature and effect of diversity, something that has bearing on how we might envision human solidarity on the broadest of scales. I am not suggesting that religious faith become a panacea or magical cure for the problem of diversity, for it is clear that religious traditions also invoke divisive mechanisms that hinder cooperative solidarity between people. Nor do I wish to introduce a new foundationalist discourse on the basis of some putatively neutral ground or common experience that can be invoked under "religious" guise to unite differences.

I wish, rather, to risk claiming that religious traditions, precisely in and through their diversity—and despite their proclivity to totalize and exclude—expose us to the possibility of something more, a beyond in the midst of life together, and thus can open an interactive space of humanization among peoples. Why? Because immanent in the give-and-take praxis of conversation or dialogue there lies a transcendent impulse, a hyperbolic modality of excess that displaces all parties and sweeps outward beyond all horizons. An unlimited, infinite, and therefore incalculable, horizon is inscribed in the performance of dwelling together, signaling a surplus at work in the relation with one's neighbor, the different, the other. Given this, the iconoclasm of the broken whole can be seen as a positive situation that rides the arc of such a surplus, giving witness to the incalculable. Moreover, perhaps it is this "incalculable" that invites the risk of faith. And if so, the witness of religious traditions may offer us ways in which to harness the promise of heterogeneity and plurality. How so? *In a double gesture that both signals a "too much" at work in the space of human relationships and provokes a hope-filled opening of new possibilities for being together.*

This, however, raises other questions. First, is it possible for positive religious attributions and affirmations to survive the trauma of the broken whole? Second, does religious talk of ultimate reality, God, or any kind of transcendent value have merit in providing resources for openness, mutuality, and even reconciliation between differences? On both accounts, I again wager so. For, especially in our present context, the contrary implies the gravest of prospects—closed borders, dispersion, and violence. In ambiguous and uncertain times, answering these questions affirmatively signals an important optimism that is needed in order to raise the banner of hope for a world caught up in peril. It also signals that there are ways for religious traditions to quell the rising tide of fundamentalisms among their constituencies.

Unpacking and legitimating such optimism, however, means undertaking a perilous journey, one that must address how it is possible to speak both of human solidarity and of religious value in light of the broken whole. After all, given the two-edged challenge of the pluralistic consciousness, is it even proper to undertake such a journey? That is, does not talk of solidarity impose a certain standard across frontiers that it cannot, or should not, traverse? Moreover, does not talk of the Ultimate or God invariably invoke a difference-denying, even violent, totalizing logic wherein alternative religious configurations of value are if not rejected, at best rubbed out or assimilated under the canopy of an absolute vision of one sort or another? If so, this hardly seems pluralistic. Rather, it appears chauvinistic and imperialistic, contrary to what would one would expect from something I am suggesting might have merit in promoting love and justice.

There is then an irony in the wagers I wish to advance, for the history of religions displays far from a litany of peace and humanization. Precisely those communities that have proclaimed to be harbingers of truth and love have often, in fact, brought colonial exploitation, violence, and untold suffering. This makes the contemporary upsurge of religious fervor in the mode of fundamentalist and militant resistance to globalization a genuine concern. For insofar as globalization exerts a homogenizing pressure on ethnic and cultural differences, religion has become part of a reactive backlash on the part of those differences, buttressing a kind of new tribalism that resists all that lies beyond narrowly conceived borders. It seems all too easy today for religions to slip into communal protectionism. And given this, any argument for solidarity in a religiously conceived pluralism must begin with extreme caution. How then should we proceed? From within the disruptive pressure of pluralism itself.

TOWARD A PRODUCTIVE WAY OF CROSSING THE BROKEN WHOLE: INSIPIENT THEOLOGY

In this book, I seek to develop a language that designates "differences in relation," and does so in a manner that opens out into a hermeneutic of religion with distinct theological potential. This involves three fundamental steps, each of which culminates in the next. First, it means examining the historical precedents and present-day features of sociocultural diversity and understanding how they impact the way in which we conceive of the issue of plurality. Chapters 1 and 2, then, function as a basic diagnosis of a contemporary postmodern and globalizing situation. Such a diagnosis sets the stage for a second, more constructive, step oriented toward answering the first basic question of this project—that of the possibility of cross-cultural solidarity. This is carried out in chapters 3 and 4. Respectively, these chapters aim to establish a philosophical-anthropological way of framing, first, the problem of human plurality in dialogical dwelling together, and second, the prospect of a pluralistic solidarity. The final step articulates a philosophical hermeneutic of religious pluralism. Chapters 5 and 6 are the capstone of the entire project in that they bring into focus a pluralistic understanding of human religiosity, justifying the plausibility of claiming that religion indeed has something at stake in our contemporary crisis. Chapters 5 and 6 pave the way for a "theological" portraiture of God, but one that must wait for further exploration, its contours as of yet outlined only in faint brush strokes.

From the onset, then, I beg of the reader a certain indulgence. For it is not my intention to make a case for pluralism "out of" a religious tradition. While I am a Christian theologian of Protestant persuasion, these pages do not contain an explicitly theological argument. That is, they do not begin from specifically Christian authorities, scriptural or otherwise. For pluralism throws into question precisely these authorities. Neither is it my aim to describe and catalogu the world's religious traditions, distilling them into a generalized set of abstractions. While such a comparative procedure might have merit in the introductory college class on religion, it would have the effect here of softening, perhaps violating, the very distinctness of differences that we seek to uphold and account for.

It is my aim instead to weave an ethically relevant and cognitively credible discourse that tilts toward the possibility of a pluralist thinking about God. In other words, I begin *from* pluralism and work toward Christian theology. To this extent, the position I advocate has a more formal and philosophical character, requiring a momentary bracketing or suspension of theological talk of God—the semantic density of which is connected to specific religious histories and their texts.[5] This is not to avoid addressing the issue. Nor do I claim to speak from a position of neutrality. To the contrary, I wish to hold open and radicalize the question of plurality. For this reason I seek to avoid what Jacque Dupuis calls a "Christian theology of religious pluralism."[6] I seek instead to develop a way of tracing those horizons of significance from which theological claims gain their credibility and relevance in a pluralistic world. Let me provide a brief rationale for taking such a tack.

Overall, I am convinced that it is through the public task of articulating pluralism in a nontheological sense that a more overtly theological project *beyond* the scope of this one will come into the clearing. If a Christian discourse about God is to make a difference, it must work with great care to create space in which such a claim can be asserted not only credibly, but in a manner that eschews vitiating the very differences it purports to champion. It is a great irony that so much theology affirms the value of difference with one hand while advancing a Christian parochialism with the other. The assumption of Christian superiority or normativity for all people vilifies religious diversity. While it may feign to "welcome" the other, it fails to acknowledge the other's unique presence as something of possible value apart from predetermined conventions and expectations. But circumnavigating this irony is not as easy as one might think.

The very talk of God involves a normative impulse that universalizes. This is a fundamental theme of Abrahamic faiths: a God that is not the God of all creation and all people is not properly God—as that ultimate beyond which nothing greater can be conceived (to invoke Anselm of Canterbury's classic phrase)—but a fiction, an idol. Speaking of God, therefore, is a boundary-transgressive act. In saying "my" or "our" God, more is invoked than a tribal deity. All people are implied. Invoking God is an interfaith gesture that cannot help but enact solidarity with humankind. And yet there are those "others" who do not pray, for example, to the Christian God, the personalistic and trinitarian theism that pervades the Christian metanarrative, and in fact envision ultimacy in quite different ways. Are these "others" then (1) idolatrous (ineffective, false, and perhaps evil); (2) well-intended errors (on the way to truth, but misguided); (3) partially true (on the way to truth, but in need of a specifically Christian fulfillment); or (4) anonymous Christians (implicitly demonstrating the truth that Christians already have explicitly)? I maintain that each of these potential Christian responses is gravely deficient in a genuinely pluralist context, a context that compels us to grant, at the very least, the *possible* viability and integrity of alternate ways of depicting ultimate reality.

While there are many scholars who would chide such an approach (for reasons that shall be examined and assessed in chapter 5),[7] bracketing explicitly theological talk of God is my attempt to avoid a hasty projection of specifically Christian meanings onto the problem. True, there is finally no such thing as objective neutrality, but we must be vigilant against the temptation to make a virtue out of a necessity. It is misguided to affirm the Christian vision because it is de facto the Christian's historical or narrative frame of reference. There is more at stake here than is alleged. Such a procedure invariably inserts into the equation a universalist discourse about God without acknowledging the interreligious context implied by doing so. Appealing to God as a normative "answer" or response "from above" the sway of pluralism can all too quickly become the privileged a priori claim of some over and against others, the few asserting their merited and authoritative access to some kind of special "revelation" that is hidden or denied to others but that beckons allegiance from all.[8] While there certainly is historical precedent for such a position in the long (and often unfortunate) tradition of Christian relations with the other, it nonetheless has the effect of hedging the complexity of the problem. One localized group extends its own particular, historically embedded, and context-bound framework of meaning either *against* or *over* all those outside the hermeneutically privileged boundaries of its own parochial perspective. Christian talk of God thereby becomes monological and "one-way"—heteronomous, tribalistic, and distortive of real difference—closing down rather than opening up the prospect of dialogical solidarity with any other "outside" of the self-authenticating Christian circle.[9]

The question then is this: is it possible to avoid this alternative and still affirm God as the ultimate, indeed universal, environing condition of all existence, the creative source and end of all creation and all peoples? Is the assertion of God hopelessly tied to a parochial universalism that in the end homogenizes and totalizes, its discourse constraining the ideal of reciprocity and conversation among differences by staking claim to the ultimate authority of a manifested divinity (whether in Christ, in the Church, or in the Bible, etc.), an appeal that imperiously stops the play of difference? If we answer in the affirmative, it seems then that any and all theological affirmations have no place in public discourse, or at least those discourses whose concern is to address pluralism. For their warrants are intracommunal and fideistic and their consequences dangerous. But if we instead answer in the negative, must the idea of God then be secularized and emptied of all meaningful content in order to appeal to irony or historicist criteria, criteria that purportedly keep differences in play but serve in their own way as intracommunal discourses? Does the relevance of God-talk for a dialogical praxis of solidarity then die the death of a thousand qualifications? This latter difficulty gets directly at the problem Berger points to in the statement quoted earlier, that religion has been drawn into a crisis characterized not only by secularity but more importantly by pluralism. *Insight into the historicity of human life forces the issue of pluralism upon any and all talk of the divine, problematizing the whole project of theology.*[10] Truly, the pluralistic consciousness is a present-day *kairos* for theological affirmation.

Where then should we begin? How is talk of God possible, or desirable at all, in a pluralist context where many religious voices claim their space and, in their differences, make seemingly disparate reality references? Addressing this requires that we begin *from* pluralistic consciousness: from below. Why? *Because being religious—that is, being Christian—already entails being "beyond" one's own local faith perspective, being interreligious. Pluralism affects religious affirmations from the root. For the presence of the heterogeneous other—its difference from the same—is already there from the start. Boundaries are already crossed and borders diffuse prior to the act of affirming one's religious identity over and against others. We are always already disturbed by something more.* This has important consequences that merit attention.

In a famous essay written late in his career, "The Significance of the History of Religions for the Systematic Theologian," theologian Paul Tillich begins to outline the contours of this response.[11] He proposes that, if it is to take seriously the question of religious diversity, theology must "break through two barriers," charting a course between two forms of reductionism: (1) traditional orthodoxy and its exclusivist claims to revelation (the "orthodox-exclusive" approach); and (2) the secularizing impulse that rejects the dimension of the divine altogether, undermining the status of the history of religions by denying it any revelatory significance (the "secular-rejective" approach).[12] While there are important resources within Christian traditions that may prove fruitful in addressing the ethical and religious quandaries of a multicultural world, genuine pluralism has the effect of shifting the center of gravity for making theological claims away from the logic of authority and strictly tradition-bound affirmations. What is now required is a taking-stock of other traditions that treats them as unique sociocultural determinations of human valuation on a par with Christianity, containing—at the very least—the possibility of distinct revelatory value.

But upon moving beyond orthodox-exclusivism in this way, as Tillich notes, the question now becomes whether the world's religious traditions, including Christianity, do in fact disclose anything transcendent and worthy of being called "divine." Is religion itself merely an illusionary projection, or worse, a distortive, divisive, and peace-thwarting way of constricting human freedom, a technique for denying and dominating differences which, for the sake of justice, requires the deconstructive and value-neutralizing tools of a relativist secular methodology? Does historicity go "all the way down," precluding any and all talk of a universal God? I think not. Indeed, I believe there are translocal criteria that might adjudicate between local perspectives and help cultivate nondistortive religious postures toward difference, opening up a positive estimation of the value of the other in a nonrelativizing sense.

Rather than hermeneutically privileging the Christian affirmation of God and "applying" it to the issues at hand from the top down, I suggest that we begin "from below," in a Tillich-like fashion, and look for traces of what might be called "God" in the broken whole. In order to substantiate not only the veracity and relevance of religious faith but also its normative import in shaping a vision of pluralism, we must first begin with historicity and what I shall call postmodern "hyper-reflexivity" (in chapter 2) and from this launchpad develop a model of pluralism that both intimates and opens out into theological territory. In the tradition of Friedrich Schleiermacher, carried on by Tillich, I maintain that theological claims must be located on the map of human existence in the world in order to become intelligible. They must be shown as blossoming forth from within and giving voice to the character and struggles of a human condition, not merely administered as something extrinsic to the hopes and aspirations that animate human life. A context of recognition is required to affirm the difference that God makes. Put in somewhat different terms, specific revelations (Offenbarung) always occur within a context of revealability (Offenbarkeit), manifesting a more originary possibility. And such a possibility must be explicated in terms wider than concrete revelations that are tied to particular traditions.

This, however, need not entail that theology become derivative in nature, an accidental and tertiary enterprise deduced from some generic human experience or essentialist foundationalism. Neither does it imply a capitulation to the relativistic temperament of postmodernity, following what is merely contemporary and in vogue in order to gain credence. To the contrary, theology at its best seeks to show how and why God-talk illuminates a human situation, a situation always already caught up within the context-bound and linguistically saturated horizons of history.[13] And our situation is the pluralism issuing from a broken whole. If it is to evoke recognition and address concrete human needs in a changing and complex world, testifying to and bearing forth redemptive power, Christian discourse about God must "correlate" in a mutually critical way with the manner in which contemporary human beings understand and live in the world, constantly revising itself to meet head-on the questions that arise out of a lived context, pointing toward personal and social transformation.[14] As faith seeking understanding (*fides quaerens intellectum*), theology is ineluctably wrapped up in the sociohistorical network of interactions that shape human existence in the world. This is precisely why this project begins, in chapters 1 and 2 respectively, with an historical analysis and a diagnostic evaluation of the contours of a contemporary situation.

Accordingly, this book seeks to lay out a broader vision of pluralism advanced philosophically and defended on public grounds, the adequacy of which can be measured by criteria drawn from a wide reflective equilibrium, from a number of relevant background theories and frameworks of adjudication, both cognitive and moral, which are not necessarily "Christian" in nature but whose relevance may be measured in Christian terms.[15] Admittedly then, this procedure is not theological, but rather a fundamental anthropology that opens into a philosophy of religion. Perhaps we might call it an "incipient theology," a theology struggling to be, trying to emerge from the thicket and give voice to a set of concerns, but doing so only piecemeal and after a detour through philosophical territory. Incipient theology recognizes the need to grapple with the presuppositions and reality references inherent in a human situation from which the question of God arises, thus giving purchase and weight to the act of witnessing the particular content of a Christian God-talk. How? In this case, by rendering the witness of faith intelligible from the standpoint of pluralistic consciousness and a potentially universal form of human solidarity, thus unleashing its capacity for redemptive power. In the end, therefore, I do not merely seek to "ground" theology in a philosophical system. I seek instead *to explore how the character of human life, in its plurality, opens up to the issue of religious meaning, such that a theological project—which begins in a revelatory moment—can become intelligible and relevant as a possibility*. I leave the careful nuance required by a pluralist theology of God open to further work.

ON MAPPING THE BROKEN WHOLE: THE VIABILITY OF A MODEL OF PLURALISM

As is apparent by now, this book is not simply about interreligious dialogue. Neither is it simply about religion as such. Rather, it seeks to clear out the semantic space for thinking about pluralism in a manner capable of invigorating the prospect of an interreligious human flourishing. My aim is to construct a model of pluralism that envisions human differences as intrinsically valuable and worthwhile, building a theoretical framework supportive of an engaged praxis of critical and freedom-making solidarity. Our increasingly interconnected and endangered world demands that we consider such an option.

Yet, if I do not advocate such a possibility by way of theological claims grounded solely in Christian traditions, neither do I present it on the basis of its "objective" validity, its referential ability to signify things in themselves. Instead, I argue for a certain model of pluralism on the basis of its productive capacity not only to portray coherently but also—speaking in pragmatic and ethical terms—to invite a robust praxis of sharing in a now planetary Mitwelt. To be sure, any understanding of human dwelling together is itself a particular interpretive configuration, functioning in a certain context to elucidate a constellation of events that seem to share enduring qualities and to display certain shapes of continuity in the midst of historical flux and flow. In the spirit of critical inquiry, such a configuration depends upon a second-order discourse that aims to represent critically and nondistortively what happens in the first-order discourses of actual communities.

A language of coherence is introduced, one that seeks to "make sense of," or illuminate, the richly complex and diverse meanings of details that exceed comprehensive grasp but that nonetheless present themselves as interpretable, suggesting possible renderings. Rather than being a literal picture with direct access to reality, however, such a language of coherence is a creative and imaginative construction. It is a provisional way of coordinating and accounting for patterns of experience that invite investigative inquiry by exhibiting a certain "force of intelligibility." By this term I mean those shapes of thought and behavior which, in the midst of the contingencies of historical flux and flow, seem to mark congruity and resemblance in a palpable set of interpretable qualities. A language of coherence therefore aims to thematize patterning events, fashioning a kind of "map" that puts forth ontological claims, claims about the character of human dwelling in the world.

But a viable mapping or ontology can never pretend to simply describe reality and state its terms outside of the sociocultural context that constitutes its hermeneutical framework. For its interpretive power emerges from that context. In view of this kind of hermeneutical circle, the model of pluralism I advocate operates unavoidably as a device enmeshed in the very thing it wishes to articulate: pluralism. It is thus heuristic rather than definitive, a provisional way of reading a certain state of affairs, presented as a living option among many others competing for viability. Such an interpretive model exists, then, somewhere between the closure of a revelatory authority, which confines inquiry to an ideological particularism, and the feigned universality of an objectivist foundationalism. This "between" zone will surface as a key theme throughout this book.

Furthermore, a model of pluralism must subject itself to the plurality it seeks to authenticate. It can never being fully finished or guaranteed, remaining open-ended, constantly in need of reevaluating its mapping tools to better take into account real historical differences, even as its puts forth genuine claims as credibly and coherently as possible in seeking to persuade. For the observation of congruities and patterns across cultural-historical boundaries can emerge only in light of genuine differences, the fact of which invariably presents important incongruities. Thus, a language of coherence must take up what Charles Taylor calls a "language of contrasts," one that temporarily coordinates differences into a comparative configuration.[16] Understanding presumes coherence, yet requires contrasts. And given such contrasts, no language of coherence can be wholly adequate or universal. Stasis is impossible. Without constantly taking into account incongruity and difference, the very comparisons and congruities illuminated by an interpretive model become themselves either vacuous or filled with the ethnocentric biases of the scholar.

At base, any model—especially one that is self-consciously pluralistic—must become rigorously explicit and self-reflexive about what it is up to, opening itself to questioning and to the productive force field of ongoing conversation. Given this, I suggest that such a model's interpretive plausibility, constructive adequacy, and possible relevance—indeed its truth-value—lies in its ability to achieve with relative sufficiency five interrelated criteria. First, a model must demonstrate internal coherence and simplicity. Its terms should be interrelated with systematic consistency. Second, it must also show an outward consistency with and/or inclusive openness toward other models and methods in a broader multidisciplinary context, engaging and taking into account other interpretive possibilities as supportive evidences of its suitability. Third, related to the second criterion, an adequate model should manifest a capacity to solve, explain, or clarify commonly perceived problems and issues across the widest of potential spectrums, its implications stretching out to address ethical and cognitive perplexities not restricted to its original domain. Fourth, accordingly, it must also demonstrate a conversational suggestibility, displaying an illuminative and productive power that engenders new and different insights about reality, insights that propel forward dialogue and that promote novel possibilities of shared interest. Finally, an adequate model withstands the conversation itself; it is temporally durable, yielding not only acknowledgment by others and extension in further dialogue, but a consensual viability among interlocutors. These five criteria—coherence, inclusive comprehensiveness, implicative stretch, suggestibility, and durability—are each conversational measurements of the epistemic gain of an interpretation, all of them played out in the back-and-forth momentum of dialogue.[17]

Truth is forged, not merely presented. It is fostered not in the solitary act of writing but in the engaged and relational context of dialogue. Perhaps in this light we should add a sixth criterion, the capacity for reflexivity and self-criticism, which is implied by the other five. Only by being called into the process of an ever-wider questioning is a model subject to the testing of its persuasive power. If there are no purely objective and neutral criteria to adjudicate between alternate construals of reality, truth can only come forth in dialogue, as many subjects engage one another and talk about realities they come to share. As we shall explore in more detail, truth is relational and ineluctably dialectical, a both-and that continually augments itself. And so, ipso facto, ontological claims become an experiment in truth, "trying themselves out" from a particular vantage point, opened up to their own shortcomings by the greater dialogical context of pluralism. Indeed, such shortcomings may turn out to be ethical failures, failures that refuse and victimize differences.

In the final analysis, the persuasive power or "proof" of a model (in this case, of pluralism) is never guaranteed; rather it lies in the matrix of conversation it generates, in the sway of a dialogical praxis of solidarity. This is precisely why I stress the need for a productive vision of pluralism, one that has constructive ethical and cognitive consequences for our lives together. Indeed, as Taylor sums it up, the "proof of a map [or model] is how well you can get around using it," that is, how well it plays out in confronting variants.[18]

In such a spirit, this book is an extended dialogue with many contemporary thinkers who have considered the character of pluralism. But I seek not simply to present their ideas; rather I wish to think with them in order to think beyond them, to dance conversationally with them in order to choreograph the issues anew. As the scope of this "conversation" unfolds, and on the basis of an understanding of religious traditions located within the purview of a kind of philosophical-anthropology, pluralism shall become a theologically saturated reality. Indeed, *as* a Christian, I believe it is God's empowering love that creates and lets-be differences as intrinsically valuable, and more, inclines us to risk the open act of welcoming other religious viewpoints. But this affirmation is not simply the property of Christians. It is a correlate of the way in which human beings are disposed to each other and to the world, and thus can play out equally as powerfully in non-Christian traditions, modified in varied shapes. Indeed, within all religious faiths there lies the possibility of dwelling nonviolently *with* other viewpoints and practices. The purpose of this book is to outline the plausibility of such a vision.

CHAPTER 1

PLURALITY AND HISTORICAL CONSCIOUSNESS: FROM HETERONOMOUS BELONGING TO A TRADITIONED BELONGING TO HISTORY

I am finite once for all, and all the categories of my sympathy are knit up with the finite world as such, *and with things that have a history.*[1]

In 1584, the self-styled Renaissance philosopher Giordano Bruno wrote a treatise, "On the Infinite Universe and Worlds," which is suggestive in its implications for thinking about pluralism in a postmodern and global context. This work, set in dialogue form, argues against the traditional Ptolemaic understanding of the universe as a finite, hierarchically structured system with the earth as its focal center. Inspired by Copernicus' criticism of the geocentric hypothesis and drawing extensively from Nicholas of Cusa's notion of the limitlessness of space, Bruno maintains that the universe is infinite both in extent and diversity, which means respectively that its center is both nowhere and everywhere. Neither boundary, hierarchy, nor center can be ascribed to an infinite space, for there is no absolute limit-position or point of reference "inside" or "outside" by which the space can be measured. All positions and centers, all insides and outsides, are fundamentally relativized. The alleged center, earth, is decentered.

Yet this does not mean that space is flat or utterly homogenized. Paradoxically, Bruno also argues that this decentering opens up automatically into an infinite polycentrism. Not one but every point in space can be regarded as either a center or part of a circumventing boundary that frames some other center point. There are an infinite number of possible worlds, which from the unique location and perspective of their position become centers of their own. Bruno muses:

> For all who posit a body of infinite size, ascribe to it neither centre nor boundary. . . . Thus the earth no more than any other world is

> at the centre; and no points constitute definite determinate poles of space for our earth, just as she herself is not a definite and determined pole to any other point of the ether, or of the world space; and the same is true of all other bodies. From various points of view these may all be regarded either as centres, or as points on the circumference, as poles, or zeniths and so forth. Thus the earth is not in the centre of the universe; it is central only to our own surrounding space.[2]

We might sum up the basic insight as follows: it is the homogeneity of infinite space that makes it heterogeneous. The universe is simultaneously acentric and polycentric, the two seemingly opposite visions being inextricably intertwined.

Bruno's idea of the relativity of centers rings with a peculiar resonance to contemporary ears sensitized to cultural and religious diversity. His radical democratization of space bears a marked resemblance to what we have gradually come to view in more sociohistorical terms as a radical democratization of human meaning and value. This has dramatic implications. Indeed, since the notion of spatial orientation, the human need to find a dwelling place to call "home," is not unrelated to the human need for meaning and value, the decentralization of cosmic order brings with it a sense of displacement, even exile. This is portrayed forcefully in the unsettling sense of value relativism that informs much of how human differences are depicted and understood in recent discussions over the issue of plurality in human life—from multiculturalism, postmodernism and postcolonial theory to religious pluralism. Viewing human languages and practices as the product of particular and local histories, which are embedded in specific cultural forms that emerge in distinct places, such value relativism implies that no human thought or practice can or should become the stable focal point for all others.

The paradox here, as in Bruno, is not just that there is no Archimedean point or center around which human forms of life ultimately congeal, but also that there are many such centers, each unique and irreducible to any all-encompassing logic or universal standard of measurement. Relativism dramatizes the polycentric, plural character of human orientation in the world. All human systems, cultures, and traditions are finite standpoints, webs of significations that are intrinsically related to given relational contexts as particular centers among many. The upshot of all this is that we dwell in human spaces that are centered and yet centerless. There is, therefore, a certain irony to the intercultural diversity of the present—an irony that I wish to address first in order to set the stage for thinking critically about religious pluralism.

Plurality itself, however, is nothing new. Human beings, in various ways, have always confronted cultural and religious diversity. Plurality is a condition of life, from the largest systems down to the smallest fragments. But as sure as plurality is a fact, it also conjures various interpretations. What makes our situation distinctive, especially in Europe and North America during the past thirty years, is the peculiar *way in which* the fact of plurality is recognized and accounted for. I suggest the following: *the experience of the simultaneous homogeneity and heterogeneity of human space is unique to our time, presenting the "challenge of difference" with unprecedented clarity and intensity.* A new kind of world-orientation has been created, revolutionizing how we thematize encounters with difference and formulate the issue of pluralism—that is, how we envision the plurality of differences as such. The intuition of simultaneous homogeneity and heterogeneity is not merely an acknowledgment that differences exist; nor is it simply the discomforting awareness of cultural conflict. Rather, it is a certain way in which cultures and histories themselves are brought into view and understood.

Particularly in Western societies, a new kind of consciousness or sensibility has emerged, one that has developed slowly yet irreversibly over the past two centuries and risen to striking prominence in the later half of the twentieth century. This consciousness has no clear-cut intentionality and points in no obvious direction, other than focusing the issue of human sociohistorical differences. In this, it presents a challenge capable of being expressed in many different trajectories and attitudes. Recent discussions that celebrate the possibility and promise of human diversity reflect and nourish its powerful hold on our perceptions, as do those discussions that move in a different direction, lamenting the carnivalesque and increasingly fragmented array of dissonant voices—cultural, ethnic, and religious—that characterize our contemporary situation. Because of the way in which it problematizes the issue of diversity and nourishes a sense of the "other," I shall call this consciousness a "pluralistic consciousness."

Put briefly, pluralistic consciousness is a peculiar modification of historical consciousness, which demonstrates a markedly postmodern disposition—one that occurs in the larger socioeconomic wake of globalization. It is neither (1) the awareness of multiple centers of meaning and value, nor (2) the experience of the lack of an overarching universal center or standard of meaning and value. Rather, it is (3) the peculiar result of both alternatives experienced together. *Pluralistic consciousness arises in the experience of being placed among and with many equally placed others without a univocal or overarching sense of place.* Here, in a progressively more interconnected and global political, economic, and cultural situation, the sheer frequency of our encounters with different ethnicities, cultures, and religions intensifies the experiences of "otherness" to such a degree that our sense of dwelling in the world becomes itself pluralized, broken open, and dispersed.

As never before, we are self-consciously aware that we come from many places in the same space, the hybrid product of many pasts and many competing loyalties in an increasingly compressed and unscripted world context. Difference is no longer remote, somewhere else; it is proximate, here in this shared, yet heterogeneous, space. Cultural interfaces are now commonplace as boundaries become more porous and overlapping, and as people inhabit varied social worlds at the same time, some of them at odds with each other. This creates a kind of disorienting multiconsciousness where differentiations are upheld, yet collapsed. From early in childhood, we are exposed through vast communications and media networks to multiple symbolic frameworks, even within one fairly isolated locale, precluding the emergence of any unified or stable sense of place.

This dramatically highlights the impression of alterity or "otherness," rupturing our sense of what it means to dwell, of what it means to be in place, by opening up a tension-filled ambiguity whose product is often ambivalence. A sense of dizzying confusion, relativistic fragmentation, nihilistic indifference, separatist isolationism, and individualistic anonymity is cultivated, the latter of these symptoms poignantly represented by the meltdown of time and place into the virtual reality of cyberspace. On a more positive front, however, pluralistic consciousness opens possibilities for new and creative ways of dwelling together in dialogical openness and mutuality, of experiencing relational co-inhabitance rather than mere indifferent co-existence or xenophobic violence. But the basic point is that pluralistic consciousness lives in the throes of a paradox, human space now perceived as both homogeneous and heterogeneous, centerless and polycentric, shared and hyperdifferentiated.

How then can we even begin to address the myriad implications of pluralistic consciousnes? In this chapter and in chapter 2, I will outline the cognitive contours of pluralistic consciousness in more detail, tracing its genesis and unpacking its salient features in an effort to delineate what it is that a constructive vision of pluralism is up against, especially a vision that takes religion seriously and that attempts to account for the particular challenges it presents. I will show how two interrelated historical developments have been instrumental in fashioning the peculiar shape of pluralistic consciousness: (1) an historicist turn in the understanding of human culture and meaning, which engendered and nurtured the so-called historical consciousness; and (2) the advent of postmodernity, with its celebration of difference. Connected with the sociohistorical phenomenon of globalization, these two developments have changed the way in which we think about cultural and religious differences. Accordingly, they become the descriptive foundations for a global and interreligious model of human community, markers outlining our present-day situation in the space of which mutual understanding and genuine dialogue between religious traditions becomes a necessary challenge. It is therefore worth highlighting this formative history in order to grasp the weight of its implications.

This chapter is a kind of preparation, dealing specifically with the rise of the historical consciousness, but in a programmatic way, setting the stage for the constructive proposals to follow. I suggest that historical consciousness, as it builds upon the critical consciousness of the Enlightenment, leads directly into the heart of Bruno's centerless polycentrism, stimulating a vigorous and irrepressible sense of sociocultural heterogeneity. Indeed, no discussion of cultural and religious pluralism can proceed very far without underscoring the drastic, even revolutionary, impact that historical methods have had on how we recognize and come to understand human differences.[3] Hans-Georg Gadamer concurs: "The appearance of historical self-consciousness is very likely the most important revolution among those we have undergone since the beginning of the modern epoch. Its spiritual magnitude probably surpasses what we recognize in the applications of natural science, applications which have so visibly transformed the surface of our planet."[4] From eighteenth-century thinkers such as Gotthold Lessing and Johann Gottfried Herder forward, a growing appreciation of the historical texture of human life has encouraged an increasingly critical and self-conscious awareness of the ever-changing, uniquely particular, contextual, and constructed nature of all human traditions and modes of discourse.

It is difficult to overestimate the power and scope of this modern historical sensibility in the West, which has had the effect of sweeping practically everything into its purview. One example of its pervasive sway is the transition from a normative-classical to an anthropological-pluralist sense of human "culture," which helped give rise to the social sciences.[5] Indeed, all human events, traditions, and texts are historical, subject to the limiting conditions of time and space. And the reverse implication follows suit: there is no fixed and final center of truth that lies outside the contingency and flux of historical life. Everything human is caught up in process.

Furthermore, and because of this, there are multiple ways of being human, multiple ways of looking at the world and deciphering the value of human life within it, each developing within distinct cultural-historical networks of meaning. It is the ripening of this focus on human historicity that fertilizes the soil from which the pluralistic consciousness emerges. Historical consciousness signifies not merely a consciousness of historical location, but a robust affirmation that consciousness itself is localized.

Thus it is that many writers in the field of interreligious dialogue emphasize the impact that historical consciousness has had on coming to grips with religious pluralism.[6] It presents a sobering challenge to authority-based traditions that claim final and universal access to the truth over and against all other traditions. Indeed, the advent of historical consciousness meant that the age of ecclesiastical authority and dogma had run its course, a major paradigm shift in Western culture.

But how did such a process begin and what are the stages of its evolution? While there is not enough space here to discuss in detail all the factors that contributed to the rise of the historical consciousness, there are wider "movements" to the story that merit attention: first, the decentering of an ecclesiastically sanctioned European unity; second, the birth of the critical consciousness of the Enlightenment; third, the emergence of history as an autonomous domain of critical inquiry; fourth, a postcritical return to tradition; and finally, the rise and consolidation of historicism. My approach to telling the story of this epochal shift will stress how each of its movements are inherently connected. Thus, rather than viewing historical consciousness simply as the rebellious child of Romanticism and its particularism, I believe that it is more accurate to see its development in terms of forces intrinsic to the critical consciousness of the Enlightenment. In fact, many of the issues highlighted by the radical historicism of the "postmodern turn" have their roots in eighteenth- and nineteenth-century thinking about history and depend in part on the very critical rationality of the Enlightenment so often dismissed by postmodernists in caricatured form. Exploring this thesis will prove to be instrumental in defining the shape of the constructive proposals to follow.

TRANSITION FROM TRADITION TO TRADITIONS

The first movement in the rise of historical consciousness involves a constellation of events in European history: the Renaissance, the Reformation, and the growth of nationalism. Certainly the Renaissance delight in the pursuits of art and exploration, in the scientific investigation of nature, and in the study and appreciation of the ideals of antiquity, all contributed to the emergence of a this-worldly focus that stressed the value of inquiry and human freedom. A new humanism challenged medieval assumptions about the function and purpose of human life in the world, which were heretofore governed by a geocentric and hierarchical vision of cosmic order, a vision in which the universe was thought to be saturated with symbolic significance and centered in the authority of the Church as the instrument of divine disclosure. With the emergence of the Renaissance, however, the productive power of human thought and the integrity of the natural world—an infinite universe governed by discoverable laws and properties—began to be appreciated as legitimate ends in themselves, subverting traditional cosmological assumptions and, by implication, decentering ecclesiastical authority.[7]

One immediate effect of this was the loosening of textual interpretation and scientific speculation from their compulsory ties to orthodox dogma. Figures like Erasmus now approached the Bible with the same reasoned interpretive methods used to explore other literature of antiquity. And even while other free thinkers such as Bruno and Galileo had their problems with religious authorities, an energetic culture of inquiry and individualism began to open up new vistas, marking a departure from the previous ecclesiastically controlled culture.

Not unrelated to this was the Reformation challenge to the Church hierarchy and to its ability to police the proper interpretation of the Bible. Despite the Reformer's best intentions to maintain Church unity, there now arose a pluralism of "orthodoxies," each proposing its own selective interpretation of scripture. As a result, Catholic orthodoxy could no longer be the taken-for-granted backdrop for theological uniformity. In place of the requisite culture of the state church there grew voluntaristic, confessional communities that made religious faith a matter of personal conviction and active choice, a key ingredient of which was the idea of the universal priesthood of all believers, which effectively rendered the role of priestly, or institutional, mediation for salvation obsolete. This is not to say that religious freedom and heterodoxy thereby became fully embraced by all, nor to say that there was no variation in biblical interpretation among Protestants, who, even as they broke from the grip of magisterial Church authority, were in many cases equally as condemnatory of religious differences as their Catholic counterparts.[8] The point is that with the Renaissance and Reformation, the social and religious cohesion of European ecclesiastical culture began to splinter apart into unavoidably independent subcultures.

Finally, on the political terrain, the growing prevalence of nationalistic fervor and territorial self-interest served to augment this situation. Bounded, autonomous, and sovereign nation-states emerged, self-consciously identifying themselves through religious association, yet no longer appealing to the institutional Church as an arbiter of disputes. Europe became a chessboard for state rivalry, inducing an era of religious wars. The unity of Christendom, which, under the canopy of ecclesiastical sanction, had woven together numerous local cultures into a broad social, political, and civilizational composite, no longer possessed its compelling and authoritative grip. Tradition broke apart into "traditions," and the grand medieval ideal of unity shattered into "many" local and heterogeneous centers of loyalty. It is this "breaking up" that helped pave the way for the religious diversity of the modern Western world.

CRITIQUE OF TRADITION AND CRITICAL CONSCIOUSNESS

In the wake of such a broad-scale transition, there developed a second constellation of events—more intellectual in nature but with powerful social and political implications—that has normally been characterized as the "European Enlightenment" or the "Age of Reason." Religious pluralism in Europe had spawned bloody conflict, and many soon saw the need for a broader, neutral, and stabilized framework for measuring the adequacy of ethical and cognitive claims, a framework based neither on the constrictive biases of tradition nor the authority-bound affirmations of faith, but rather on objective and universal truths available to all persons. The newfound success of the sciences and mathematics seemed like ideal frameworks from which to pursue such objectivity. Though the Enlightenment was a far more complex and multifaceted phenomenon than can be represented here, certain key features are worth pointing out because of their instrumental role in shaping the modern world and historical consciousness.

The Scope of the Enlightenment Heritage

By extending and radicalizing the this-worldly humanistic spirit of the Renaissance, with its thrust toward inquiry and scientific investigation, and the ideas of free conviction and universal priesthood characteristic of the Reformation, the Enlightenment launched a devastating critique of ecclesiastical authority and dogma. In place of divine revelation as the primary court of appeal there arose a confidence in the ability of individual reason and conscience to adjudicate matters of belief and behavior. Human inquiry could discover the truth without recourse to external or imposed standards of meaning and value dependent on custom or tradition, whether God-breathed or not. The "true" and "right" were no longer arbitrary sanctions from the "outside," assent to them compelled by the authority of the Bible or Church alone; instead, truth and rightness were now thought to emerge from human inquiry, through autonomous questioning and critical examination, the telos of which is independent and free rational conviction. Consequently, revelation stood no longer on its own, self-authenticating and absolute, but only as it was subjected to rational criteria in the court of reason. The model of the burgeoning sciences thus became the dominant vehicle for assessing the world and humanity's place in it.

One crucial result of this process was a worldview in which nature was understood as an interconnected nexus of causes, a self-contained and autonomous whole whose laws had the lucidity and validity of mathematical axioms, thus emptying the world of the need for special interventions of the divine (i.e., miracles). In this mode of thinking, all events are analogous and homogeneous, demonstrating a regularity that renders them capable of being examined vis-à-vis their connections with other similar events; no events are special, originating from outside the matrix of interrelationships that comprises the world. And so, a nonhierarchical and acentric cosmology not unlike Bruno's came into prominence, wedging a yawning rift between the newfound ideals of rational inquiry—such as objectivity and universality—and those more prejudicial, particular, and exclusivist norms governing traditions built on supernatural revelation and divinely ordained faith. In fact, this perceived distance between the truths of reason and of tradition produced a *critical consciousness* in the minds of European thinkers that not only made suspect the intellectual credibility of the Christian worldview, but also effectively removed social and political institutions from ecclesiastical control. Society and culture could no longer simply be a matter of remembering and embodying an absolute or exemplary past, for this restricted rational autonomy and reduced human thinking and behavior to mere repetition.

Dissociating itself from the normative past, the future thereby became a place of promise, a horizon of expectation. By sifting through and weighing the evidence, rational criticism could weed out fact from fiction, necessary truth from contingent opinion, to determine general laws of thought and action; and these laws could dispel the clouds of ignorance, error, and superstition and, in their stead, promote the furtherance of enlightenment, emancipation, tolerance, and well-being. Thus began a way of living and thinking that was "secular" and "modern" in character, liberated from submission to the past-ward looking prejudices of tradition and opened up to the progressive advancement of humankind through human effort alone. In a broad sense, the Enlightenment project meant a self-conscious critique of, and distancing from, tradition(s).

Identifying the Enlightenment Project in Three Moments

If we begin to unpack the basic constituents of the general description in the previous section, three interwoven ingredients of the Enlightenment project can be identified, each an inner moment of the landmark effort to "distance" the fabric of human meaning and value from the constrictive, even debilitating, sway of tradition. First, and perhaps most significantly, critical consciousness involves an emancipatory and liberative thrust. The point is powerfully represented in Immanuel Kant's famous dictum, "Enlightenment is man's release from his self-incurred tutelage," a release from heteronomy and authority—that is, the nonrational forces of convention, fear, ignorance, and superstition—through the use of reason as an engine of critique. And the ultimate goal is freedom, "freedom to make public use of one's reason at every point."[9] Here, Kant affirms a moment of critique that castigates, and severs itself from, those frameworks and institutions that restrict or subvert individual rational autonomy and thus distort the natural integrity of human experience. Enlightenment, then, is not just a cognitive affair, but the creation of social conditions that promote the self-determination of thought. Only free thinking can be critical thinking.

This freedom-making standpoint of critique is what we might call a "first moment" in the Enlightenment project. Its aim is liberative and emancipatory, to free us from being forced—overtly or otherwise—to become something we do not will of our own volition and power.[10] Such an endeavor, then, is the fulcrum of egalitarian individualism, empowering the affirmation of individual dignity against authority-based systems whose normativity was based upon custom, superstition, or prejudice. But how is such a liberative project to be carried through?

The answer, of course, is that it cannot be carried through without supplementation from another dimension, a *second moment*, so to speak, in which "freedom from" the past takes the shape of a "freedom for" the present opened up to its own possibility. The Enlightenment project inaugurates a new posture toward the present, what I will call, drawing from Anthony Giddens, "reflexivity."[11] Reflexivity consists of a dynamic feedback loop whereby one's own moment or position in history is brought into reflective awareness. A truly critical consciousness, one that is self-determining and does not simply repristinate the past, borrowing its orientation from conventions or habits sanctioned by an authoritative heritage, is one that must become critically self-aware, casting its gaze productively back upon itself. Attaining critical distance from the immediacy of tradition requires a new form of time-consciousness that views the present as an authentic horizon of expectation released toward the future: as "modern." In posing as a way out of the "self-incurred" social impositions and doxic assumptions of the past, critical reflection thus becomes a reflexive self-relation that is conscious of the need to establish its temporal novelty, its individuality, and its difference.[12] As Michel Foucault suggests, however, echoing Charles-Pierre Baudelaire, this is not merely a glorification, or "heroizing," of the present "as sacred in order to try to maintain or perpetuate it," but rather it is an effort to "imagine it otherwise than it is, and to transform it not by destroying it but by grasping it in what it is," thereby problematizing the present and necessitating a "critical ontology of ourselves," of our historical moment in time.[13]

Disengagement from the models of knowledge and action supplied by another epoch mandates that the present define and constitute itself, and even more, in the words of Jürgen Habermas, "create its normativity out of itself."[14] Accordingly, in its reflexivity, critical reflection analyzes itself even as it legislates and defines the world; that is, it thematizes its own self-determination. Foucault states the point more radically, claiming that the modern human being is not liberated merely by virtue of the present or by mere self-discovery, but through the ongoing task of "producing" and "inventing" herself, or in other words, by effecting a critically reflexive self-creativity.[15] Thus it is that the first two moments of the Enlightenment project are inherently intertwined, and in such a way that they necessarily invoke yet a *third moment.*

The emancipatory and reflexive character of critical consciousness automatically opens up the issue of the means of its procedure. After all, precisely *what* is it that should replace the past and provide the means by which the integrity of the present can be opened up toward its own possibility? This is where the (now dubious) legacy of the Enlightenment emerges in the ideal of an impartial and universalizing rationalism. The operative model of rationality employed by the sciences, which discerns uniformity and regularity in nature, begins to be applied as a reflexive mechanism to determine, order, and judge human values, behaviors, and institutions. For example, the animating force behind René Descartes' program in the *Meditations* is an aim to establish an indubitable and objective ground of the sciences unencumbered by opinion, prejudice, or any external authority other than reason's own self-guaranteeing methodical doubt.[16] The regularity and uniformity of the natural world in this way becomes the paradigmatic model driving the larger modern project, determining the manner by which human reality is understood and ordered. Hence, thinkers like Descartes and Kant baptize reason as the formally entitled and empowering subject of critical consciousness. Reason is the engine propelling critique, giving critique its leverage.

It is no accident that the move toward the objective and universal meant an advance over the partial, the particular, and the contingent, which demonstrate inconsistency and error. In this third moment, reason is exalted as the highest court of appeal in determining what is right, true, and just. Only reason is qualified to dismantle the old and to provide the foundation and normative structure required for modernity to launch itself self-creatively into the future. Kant's categorical imperative stands as a classic example, compelling humans to act in the most impartial and universalizable manner possible in every instance, in every context. In fact, elsewhere Kant describes the "universal man" as one who has a "*broadened way of thinking* if he overrides the private subjective conditions of his judgment, into which so many others are locked, as it were, and reflects on his own judgment from a *universal standpoint* (which he can determine only by transferring himself to the standpoint of others)."[17]

Thus, in place of varied and conflicting traditions, based as they are on contingent and local discourses perpetuated by appeals to custom and authority, there now stands the homogeneous and impartial ideals of reason that bring the discord of multiple standpoints into harmonious relation under a univocal mode of objective discourse. Objective truth is transregional and universal, an inclusive framework for measuring human life in all of its variances. The ideal then is a kind of rational, homogeneous metatradition of sorts that functions to disembed and relocate all local differences in terms of a single, rational, and unitary standpoint. An example of this is the Enlightenment concern for a "natural religion" purified from ignorance and superstitious baggage, founded not in the particulars of tradition but in general rational principles upon which all thinking persons can agree, and therefore able to promote universal tolerance rather than exclusivist bigotry.[18] In the mind-set of the Enlightenment, as Steven Toulmin quips, "abstract axioms were in, concrete diversity was out."[19]

In sum, beyond its freedom-making power, reason also is reflexive, self-critical, and self-defining, capable of grounding itself apodictically (Descartes), setting limits to its proper purview (Kant), or uniting the ruptures and contradictions of contingency in its sweep as an integrative power (G. W. F. Hegel). In Kant, the knowing subject becomes a transcendental subject, the object of its own critique, in order to establish the possibility of knowledge, human freedom, and morality. Hegel's notion of subjectivity, of the rational freedom of self-relation, goes further, bringing together the emancipatory and reflexive moments of the Enlightenment project in the shape of an idealist metaphysics, by which modernity comes to terms with and completes its own historical dynamic.[20] Striving against the rhetoric of coercion that defined ages past, the ideal of rational unanimity and a universal standpoint of critique propels the Enlightenment project toward inculcating an essentially utopian vision, where, as Christoph Martin Wieland advocated, all civilized minds are obligated to "do the great work to which we have been called: to cultivate, enlighten and ennoble the human race."[21] Freedom *from* the past thus entails a reflexively constituted freedom *for* innovation and progress via the enabling power of critical reason. But how is the Enlightenment project carried through and what are it implications?

Diving Deeper: Universality as the Detraditioning of Tradition through the Power of Reflexivity

Reason's putatively universal standpoint involves what might be called the "detraditioning" of tradition, a decontextualization process that abstracts, or disembeds value from, its concrete sociohistorical location and reconfigures it against a broader, standardized universal context. After the means of preserving tradition by appealing to some direct link to the divine (whether textual or institutional) are discredited, traditions become transparent and show themselves as humanly originated and not absolute. Their real value becomes grounded not in themselves but rather in their potential to display a nonparochial, standardized economy of rational virtue and truth.

A lucid account of this detraditioning process and its social significance is given by Anthony Giddens.[22] In modernity, he notes, time and space become separated from any privileged connection to the distinctive vantage point of a certain group of people, events, or customs. With the invention of abstract time, symbolized by the advent of the mechanical clock, events are coordinated according to a uniform measurement without reference to any specific sociospacial markers or traditions. According to Giddens, this emptying of time is also tied to the emptying of space: the dislocation of space from its lived relation to "place" or geographic locale, which standardizes and renders it boundaryless and substitutable, a point on the global map independent of the peculiar happenings in that locality. Separating time and space into abstract dimensions is the prime ingredient for what Giddens calls "disembedding," a process by which values and social relations become "lifted out" or disengaged from local contexts of interaction and reconfigured rationally across indefinite and noncentric spans of time and space.

Besides opening up the possibilities for genuine change and mobility in a transregional world context, this type of delocalization of truth makes possible the instantiation of universal values and institutions that are not embedded in particular geographic locations and specific historical traditions but extend across and link them. Provincial boundaries become practically inconsequential. They hold no binding power within the sway of mechanisms that transgress the local and standardize time and space into routine units of rational management and technical control.[23] No tradition remains insular. Through this kind of detraditioning of traditions, the critical consciousness of the Enlightenment creates a genuinely global and world-historical framework of action and experience.[24] Knowledge of truth is (in principle) not the privilege of one locality, but is exchangeable across boundaries because it is disembedded and homogeneous, available to all. Rational discourse is the anonymous discourse of a universal standpoint. Knowledge is a universal currency.

The universalizing-disembedding process of rationalization can be further understood by noting its kinship with the dynamic of *reflexivity*.[25] Reflexivity is where modernity's inherent contrast with tradition stands out with bold clarity, for, as noted earlier, it denotes a way of disengaging from a lived situation and thinking about it from an objectivizing distance, without appeal to an authoritative past. While the reflexive monitoring of ideas and actions is present in tradition-oriented societies, it is largely focused on perpetuating the continuity of past, present, and future in recurring practices that reinterpret and clarify cultural inheritances in a given location. With the advent of critical consciousness, though, reflexivity takes a different twist, focusing not on time-space continuity but on the production of autonomous knowledge to be appropriated and fed back into the system, accordingly shaping the further production of still more knowledge.

Detraditioned universality and reflexivity feed on each other, their interplay energizing self-reflective autonomy. As Giddens notes, modern rationalism introduces reflexivity "into the very basis of system reproduction, such that thought and action are constantly refracted back upon one another." Thus an idea, practice, or institution cannot be sanctioned simply because it represents tradition: "tradition can be justified, but only in the light of knowledge which is not itself authenticated by tradition."[26] Knowledge is decontextualized and self-critical. This kind of autonomy is epitomized in the transcendental philosophy of Kant's first "Critique," wherein reason bends back on itself in order to examine, limit, and ground its own activity, speculatively establishing its own purview.[27] And this is why, distanced from tradition, modern reflexivity engenders the need for reason to authenticate itself, to create norms within itself.[28]

Instabilities within the Enlightenment Project: Opening to an Historical Sensibility

It is my contention that the first two moments of the Enlightenment project—that is, its freedom-making and reflexive thrust—invoke unsettling implications which, despite themselves, begin to subvert the ideals of reason as an objective and universal currency. When the claims of science and reason replace those of tradition, they appear to offer greater certainty and stability, yet they too are constituted in and through the forward momentum of reflexively applied knowledge, engulfed in a process of constant revision and adaptation.[29] The Enlightenment apotheosis of reason thus contains the seeds of its own undoing, and this is played out in the following series of self-limiting components.

Modernity is a dynamism that seeks to become conscious of itself as self-grounding, fashioning its own historical identity with an eye toward the forward thrust of history—the future—rather than toward the past.[30] Yet, as Louis Dupré points out, where human action is set free to influence the future through innovation and modification, "the idea of history as indefinite progress follows," which envisions a future always capable of further production and perfection.[31] To a certain degree, then, this relativizes and limits the rational endeavors and accomplishments of the present. For it directs the human project forward "toward a concrete, historical goal attainable in time yet implicitly denies that it can ever be reached."[32] The "not-yet" renders the present open-ended and incomplete, requiring a constant reinterpretation of the past. In order to render the ideals of progress acceptable, the new must legitimate itself in relation to the old, invalidating the past's authority in order to thematize the authenticity of the present and to open up the future. But the present always displays a lack of self-grounding, for it is ever unfinished. The objective surety of reason is never quite realized. Accordingly, the notion of reason as self-contained and autonomous implodes.

Because of this, furthermore, the present must be continually unmasked as potentially heteronomous, even hegemonic. This is why modernity must cast its gaze back on itself. Breaking from a normative past necessitates that critical consciousness create and legitimate its own autonomy, granting its normative impulse as something that stems from itself. But this type of reflexivity introduces the prospect of a relentless and even paralyzing self-criticism. Launching a critique that functions to historicize tradition, exposing its human partiality and limitations, requires the critique itself to turn back on itself, caught up in a momentum that forces it inevitably to historicize itself—to see itself connected to the very tradition it critiques. In this, the ideals of universality and impartiality begin to collapse.

This dynamic becomes intensified by yet another difficulty. Because the general laws of thought are seen as homogeneous, objective, and universal, modernity presumes that knowledge across different fields of inquiry must accordingly correlate. Thus, objects in the variable and changing world of human events should mirror or indicate something analogous to those examined by the natural sciences, at least if they are to be suggestive of the uniformity of truth yielded by genuine rational inquiry. Descartes' model, for instance, axiomatically assumes that human reason—in all of its endeavors—remains one and the same. Ernst Cassirer sums up the point: "No matter how heterogeneous the objects of human knowledge may be, the forms of knowledge always show an inner unity and a logical homogeneity."[33] The methodological premises of the natural sciences, therefore, should be translatable into the realms of politics, the arts, and morality, indeed history. But an aporia is created. Where do we find the logic, regularity, and permanence characteristic of truth within the flux and flow of human life? Does human life exhibit the same order as does nature, capable of being reduced to predictable laws and axioms? Can that which is historically unique and transient ever be recognized as something with universal and unchanging significance?

These kinds of issues problematize certain strains in the process of thinking rationally about human affairs. And the third moment of the Enlightenment project begins to unravel from the inside. This becomes manifest in a growing and inescapable concern for the relevance of history.[34] It is the dynamism of freedom-making reflexivity that challenges and helps transform the critique of tradition into a new attitude toward the past, not as an exemplar to which inquiry must conform but as an ongoing present, an objective fact capable of bearing questions and rational interrogation. Tradition is thereby turned into history—a purely human and contingent field of events perpetually carrying humanity into the future. It is this development that eventuates into a full-blown historical consciousness. We now turn our attention to this process, but will highlight only certain themes and figures as they are important for this study.

THE RISE OF HISTORICAL CONSCIOUSNESS

First of all, the foregoing analysis suggests, contrary to popular "postmodern" wisdom, that the Enlightenment project itself should not be seen as patently unhistorical in its quest for the necessary, objective, and universally true.[35] In fact, the reflexivity of rational criticism contributed to the rise of scientific historical method, encouraging a sensitivity to history that paved the way for historical consciousness.[36] Such a process can be narrated in several key steps, leading to an historicism that effectively undercuts the third moment of critical consciousness, universal reason, by sweeping it into a reflexive mode wherein reason itself become decentered and contextualized, made relative to historical effect.

From Tradition to History

As illustrated earlier, the Enlightenment critique of tradition hinges upon advances in the sciences, which render nature an autonomous and interconnected realm of self-contained, efficient causality. This undermines any special claim to divinely granted authority by dismantling the supernaturalist interventionalism upon which those claims are based. The result frees allegedly privileged human events and meanings from their direct link with divine intention or activity. Without its divinely ordained pillars to hold it up, the "house of authority" collapses.[37] Here then is the important point: rather than akin to the divine and tethered to revelation, tradition now becomes a constellation of transitory human events on a par with others, intertwined with, and part of, the ordinary empirical world and therefore open to critical examination.

Tradition becomes history, factual rather than paradigmatic, and the implications of this are radical. Freed from the dogmatic bonds of authority, history can be investigated as impartially, methodically, and systematically as the physical sciences investigate nature. The goal is not merely to recover the past in order to conform to it, but to survey and examine it as a mundane, causally interconnected series of human activities and influences. And in this task, one cannot simply accept the authoritative testimony of someone else and treat it as a reliable or authentic account; one must apply methodical doubt and examine such testimony with a discriminating eye, weighing evidences and exercising considered judgments so as to determine what really happened and wherein its significance lies. A rigorous empiricism toward the historical world is opened up.

An excellent example of such rigor is the *Historical and Critical Dictionary* (1695), by Pierre Bayle, perhaps the first modern thinker to decry the obscuring consequences of traditionalist, uncritical, and nonhistorical thinking and to formulate a scientific approach to history as objective fact—fact emancipated from prejudice and distortion by religious or political bias.[38] For Bayle, autonomous reflection and methodological skepticism yields true historical knowledge; just as in the sciences, authority is conferred upon sources (rather than assumed) by evaluating their credibility, authenticity, and integrity, in the end (re)constructing by inference a sequence of events and/or meanings that best accounts for their intentionality and significance as facts.[39]

The keystones of this germinating historical method, therefore, are the ideals of critical reason: investigative autonomy, impartiality, and objectivity in discovering and displaying the truth. However, the truth is revealed not through homogeneous, necessary, and universal axioms or laws, as in the natural sciences, but through detailed expositions of "what really happened." Fact is not the starting point, but the goal, discovered by scrupulous analysis of the historical evidences. The basis for this approach is the sense that human events and meanings are "historical" not merely because they recount or narrate a sequence of occurrences, but because they spring from, and are inherently related to, a particular horizon of circumstances and intentions that can be rigorously explored and illuminated. Thus begins modern historiography.

This latter point, however, proves to be problematic for thinkers operating out of Cartesian rationalism, for whom the particular and factual, which includes history, is not the proper domain of universal and necessary truth. From such a standpoint, reality is rational insofar as it is capable of being brought under laws grounded in timeless and general concepts. But while it appears unhistorical at face value, such an attitude actually served to fuel new interpretations of historical events and sources. As Cassirer notes, "Consideration of the eternal and immutable norms of reason must go hand in hand with consideration of the manner in which they unfold historically, in which they have been realized in the course of empirical historical development."[40]

Biblical criticism in Germany, for example, represented an attempt to treat biblical texts as historical material, as objects of critical scientific inquiry, while at the same time revelatory significations of eternal truths. These eternal truths, however, were not dogmatic or tradition-bound; they were reflective of the natural religion of reason, with its focus on self-evident moral and spiritual truths. Neologian J. S. Semler, considered by many the progenitor of modern historical critical study of the Bible (although its trajectory can be traced back through Benedict de Spinoza to Desiderrus Erasmus), called for a purely historical approach to the Bible without concern for edification or orthodoxy, seeing the work as a compilation of texts revealing not infallible and verbally inspired truths but contingent religious worldviews representative of the varied circumstances in which they were written. Impartial historical inquiry leads to the viewpoint that the Bible is a literary source not unlike others. It is written by human beings and is a product of its times. H. S. Reimarus took this even further, claiming that the idealized Christ of Christian tradition is a corruption that has no genuine connection with the historical evidence relating to the actual person, Jesus of Nazareth.[41]

This brings into striking focus the problem of relating the homogeneity and disembeddedness of rational truth to the particular contingencies of history. If truth is rational and universal, how is it manifest in the transitory particulars of history? With this question, the growing sensitivity to history is raised to the level of historical consciousness.

The Beginnings of Historical Consciousness: Introducing Reason into History

It was Gotthold Lessing who rendered explicit the full weight of this tension between reason and history, highlighting its significance particularly with regard to religion. Other thinkers—like Giambattista Vico, Charles Louis Montesquieu, and François-Marie Voltaire—had in various ways already struggled to treat history scientifically, making efforts to discern patterns and hidden laws at work in the myriad religious, political, and cultural forms of the human past. The result was an understanding of human history as a progressive teleological development toward the instanciation of a rational ideal.[42] Reflective of permanent aspects of human nature and inclusive of all humanity, this universal rational teleology proved to be the Enlightenment's trump card in employing critical historical method without recourse to the supernaturalism and exclusivism of traditional salvation history. Thus the process by which uniform patterns and laws emerge empirically came to represent the ideal and universal meaning of history, revealing the unity in multiplicity, the eternal in time—not as an actualized identity between the two, for this would be tantamount to a return to the authority-based absolutism of the principle of identity, but as a gradual program of development in which the abstract Enlightenment ideals of tolerance, freedom, moral virtue, and rational discourse could be increasingly discovered and actualized. History, here, becomes seen as a vehicle progressively revelatory of the homogeneous and disembedded truths of reason.

Gotthold Lessing broadly adopted this viewpoint but with more sophisticated historical nuance. In his view, which adopted Leibniz's distinction between the necessary truths of reason and the contingent truths of fact, the study of history can neither establish the absolute truth of a particular historical configuration nor act as a vehicle portraying the indubitable and suprahistorical truths of reason. Historical truths themselves can never be demonstrated because they depend on the testimony of others, whose reliability can be questioned, thus rendering the knowledge of historical occurrences a matter of degrees of probability. In asserting this Lessing both refutes the certainty that traditional Christianity assigns to reports of prophecy and miracles and rejects the idea that any historical event can ever do more than indirectly infer a moral or metaphysical truth of reason. As he succinctly put it in his famous dictum, "If no historical truth can be demonstrated, then nothing can be demonstrated by means of historical truths. That is: Accidental truths of history can never become the proof of necessary truths of reason."[43] Here is the "wide, ugly ditch" between history and truth over which Lessing said he could not jump.[44]

Lessing's way of addressing this problem represents an important move beyond the more rationalist confines of the Enlightenment view. He did not share the Cartesian disdain for the messiness of history. For Lessing, the contingencies of history become a progressive means by which rational truths are made concretely manifest, disclosed provisionally in a way that autonomous reason, left alone in its disembedded anonymity, might never approximate. Reason *needs* to become subject to historical process in order to be appropriated and temporally realized not abstractly but as lived truth. In contrast to the abstract formalism of the Enlightenment, which seeks to extract the universal as an inference *from* concrete worldly life, Lessing shifted the focus to discovering the universal *within* the ever-changing textures and variations of historical life. The idea of teleological historical development allowed him in the end to affirm that there is no radical discontinuity between the rational and the historical, between the necessary/eternal and the contingent/temporal.

This mediation between the historical and the rational plays out with peculiar significance in the history of religion. In "The Education of the Human Race," Lessing developed the idea that, while limited in scope, positive historical revelation is necessary for the world-historical development of humanity toward the truly rational religion. Although an early passage in the text states that "Revelation gives nothing to the human race which human reason could not arrive at on its own," it seems clear from later statements that Lessing believed that human reason needs the aid of historical revelation to "win by experience" those universal and immutable truths it aspires to through a teleological process of "education."[45] Reason alone is unable to attain divine and necessary truth; it needs the providential guidance of historical revelation to unfold properly and become actualized.[46] To be sure, the goal of revelatory events and meanings is "the development of revealed truths into truths of reason," but this is a goal that "human reason would never have reached on its own."[47] Rational religion was for Lessing the ultimate truth, but rather than depicting historical religions as unfortunate but inevitable additions to, or distortions of, this original and pure focus, gradually overcome through time, he considered them necessary for the development of a religious consciousness in a perpetual striving for a future ideal focus, which perhaps could never be fully realized.[48] Each positive religion is a partial yet legitimate disclosure of ultimate truth, expressing its truth with a distinctiveness appropriate to its own historical context and stage of development.[49]

Finite human history is the framework for truth's appropriation in the temporal process of becoming, and it is precisely this fact that thoroughly historicizes both reason and religion, reembedding the homogeneity of truth in the finite conditionalities and heterogeneous contexts of history.[50] History is not simply the past, a collection of facts to be scientifically examined, but rather the way in which the permanence of the real perpetually unfolds in fluid, limited, and diverse forms, no age to be viewed without its own relative virtue. While Lessing did show an Enlightenment propensity toward the natural religion of reason, his sensitivity to the character of history led him to a deeper understanding of the historicity of religion and of human life as a whole, marking in bold the transition from rationalism to historical consciousness.

Into the Sway of Historical Consciousness: From History to a Postcritical Return to Tradition

It was Lessing's contemporary, Johann Gottfried Herder, who even further radicalized the implications of history by underscoring the heterogeneous and contextual nature of all human value and truth. In Herder, there is not the strong sense of teleological development in human history that we find in Lessing, nor is there a concern for diverse religions to eventuate in the necessary truths of enlightened rational reflection. Instead, there is a celebration of the varied and distinct forms in which human life flowers because of its inherently embedded and historical character. Herder saw in history, rather than in disembedded reason, the vital integrity of all truth and value, and this central insight becomes a wellspring out of which genuine historical consciousness emerges for the first time.

Rejecting the suggestion that ideal reason is autonomous, anonymous, and pure, a faculty that stands isolated from the qualifications of time and space, Herder's conception of history trades on a contextual holism, reflecting a keen sense of the unavoidably conditioned, temporal, and local character of all human life—that is, its historical embeddedness or historicity. The historical implies relationship, for no event exists in isolation, separate from a context. And as language signifies an interdependency between the individual and the social-linguistic context, so too is history intrinsically interdependent. Building upon the idea that history exhibits a dynamic relationality, Herder claims that "everything in history" points to a "dependence on others" for the development of human features, not to a self-made, isolated, and all-sufficient center of subjectivity.[51] He makes use of the word tradition (Bildung) to describe such dependency, for the process of human formation and cultivation relies on the "transmission" of the values and ideas of those who have come before, linking the individual to parents, teachers, and friends, to the circumstances of that individual's life and her surrounding culture and people, implying both the history of that culture and its interaction with other cultures in the past and present.[52] But this is not mere slavish imitation or backward-looking repetition, for Herder also stresses that through what he calls "organic powers" humans assimilate and apply what is transmitted in ways that make it uniquely their own according to the exigencies of time and place, promoting genuine historical change.[53] While not absolute, tradition is a given, a fact denoting the historical nature of human life, with its temporal and local situatedness. Tradition is a dynamically relational force-field of interdependency.

Such a conception of history is the product of a reflexive move. Stressing the uniqueness and individuality of cultures, Herder turns reflexively back through history to a postcritical affirmation of tradition, not as "the" exemplary past, but as a conditioned repository of human flourishing. We do not just have a history, we belong to our history, a sociocultural and traditioned context in which we become who we are. Put differently, the historical horizon of tradition is not merely a heteronomous imposition that blindsides rational reflection, preventing us from seeing clearly; rather, it is in fact the linguistically saturated condition for rational reflection, permitting sight in the first place.

This brings us to a place where Herder's move beyond Lessing becomes even more pronounced. Herder finds a way to articulate the idea of history as a realm of concrete individualization. History is not only a horizon of dynamically relational interdependence; it is a horizon of interdependence that flowers in novel and richly diverse individual ways. Contextual holism implies that each historical moment is irreducibly unique, having an intrinsic integrity developed in consonance with its own peculiar temporal and spatial exigencies. In the way that each person has his or her own inexpressibly unique way of experiencing the world, so too does each social group in each period in history.[54] Every age, nation, culture, or religion has a distinctly individual character, its own "center of gravity," which is always in the process of development according to its own organic profile, whether growing or decaying.[55] And it is the multiple shapes in which this distinctiveness blossoms across the human landscape that creates the fertile and heterogeneous mosaic of history, as "no two moments in the world are ever identical."[56]

This being so, "rational uniformity" and "human history" are, for Herder, contradictory terms. The historical is a dynamism that by nature inclines toward novelty, individuality, and variation, rendering it vanity to reduce the inexhaustible differences of specific cultures and traditions to some disembedded or abstract ideal of comparison or measurement.[57] Each must be seen in light of its own sociohistorical context and center of gravity in order to be truly understood. For Herder, as Hans-Georg Gadamer points out, "To think historically now means to acknowledge that each period has its own right to exist, its own perfection," its own inherent integrity irrespective of standardized external criteria.[58] It is precisely in the two interrelated ideas of dynamic relationality and concrete individualization that Herder's contextual holism blossoms into a pluralistic vision of human historical life.

Thus, the complex diversity and messiness of the drama of history resists not only the disembedded rationalism of the Enlightenment, but even the more historically sensitive notion of teleological development according to a collection of universal standards. Why? Because, I suggest, Herder has allowed full sway to the first two moments of the Enlightenment project, its freedom-making and reflexive elements. Each culture, each epoch, is free and reflexively self-constituting, including our own. Herder condemns the ideal of a uniform blueprint of progress as an illusion, for this would not only obliterate real differences, reintroducing a new heteronomy, but also deny the historical character of language and reason itself.[59] In order to free history, Herder historicizes the engine of rational inquiry.

HISTORICISM AND THE FULL WEIGHT OF HUMAN HISTORICITY

Though Herder was not a systematic thinker and did not take his program to its potentially more radical conclusions, his importance for the development of a historical consciousness in the modern world should not be overlooked.[60] Through his philosophy of history, as Georg G. Iggers opines, "Herder had laid the foundations for a historicism which spread far beyond the German boundaries."[61] In Herder, not the disincarnate or transcendental forms of reason, but rather history becomes the source of real value; all that is true and genuine about humanity emerges in the conditioned flow of time and place. Following Lessing, Herder did more than simply apply scientific methods of thought to historical matters of fact; he developed a sense for history as the temporal and contextual play of particular forms of life. Yet moving beyond Lessing, for whom history is focused progressively on the realization of axiomatic, rational ideals as the perfection of humanity, Herder sees history as an interdependent yet individualizing process of development instantiated only in the fecundity and multiplicity of sociocultural differences. Variety, not uniformity, is primary. This embodies the emancipatory and reflexive moments of the Enlightenment project while subverting universal reason.

According to historian Friedrich Meinecke, this "individualizing" view of history, in contradistinction to one that "generalizes" and holds hostage particularity to universality, introduces the theme of historicism (Historismus).[62] While the term has been used variously, "historicism" on the whole reflects a methodological resistance to subsuming the historical under timeless and absolutely valid truths or laws reflecting the uniformity of the universe. The historicist outlook hinges upon the assumption that human history exhibits fundamentally different characteristics than does nature; history is comprised of temporal, unrepeatable, and unique acts of collective individuality and intentionality rather than permanent and uniform laws devoid of consciousness.[63]

What I have called "contextual holism," with its dynamic relationalism and concrete individualization, is at the heart of historicism. And, as Herder's perspective on history suggests, three interrelated implications follow: (1) to study humanity one must study history; (2) history shows that human nature is not constant, eternal, and singular—that is, a standardized rationality that always and everywhere speaks with the same voice—but rather a mutable substance, constantly taking new and individual shapes; and (3) human ideas, values, and practices are always already embedded in a temporal and spacial sociocultural context, one that forms and is informed by tradition and language. These indicate a fundamental shift in the way in which human life is envisioned and understood, the effects of which send epistemological, ethical, theological, and metaphysical ripples through any and all thinking about human life. Historical method, when its sail is fully opened, almost invariably launches a wider and sharper historicist view of human existence, engendering an acute form of "historical consciousness."

Perhaps this more radicalized historical consciousness is most fully embodied in the idea of human historicity. "Historicity" alludes to the fact that humans are temporally constituted beings, linguistically related to others in an intersubjective world conditioned by determinate sociocultural configurations. There is, however, an important way in which this concept goes beyond Herder's program. For it acknowledges that the inquiring subject holds no special exemption from historical influence, but is—like all events—conditioned by historical forces, an intractable part of the flow of events being investigated. While Herder recognizes that all human events and meanings are contextually based, he does not go so far as to historicize the historian's act of knowing as such, a fact that betrays his proximity to the critical consciousness of the Enlightenment.

This notion of historicity, however, leads to a problem. Given the embeddedness of the subject in a sociohistorical context, how can objectively valid knowledge be ascertained? Answering this question took two distinct directions in the nineteenth century, creating a dividing line between (1) those who held to a teleologically framed, idealist metaphysic of history as a means to universal and objective truth (i.e., Hegel); and (2) those whose focus was directed toward historical individuality, raising contextual holism to the level of the hermeneutical problem of historical understanding and the articulation of universal values (i.e., Dilthey). Space does not allow for a treatment of these developments. Suffice it to say, however, that out of the second view an even more extreme form of historicism emerged, leading directly into pluralistic consciousness by subsuming into finite history the very process of understanding itself.

The fact of human historicity radicalizes the problem of relating the always already local and particular to the translocal and universal. As Wilhelm Dilthey himself noted, the meaning of a whole can only be seen from the contingent perspective of its parts, rendering all thinking about universality inescapably particular and local in its jurisdiction, including that of the historian.[64] The collapse of everything human into history unavoidably undermines the human penchant (the Cartesian ideal) for immediate access to the objective and universally valid. All thinking that prioritizes the historicity of human life runs aground while trying to advocate objectively valid truths. Historical knowledge is mediated knowledge. Thus, historical consciousness revolutionizes the way in which human beings look at themselves, unveiling the spatiotemporal relativity and contextuality of all knowledge and meaning. As Gadamer concludes, this is both a privilege and a burden, "the like of which has never been imposed on any previous generation."[65]

It is therefore in the historical consciousness that the reflexive turn of the modern spirit, engendered by the Enlightenment critical consciousness, becomes fully manifest.[66] Cognizant of the sociocultural contextuality of all human perspectives, modern human beings have been inducted into the "full awareness of the historicity of everything present and the relativity of all opinions."[67] This involves a reflexive *double critique*, on the one hand carrying forth the liberative moment of Enlightenment critique against the house of authority, undermining heteronomy and any protective appeal to tradition as absolute, and on the other, leveling against the third moment of the Enlightenment project an historicist critique of disembedding rationalism, rationalism that tends toward an abstract uniformity and homogeneity distortive of historical life. By underscoring the fact that there is no Cartesian view from nowhere, no permanent, timeless, and universal truths distinct from the local and temporal processes and situations that express them, reflexivity in the shape of historical consciousness is inescapably self-critical.

A kind of intertextuality pervades all levels of human life. Every position, including that of the inquirer, is embedded in an intensely fluid temporal continuum, conditioned by intrinsic relation to other such positions and therefore contingent upon them. The processes of historical life are *productive* of meanings disclosed therein, not *reflective* of some homogeneous transhistorical universality. History is not an accidental accretion to an otherwise timeless essence; human nature is historical. Human beings and their endeavors are defined by the traditions in which they live, traditions that themselves are organic, integrative, and contextual matrices of meaning and valuation limited by the exigencies of time and place. Historical consciousness thus means that modern human beings are relentlessly self-aware, perceiving their own cultural-historical achievements as finite configurations of meaning and practice.

In sum, the critical historicizing of tradition leads criticism itself down a path to the acknowledgment of its own historicity. The double critique of historical consciousness radicalizes the Enlightenment moment of reflexivity. The self-grounding normativity of the present is not accessible via rationalism, but only via an ironic process that historicizes all human meaning and value, including that of the present. Perhaps this chapter's epigraph by William James puts it best, reminding us that we are finite and tied to things that have a history. And it is this reflexivity of historical consciousness that opens up a diversity of finite, relative, culturally bound, and plural worlds. A new horizon is formed, one that might be depicted developmentally as the gradual yet revolutionary transition from *heteronomous belonging to a tradition* to a *traditioned belongingness to history*.

CONCLUSION: PROMISES AND PERILS

This acute sense of belonging to history brings the discussion back to the paradoxical character of Bruno's universe (or should I equally say "pluriverse") introduced at the beginning of this chapter. For like Bruno's cosmos, history is simultaneously centerless and polycentric, both aspects dialectically intertwined. Sensitivity to history cannot help but germinate an appreciation for the fact that human events and meanings do not present themselves in monotone and stable forms. History is polyphonic and always already overdetermined in specific configurations irreducible to uniform characterization, only emerging in heterogeneous shapes. Yet this very acknowledgment implicitly signifies the homogeneous character of history as a democratized playing field of human differences. Indeed, it is the recognition of the homogeneity of history, its integral continuity, that carries out the Enlightenment project in historical consciousness.[68] The critical distance between universal truth and historical tradition is maintained, but in an historicist form that treats concepts and values as captives of finite sociocultural processes. History is a level playing field, a realm of homogeneous neutrality where all events are in principle analogous.

This recognition is a privilege in that it promotes a consciousness of what might be called "positional finitude," which helps break the hold of absolutist commitments, whether dogmatic or rationalist. It enables us to thematize diversity in a new way and to encounter differences with full respect for their own integral sense. Moreover, it supports injunctions against ethnocentrism and cultural imperialism in favor of cosmopolitan ideals such as tolerance and cross-cultural mutuality. No culture contains permanently valid meanings capable of being normative for all others, for such meanings depend upon historical context. From different points of view, as Bruno suggests, all points in space, all historical perspectives, can in their own right be considered centers or boundaries, marked on the map of existence in terms of some framework or another. Thus, it is the acentric homogeneity of history that makes it heterogeneous and polycentric, opening up a new kind of pluralism that thematizes differences in sociocultural and historical terms. We are similar in our differences in one respect: our historicity.

But this recognition of human historicity is also a burden in that what it gives with one hand it takes away with the other, consequently threatening to unravel any and all claims to the worthwhileness of life. Cultural-historical differences, in effect, cancel each other out in an unqualified cultural relativism that leaves each paralyzed within its own vantage point, unable to address a shared world beyond the confines of its particular purview. Disturbingly, the homogeneity of history thereby becomes a meaningless anarchic vacuum in which localized particular meanings are not simply decentered, but ironically displaced, even dissolved. All value is democratized and flattened. Does pluralistic belonging-to-history then negate the very individuality it aims to uphold, introducing a skeptical disenchantment with all forms of meaningful valuation? While it compels acknowledgment of the facticity of sociocultural differences, is it able to ground the positive value of such difference? These questions set up the dilemma that chapter 2 will address.

For now it is enough that the story of the historical consciousness has been traced and its implications discussed. If it is not already, it will soon become clear that the material outlined in this chapter is fundamental to thinking about pluralism in the present-day context. In fact, much of what postmodernity advocates stems from the conjoined seeds of the critical consciousness of the Enlightenment and the historical consciousness that followed. Thus far, I have intentionally focused on the historical preparation for "pluralism," only lightly touching on the implied consequences. My hope in this was to establish a broader framework through an examination of historical consciousness, the fruits of which will become evident as the argument of this book unfolds.

CHAPTER 2

PLURALISTIC CONSCIOUSNESS: FROM HISTORICAL BELONGING TO THE CHALLENGE OF RADICAL CONTINGENCY AND DIFFERENCE

The play will be all, after all.[1]

As chapter 1 concluded, the radical consequences of the historicist turn had begun to emerge in bold clarity, dramatizing the polycentric and plural character of human dwelling in the world by representing all events and significations as finite products of exigencies bound to particular times and places. I suggested there that what Giordano Bruno's centerless polycentrism does to our sense of space, the leveling play of historical consciousness does to our perception of meaning and value, relativizing and democratizing any and all such expressions as sociocultural productions. I will now draw out in more detail the implications of the concluding statements of chapter 1.

As Hans-Georg Gadamer suggests, historical consciousness is paradoxically both a privilege and a burden.[2] On the one hand, it is a monumental achievement that provides a starting point for appreciating diversity as an ineluctable fact of human life, one that reflects the historicity of reason and thereby opens up the possibility for new forms of understanding. The lens of historical consciousness directs our attention anew to myriad cultural forms and shapes, refracting and magnifying their differences as they present themselves in their own multivalent life-contexts. With its double critique, this "nonevaluative" approach stands as an alternative both to the distortive lens of ethnocentrism, which swallows differences into parochialisms of one sort or another, and to the disembedding objectivism of Enlightenment rationality, which, in the mode of epistemic imperialism, all too quickly instrumentalizes the particular as a means to approach the universal. The end product is a democratic ethos of particularism.

On the other hand, historical consciousness ironically engenders a sensibility that threatens to vitiate the very particularity it so powerfully yields. In effect, it trivializes cultural-historical differences by reducing all local positions to equivocation and homogeneity. All are interchangeable, endowed—in principle—with the "same" value as centers of significance in their own right. History knows no privileged point of origin; it is a realm of centerless neutrality. There are no unmitigated principles of uniformity around which differences might cohere and come to be judged. All particular viewpoints thus have an identical stake in the play of plurality. While this foments a "democratic" acknowledgment of difference, it winds up reducing differences to depthless equivalence as well, flattening out and leveling all historical life into banal artifacts cut loose on a vast and empty sea of polycentric indifference. For there exist no transhistorical criteria whereby each center can be made to recognize, value, and preserve the genuine differences of others. Not only does this preclude critical judgment by granting a priori equal status to all standards and perspectives, regardless of their ethical adequacy, but it also amounts to not taking seriously the positive value of differences.[3]

Reacting nobly, as it does, against imperialist claims of cultural superiority, historical consciousness can end up invoking rhetorics of parochialist exclusion, disintegration, fragmentation, ironist indifference, and even nihilism, all of which presume that every viewpoint and practice carries the same weight. This fact is well exemplified in the statement, "you do your (sociocultural) thing, I'll do mine." Charles Taylor, in acknowledging the need for a multicultural politics of "mutual recognition," warns that the "peremptory demand for favorable judgments of worth is paradoxically—perhaps one should say tragically—homogenizing."[4] In granting a kaleidoscopic and irreducible plurality, it seems that historical consciousness (despite itself) induces a kind of homogenizing spectator-like neutrality toward the very differences that constitute this plurality. The danger is a kind of *empty universalism*, a vacuous monism of sorts that would nullify the integrity of genuine heterogeneity.

This sobering paradox, harkening back to Giordano Bruno, gets to the heart of the problem of historicism, and of the relativism that accompanies it. It also emerges as a dominant twentieth-century motif in the West, seeping into the broader cognitive and ethical horizons of various discourses—from cultural anthropology to the philosophy of language to postempiricist theories of science to both revisionist and postliberal theologies to the politics of difference. In point of fact, it has become part and parcel of the "postmodern," which is less a moment in time than a certain mood that stretches modernity to its breaking point. As we have seen, historicism surfaces as a consequence of Johann Gottfried Herder's philosophy even though it remains relatively unproblematized in his own thought. Nonetheless, the seeds of relativism are present, energizing an aftermath that leans heavily toward a critical skepticism, even disenchantment, which in principle deems all constructions of value and meaning incapable of providing objective resources for thought and action and therefore irrelevant. The gulf thus widens between fact and value, and Gotthold Lessing's "ugly ditch" makes its appearance again, opening up what has been called the "crisis of historicism." Put baldly, this crisis signifies the collapse of rational knowledge into contingent historical knowledge.[5] As Wilhelm Dilthey himself perceived, historicism leads ineluctably toward the question of how objective knowledge and judgment, truth and value, are possible at all if human knowing is local and contextual, historically and culturally conditioned.

Consequently, we can say that what historical consciousness gives with one hand it threatens to take away with the other, creating an unstable aporia that can be appraised in many ways. Some revel in the collapse of rational objectivism, turning the centerless and anarchic free-play of relativism into a kind of virtue (e.g., Friedrich Nietzsche and those who take up his mantle). Others lament the bankruptcy of contemporary cultural forms and look forward with nostalgia to the reappearance of a lost ideal (e.g., the later Martin Heidegger and Allen Bloom). Others strive against the specter of relativism in a more conservative and perhaps reactionary posture, reaffirming the importance of tradition through a postcritical return to premodern values (e.g., Alister MacIntyre or the radical orthodoxy of John Milbank). Still others—and I think appropriately—seek to resist radical historicism by rethinking rationality in a way that is historically conscious yet able to sustain the need for dialogic truth claims (e.g., Gadamer, Charles Taylor, and Jürgen Habermas). Whatever their peculiar thrust, however, each of these approaches assumes a similar starting predicament: the centerless polycentricism mobilized by historical consciousness, which simultaneously establishes yet annuls the centrifugal force of all finite perspectives. Indeed, it is this kind of Brunoesque two-sidedness that gives historical consciousness its peculiar sting, creating space for the emergence of a postmodern "pluralistic consciousness." The following discussion, then, will be directed toward illuminating the various elements and processes that contribute to the radicalization of historical consciousness into pluralistic consciousness, thus setting the stage for the constructive claims that will follow in chapters 3 and 4.

By canvassing certain intellectual and sociohistorical currents in the twentieth century, this chapter will depict how the contemporary pluralistic consciousness, as an outgrowth of the aporias of historicism, problematizes the issue of difference and pluralism with unprecedented vigor. My general thesis is this: *pluralistic consciousness entails a polyvalent and destablizing sense of "otherness"—one that is engendered by a cognitive and ethical privileging of difference vis-à-vis a postmodern extension of the historicist turn.* When the reality of globalization is refracted through such a "privileging of difference," a distinct kind of sensibility is created, exacerbating the issue of sociocultural relativism.[6] Put simply, pluralistic consciousness is historical consciousness in a postmodern shape: the experience of being placed contingently among equally placed others without a univocal or shared sense of place. As seen through the pluralistic consciousness, diversity is not merely the acknowledgment of numerical plurality, but the more trenchant recognition that there are many "centers" that are unobjectifiable and irreducible. Accordingly, the experience of the "other"—its foreign quality and difference from the "same"—has become the hallmark of present-day diversity.

And it is precisely this that allows us to speak of the differentiation of the many in our contemporary situation as a genuine "plurality." Noting how the "discovery of the plurality of cultures is never a harmless experience," Paul Ricoeur, writing in 1962, perceptively describes the traumatic effect of such an awareness:

> When we discover that there are several cultures instead of just one and consequently at the time when we acknowledge the end of a sort of cultural monopoly, be it illusory or real, we are threatened with the destruction of our own discovery. Suddenly it becomes possible that there are just *others*, that we ourselves are an "other" among others. All meaning and every goal having disappeared, it becomes possible to wander through civilizations as if through vestiges and ruins . . . in an interminable, aimless voyage.[7]

Pluralistic consciousness locates one's viewpoint and way of dwelling in the world as an "other among others," the symptom of an increasingly intertwined yet differentiated world, magnifying the centerless polycentrism brought on by historical consciousness. This involves a certain displacement of one's identity.

But the negative word is not the last word. I wish to suggest that intrinsic to this shocking and decentering experience there lies the promise of possibility—namely, the openness to, and practice of, genuine conversation or dialogue among differences, a conversation that itself displays and enacts human solidarity. Indeed, Ricoeur goes on to say that the experience of being an "other among others" is not fatal to all meaning and value, for while we can no longer practice the dogmatism of a single overarching truth or continue to encounter others by means of the logic of conquest or domination, we can indeed engage others communicatively through "a dramatic relation in which I affirm myself in my origins and give myself to another's imagination in accordance with his different civilization." The passage I refer to then concludes with a powerfully prophetic element:

> Human truth lies only in this process in which civilizations confront each other more and more with what is most living and creative in them. Man's history will progressively become a vast explanation in which each civilization will work out its perception of the world by confronting all others. But this process has hardly begun. It is probably the great task of generations to come.[8]

It is this kind of vision, which now more than ever challenges us toward an efficacious dialogical praxis of recognition, reciprocity, and reconciliation among differences, that I wish to draw out of pluralistic consciousness as a constructive project. Thus, I shall speak not simply of plurality, but of *pluralism*, an ethical vision of human dwelling together in and through varied sociocultural configurations.

With this larger aim in mind, the present chapter continues the story begun in chapter 1, making several diagnostic evaluations along the way. These, in turn, will lead into the more constructive and prescriptive arguments of chapters 3 and 4, which develop with an eye toward not only recognizing, as social theorist Craig Calhoun puts it, "fundamental differences of value," but also, and more importantly, appreciating the "positive value of difference."[9] Subsequently, chapters 5 and 6 shall bring this to a crescendo in terms of a philosophy of religious pluralism.

While it seems that we often seek to differentiate ourselves against the identitarian logic of sameness, it would also seem to be true that we seek to share, to belong, to establish fruitful connections of solidarity with others. Indeed, there is no recognizable difference not related to some background of common recognition; and there is no identity that forms itself without reference to some shared horizon of values.[10] Yet the postmodern sensibility calls this supposition into question. The challenge then is twofold: to envision (1) heterogeneous variety without yielding fragmentation and insularity and (2) solidarity and interconnectedness without yielding totalizing homogeneity. One thing is clear: pluralism is not so much a fact as it is a task to be achieved. And this task requires a thorough engagement with the postmodern.

HYPER-REFLEXIVITY: SITUATING FINITE REASON

Through its inherent double critique, which on the one hand dismantles the precritical house of authority and on the other reproaches the Enlightenment ideal of decontextualized reason, historical consciousness generates a vigorous momentum that carries out, and increasingly radicalizes, the critical and emancipatory project inaugurated by the Enlightenment, culminating in a posture of "hyper-reflexivity." Hyper-reflexivity is a critical historicist orientation that is relentlessly conscious of all standpoints, but most pointedly its own, as locally positioned in the ever-mobile flux and flow of historical life.[11] With the sharpest acumen, it underscores what Karl Marx called the "this-sidedness" of thinking, namely, that thought is socially constructed and related to historical circumstance and practice.[12] A self-subverting sense of irony thus befuddles any and all attempts to maintain cultural superiority or find any kind of privileged, final closure from one particular position within the currents of historical life. Correspondingly, hyper-reflexivity implies a devastating critique of the objectivist and universalist thrust of Enlightenment rationality. Just as no tradition can be absolute, neither can reason alone claim total jurisdiction over all discourse.

A crucial consequence follows: gone is the strict opposition between reason and tradition, objectivity and prejudice, truth and myth that characterized the Enlightenment's desire to inculcate rational autonomy. Gadamer succinctly demonstrates this kind of hyper-reflexive move in stating: "Real historical thinking must take account of its own historicity."[13] This self-referential "taking account of" has occupied the minds of the widest variety of thinkers throughout the past century and a half—from Dilthey, Karl Marx, and Nietzsche through Edmund Husserl, Max Weber, Heidegger, John Dewey and Ludwig Wittgenstein to Michel Foucault, Jacques Derrida, and Richard Rorty. As Susan Sontag acknowledges: "Perhaps once a marginal tic of consciousness, [the historicizing perspective is] now a gigantic, uncontrollable gesture—the gesture whereby man indefatigably patronizes himself."[14] Whether or not hyper-reflexivity constitutes a self-patronizing gesture, it is clear that Herder's organic contextual holism of meaning has become radicalized. An inevitable self-referentiality precludes any sure foundation or final closure, breaking reason itself open into a nonreducible and discontinuous plurality of determinate value-producing horizons of signification or multiverse: that is, the relativism of historicism in full-bloom.

The description of historicist hyper-reflexivity in the preceding paragraphs may resonate with familiarity to postmodern ears, and for good reasons, but we should be cautious about reading this as an exhaustion of all three moments of the Enlightenment project—that is (1) its emancipatory thrust, (2) its reflexivity, and (3) its claim to objective universality through reason. There are several reasons why.

First, while at odds with the disembedded rationalism of the third moment, the double critique of historical consciousness actually advances the first moment of the Enlightenment project in its freedom-making critique of normalizing heteronomy. For no point in history, no culture or tradition, can claim the privileged status of inevitability and superiority, of being a point of departure for measuring all other points. This is why Herder could speak out against the vicissitudes of colonialism; it betrayed an overt Eurocentrism that denigrated the intrinsic worth of other cultures.[15] Stimulated by historical consciousness, the rise of cultural anthropology trades on, as Kathryn Tanner puts it, the promotion of a "nonevaluative alternative to ethnocentrism" that in the end "furthers a humanistic project of social criticism."[16] This project, as we shall soon see, unfolds into a critique of totalizing discourses that seeks to expose and disrupt those systems that corrupt the genuine recognition of sociocultural differences. The consequences of this critique, in turn, spill over quite naturally into praxis-orientated sociopolitical approaches (e.g., Marxist and neo-Marxist). The process of unmasking and demystifying suppressive taken-for-granted conventions and norms is connected with the empowerment of those voices that have been subjugated or marginalized, and both activities embody the critical-emancipatory spirit of the Enlightenment project.

Second, as I pointed out in chapter 1, it is through the moment of reflexivity and self-criticism in the Enlightenment project that an awareness of, and sensitivity to, the contingencies of historical life is generated, increasingly pushing critical consciousness in the direction of an historical consciousness that begins to unravel—from the inside out—the ideal of a decontextualized and universal rational standpoint. Hyper-reflexivity is an extension of the same dynamism wherein critical reason extends a critique of itself, an interrogation which, as Foucault puts it, "simultaneously problematizes man's relation to the present, man's historical mode of being, and the constitution of the self as an autonomous subject," all of which are "rooted in the Enlightenment."[17] Struggling to become conscious of, define, and indeed create itself against the rejected past in order to direct its own expectation toward the horizon of the future, the reflexivity of the Enlightenment project becomes acutely aware of its own historical position, creating the need for a "critical ontology" of the present. This is most fruitfully conceived of not as a theory or body of doctrines but as "an attitude, an ethos, a philosophical life in which the critique of what we are is at one and the same time the historical analysis of the limits that are imposed on us and an experiment with the possibility of going beyond them."[18] The end product of such reflexivity, as Dilthey recognized, is an increased emphasis on human historicity, or in the words of Foucault, a raising of "the question of the historicity of thinking about the universal."[19] Rather than being objective, reason becomes contingent and contextual, a vehicle not for "discovering" truths that in principle tie all together, but for interpretively "constructing" truths relative to some sociocultural location.

Third, when joined together, the first and second moments of the Enlightenment project function progressively to call into question its third moment. The critique of Enlightenment reason emerges from within the Enlightenment project itself. Recognizing the contingency of all rational reflection yields the admission that reason itself, contrary to the hopes of the *philosophes* and Aufklärer, can serve and has actually served to mask violence and the repression of difference, providing rationale for imperialism and colonialism and thereby becoming an instrument of the very discourse it claims to reject. The noble ideals of reason are themselves contextual (not objective) and express a particular (not universal) worldview. Such ideals can become dangerous ideological tools of oppression when "objectivity" and "universality" are claimed ostensibly for the many but in reality legitimate the privileged priority of the few. One needs only to look at the history of the twentieth century to see that when touted as a foundational source of solidarity linking all provincialisms to one framework (cf. Kant's "universal standpoint"), reason can become totalitarian and difference-dissolving, negating the liberative and self-critical moments of the Enlightenment project.

By masquerading as what it is not and feigning neutrality, reason in effect becomes just one more manipulative and heteronomous tradition disguising the localized agenda of particular power-claims in the worst form of hypocrisy, invoking slavery in the name of freedom. Moreover, when absolutized under the banner of mastery and control, a decontextualized and disembedding reason suppresses the concrete and plural dimensions of human life, reducing everything to an identity that empties the world of all but instrumental value. Whether as state socialism, fascism, capitalism, or the empirical sciences, rationalist formalism—and its sibling, technocratic proceduralism—has the capacity to systematically impose itself on and reify reality.[20] Thus, there is a paradoxical tension built into critical consciousness between its liberative and self-critical moments, on the one hand, and its rationalizing and universalizing moment, on the other.[21] And the dramatic release of this tension culminates, I suggest, in the basic temperament of postmodernity.[22]

POSTMODERNITY: RADICAL ONTOLOGICAL CONTINGENCY AND THE CRITIQUE OF TOTALITY

Postmodern discourse represents a celebration of the first two moments of the Enlightenment project over and against the distortions of the third.[23] It is a consummation of the freedom-making and reflexive impulses of the critical consciousness originally linked to and empowered by Enlightenment rationalism; however, the privileging of universal and objective discourses is now replaced by a privileging of particularity through critical hyper-reflexivity, marking an abandonment of the

Enlightenment concept of reason. This privileging occurs in two interrelated impulses, each an inverse image of the other.

First, in the mode of affirmation, postmodernity involves an exaltation of radical contingency, historicity, and the resulting polycentrism. Existing self-consciously in the alleged "aftermath" of the collapse of Cartesian-Kantian foundationalism (Rorty) and the overcoming of metaphysics and its legacy of logocentrism (Heidegger and Derrida), postmodernity accents the constructed, socially conditioned, linguistically saturated, temporal, pragmatic, power-related, fluid, discontinuous, and pluriform—perhaps even indeterminate and fragmentary—character of truth.[24] For reason is finite and wholly immanent, subject to material and linguistic practices always already embedded concretely in heterogeneous sociohistorical horizons. The problem of Lessing's ugly, broad ditch vanishes, for in the end there are only the accidental truths of history. Necessary truths are usurped by the flux of finitude, with the exception of purely formal truths—that is, definition and tautology.

For this reason some see postmodernity as a "new historicism," a thinking of sociocultural difference and otherness in the postmetaphysical context of a polycentrism in which contingency has the last word.[25] In such a situation, there arises the need for what John D. Caputo calls a "radical hermeneutics," one that redescribes reason as a groundless and playful means of attending to difference, cultivating "an acute sense of the contingency of all social, historical, linguistic structures, an appreciation of their constituted character, their character as effects."[26]

Second, and correspondingly, the mood of postmodernity takes the negative shape of a resistance—a posture of incredulity, distrust, or even hostility toward universalizing and totalizing discourses, not simply because they are false, but because they are insidious, serving to suppress the play of difference and to exclude voices of otherness.[27] This resistance amounts to an ethically configured protest against the violence perpetrated by absolutizing and homogenizing depictions of truth. Its intended goal is to recognize, legitimate, and open up free-space for the local and particular to present itself as "other." Perhaps the best-known exemplification of this ethos of contestation is Jean-François Lyotard's definition of the postmodern as an "incredulity toward metanarratives"—meaning not merely a loss of faith in, but an attitude of suspicion toward those large-scale discourses that distinguish the modern, discourses that ostensibly operate as comprehensive interpretive frameworks for discerning the real but instead, argues Lyotard, tend to impose an artificial order on the genuine heterogeneity of things—whether as God, the ideal of progress, scientific positivism, or the ideology of Marxism or capitalism.[28]

Characterizing this sentiment as a "rage against reason," Richard J. Bernstein marks the increasing focus among twentieth-century authors on "images of domination, oppression, repression, patriarchy, sterility, violence, totality, totalitarianism, and even terror" in connection with what not so long ago "elicited associations with autonomy, freedom, justice, equality, happiness, and peace."[29] Such a "rage" is a critical response to misguided or corrupted identifications of (and here is Lessing again) accidental truths of history with truths of reason, the cost of which is a distortion and negation of the former. Caputo expresses this in the shape of an "ethics of dissemination," an ethics "directed at constellations of power, centers of control and manipulation, which systematically dominate, regulate, exclude," the intention of which is to "disrupt that momentum (of power), to assert difference."[30]

However construed, postmodernity in the posture of resistance involves a vigorous corrective therapy designed to "break the hold of" or "overcome" totalizing conceptions of reason, discourses of mastery and control, and to liberate authentic difference from the essentialist logic of the Same, a procedure embodying what Lyotard, perhaps not overdramatically, calls a "war on totality."[31] What is left over, then, is the free space of discontinuity and centerlessness, where the disintegration of heterogeneity blossoms into the unrepresentable and ever fluid shape of, as Foucault calls it, a "heterotopia."[32]

In both its celebrative and resistant impulses, the cognitive style of postmodernity entails a privileging of difference that amplifies the reality of pluralism, or in the words of Lyotard, "refines our sensitivity to differences and reinforces our ability to tolerate the incommensurable."[33] In this, postmodernity carries forth the double critique of a now hyper-reflexive historical consciousness. Simultaneously, hyper-reflexivity shapes the double-edged sword of postmodernity: it proffers both an acknowledgment of the radical ontological contingency of human life and a critique of those reductive discourses that threaten to repress the dignity of difference. Charles Jencks captures it succinctly: "Post-modernism means the end of a single world view and, by extension, 'a war on totality,' a resistance to single explanations, a respect for difference and a celebration of the regional, local and particular."[34] Obviously, as Lyotard observes, this implies "a major shift in the notion of reason. . . . The principle of a universal metalanguage is replaced by the principle of a plurality of formal and axiomatic systems."[35]

This does not, however, negate the Enlightenment project *tout court*; rather it is its continuation and reworking, perhaps even its radicalization. Lyotard himself agrees that the postmodern "is undoubtedly part of the modern."[36] And Anthony Giddens helps us understand why: "Rather than these developments [of postmodernity] taking us 'beyond modernity,' they provide a fuller understanding of the reflexivity inherent in modernity itself. Modernity is not only unsettling because of the circularity of reason, but because the nature of the circularity is ultimately puzzling. . . . Modernity turns out to be enigmatic to its core."[37] This "enigmatic" quality, I suggest, intimates the tension between the first two moments and the third moment of the Enlightenment project. Modernity's claim to normativity, objectivity, and universality becomes, through its own liberative and critically self-referential dynamic, increasingly questionable. Hyper-reflexivity is Enlightenment turned against itself.

The problem, however, is that the Enlightenment project stands or falls as one piece, as a threefold unit. That is, without some notion of an empowering and shared rationality—that is, a third moment—the first and second moments of the Enlightenment project lose their weight and efficacy. From what standpoint, then, should the freedom-making critique of heteronomy proceed? And by what standards should reflexive self-criticism proceed, or self-referential normativity be constituted? We seem to be caught in the throes of an insurmountable paradox. My contention is that, left to itself, the dynamism of hyper-reflexivity runs aground in a performative contradiction that undermines the positive value of difference, consequently thwarting the very pluralism it inaugurates. We can see how this occurs through a further examination of the twin impulses of postmodernity.

Radical Ontological Contingency

The affirmation of radical ontological contingency has its genesis, as just noted, in the rise of historical consciousness, but it becomes a major theme unifying various twentieth-century currents of thought as historical consciousness blossoms into hyper-reflexivity. There are numerous examples: the constructivism of Friedrich Nietzsche; the turn to ontological situatedness represented by Edmund Husserl's concept of the "life-world," and Martin Heidegger's understanding of *Dasein* as "Being-in-the-world"; the highlighting of the social as a primary locus of human practice and meaning characteristic of Karl Marx, Emile Durkheim, Max Weber, Karl Mannheim, Alfred Schutz, Peter L. Berger, and Thomas Luckmann; the so-called linguistic turn of Ludwig Wittgenstein and the philosophy of language; the hermeneutical programs of Hans-Georg Gadamer and Paul Ricoeur; the emergence of postpositivist theories of science in Thomas Kuhn and Paul Feyerabend; structuralist and poststructuralist thought in France, from Ferdinand de Saussure to Michel Foucault and Jacques Derrida; and the pragmatism of William James, through John Dewey, to the neopragmatism of Richard Rorty. In all of these, the dimension of finitude and contextuality in human life is thematized with unprecedented clarity as a post-metaphysical move away from objectivist and universalizing rationality. Jürgen Habermas summarizes the situation: "contextualism has become a manifestation of the spirit of the times. . . . [T]he experience of contingency is [today] a whirlpool into which everything is pulled: everything could also be otherwise, the categories of the understanding, the principles of socialization and of morals, the constitution of subjectivity, the foundation of rationality itself."[38]

For the purposes of the discussion in this chapter, however, I want briefly to center on the contributions of Rorty. Rorty is significant because he starkly expresses and pulls together many of the more radical implications of hyper-reflexivity, gathering motifs from Nietzsche, Heidegger, Wittgenstein, Kuhn, and Derrida—to name a few—and assembling them into a compelling, if not problematic, nonfoundationalist vision of radical ontological contingency. Rorty is also important because he provides us with a rich model of "conversation" that will prove instrumental—vis-à-vis Gadamer—in shaping the discussions throughout the remainder of this book.

Rorty presents a thoroughgoing contructivist contextual holism in the modality of an iconoclastic pragmatism. Beginning with his monumental *Philosophy and the Mirror of Nature*, Rorty attacks the ahistorical foundationalism of "traditional philosophy," which sees truth and rationality in the form of representational immediacy, as direct mirrors of the way things actually are, and in its stead promotes a nominalist and historicist picture of philosophy as "edifying," trained not on obtaining objective validity but rather on resisting closure and "keeping the conversation going" among varied interpretations.[39] Thus, in the absence of foundations, epistemology gives way to hermeneutics, the conversational art of interpretation being the best example of the open-ended give-and-take process that distinguishes truly Socratic philosophy. For there is no correspondence between word and reality that is not already the finite product of conventional usages and habits that are themselves caught up linguistic and social webs of relation.[40]

It is therefore useless to search for a vocabulary "closer" to the way things are in order to resolve conflicting assertions; interpretation goes "all the way down." Echoing Nietzsche's claim that "the value of the world lies in our interpretations . . . for—there is no 'truth,' "[41] Rorty states pointedly that "there is nothing deep-down inside us except what we have put there ourselves, no criterion that we have not created in the course of creating a practice, no standard of rationality that is not an appeal to such a criterion, no rigorous argumentation that is not obedience to our own conventions."[42] And precisely because truth is made rather than found, the perspectival and multivoiced nature of *conversation*, rather than the neutral and univoiced adjudications of reason, becomes significant, its success measured not by any pre-given standards or goals but by its continuance as an end in itself.[43]

"Truth," then, might be better cast in the pragmatist terms of what Rorty calls "solidarity"—that is, in shared habits and communal agreements, not in the realist sense of objectivity. Truth as solidarity is that which gains a certain amount of collective weight among interpreters during the ever-shifting procedure of conversation, rather than something that happens outside and regardless of such conversation.[44] Thus, solidarity is not achieved by being grounded in something more essential or objective, a common human nature, but by the reverse: "For pragmatists, the desire for objectivity is not the desire to escape the limitations of one's community, but simply the desire for as much intersubjective agreement as possible, the desire to extend the reference of 'us' as far as we can."[45] The "us" of community is both the starting and ending point. It is always a socially constructed consensus governed by time and chance, produced in the course of history, contingent and contextual, indeed, parochial and ethnocentric—that is, subject to the intersubjective practices that define an "us."[46]

Developing these themes further in his *Contingency, Irony, and Solidarity*, Rorty emphasizes the utter contingency of human language, selfhood, and community, but in a way that leads him to the positive vision of a public "liberal utopia" composed of private "ironists." Noting that all "human beings carry about a set of words which they employ to justify their actions, their beliefs, and their lives," which he calls their "final vocabulary," Rorty goes on to describe the ironist as one who "has radical and continuing doubts about the final vocabulary she currently uses, because she has been impressed by other (such) vocabularies," who "realizes that argument phrased in her present vocabulary can neither underwrite nor dissolve these doubts," and who "does not think that her vocabulary is closer to reality than others, that it is in touch with a power not herself."[47] Final vocabularies are necessary vehicles for making sense of, coping with, and functioning in the world; they inform our deepest convictions and most meaningful practices, defining our "selves" and our "cultures." But here's the rub: they are "final" in that there is *no noncircular recourse to anything beyond them*; they are as far one can go with language.[48]

It is the recognition of their final vocabulary's radical historical contingency, its unnecessaryness, which makes ironists so different from what Rorty calls "metaphysicians," those who seek to ensure validity for their final vocabulary by connecting it to some "single permanent reality to be found behind the many temporary appearances," vindicating finality not just for themselves but for all people. Ironists recognize that anything can be made to "look good or bad by being redescribed," and are "never quite able to take themselves seriously because [they are] always aware that the terms in which they describe themselves are subject to change, always aware of the contingency and fragility of their final vocabularies, and thus of their selves."[49] Because, as the later Wittgenstein suggests, language, selfhood, and community are finite and provisional constructions informed by particular "language-games" and connected to distinct sociocultural "forms of life," Rorty's ironist must be intensely self-conscious.[50] An ironist is hyper-reflexive.

Furthermore, an ironist must be self-creative. Why? Because the criterion for resolving doubts about one's final vocabulary is "autonomy." An ironist is one who tries "to get out from under inherited contingencies and make his own contingencies, get out from under an old final vocabulary and fashion one which will be all his own," redescribing the past in new terms, "thereby becoming able to say, 'Thus I willed it.' "[51] And we accomplish this by "enlargening our acquaintance," imaginatively engaging other vocabularies and playing vocabularies off one another dialectically, thereby redescribing ourselves in light of other vocabularies.[52] In this way, Rorty takes up the first and second moments of the Enlightenment project while eschewing the normative content of the third, viewing final vocabularies as imaginative "poetic achievements" rather than the fruits of argument or diligent inquiry into an objective truth independent of language.[53] Reflexive self-description in the form of a will-to-power now takes the place of rational foundations.[54] In fact, the poet is the visionary and cultural hero who is able to redescribe her or his final vocabulary, imagining new kinds of self-descriptions and empowering new vistas of human possibility.[55] Logos becomes mythos in the name of poetic freedom. But how does this lead to a vision of a public and liberal utopia?

Rorty's thesis is that there is a crucial freedom gained in the ironic recognition of the contingency of all final vocabularies, a freedom that conjures a certain kind of society. He cites with approval Isaiah Berlin's use of Joseph Schumpeter, who said, "To realize the relative validity of one's convictions and yet stand for them unflinchingly, is what distinguishes a civilized man from a barbarian." Rorty capitalizes then on Berlin's follow-up comment, "To demand more than this is perhaps a deep and incurable metaphysical need; but to allow it to determine one's practice is a symptom of an equally deep, and more dangerous, moral and political immaturity."[56] For Rorty, the virtue of the ironist posture is its therapeutic corrective against the propensity of "metaphysical need" to evade contingency. Irony gives up the hope for a universal rational standpoint, which fails to promote genuine solidarity because it cannot help but bring conversation to an artificial closure, endowing one finite and situated interpretation among many with an unwieldy authority. In his *The Consequences of Pragmatism*, Rorty states succinctly what this entails:

> To accept the contingency of starting-points is to accept our inheritance from, and our conversation with, our fellow-human as our only source of guidance. . . . If we give up this hope [to find one axiomatic starting-point for determining practice], we shall lose what Nietzsche called "metaphysical comfort," but we may gain a renewed sense of community. Our identification with our community—our society, our political tradition, our intellectual heritage—is heightened when we see this community as *ours* rather than *nature's*, *shaped* rather than *found*, one among many which men have made. In the end, the pragmatists tell us, what matters is our loyalty to other human beings clinging together against the dark, not our hope of getting things right.[57]

Irony, thus, is not a call for despair, but for a kind of virtue that reinvigorates our desire for community, opening up free space for conversation through a reflexive acknowledgment of the "relative validity" of all final vocabularies.

This is why Rorty advocates the "Socratic virtues—willingness to talk, to listen to other people, to weigh the consequences of our actions upon other people."[58] For they engender a certain kind of society: one bound by no (Platonic) metadiscourses or transcendent rules, no mandates of Truth or Reason, a community of free inquirers held together only by ongoing conversational encounters, where open-mindedness is fostered for its own sake and consensus emerges by persuasion, not force.[59] Such a society, a foundationless pragmatist paradise, is what Rorty calls a "liberal utopia":

> A liberal society . . . is one which has no purpose except freedom, no goal except willingness to see how such encounters go and to abide by the outcome. . . . To sum up, the citizens of my liberal utopia would be people who had a sense of the contingency of their language of moral deliberation, and thus of their consciences, and thus of their community. They would be liberal ironists—people . . . who combined commitment with a sense of the contingency of their own commitment.[60]

Thus Rorty's private ironist is a public liberal, an anti-authoritarian whose social hope lies in the ad hoc solidarity forged not by something we all have in common, but by happenstance communities of conversation.[61]

It is clear, then, that Rorty advocates a contextual holism—what he somewhat wryly, perhaps even surreptitiously, calls an "ethnocentric" parochialism—that nourishes and explicitly seeks to maintain a thoroughgoing pluralism. For it is impossible to speak from anywhere but one's own local tradition with its contingent vocabulary: from the "us" of a community.[62] Because there is no ahistorical and universal standpoint, pragmatist Rorty believes that we cannot help but "attach a special privilege to our own community," unable to avoid being methodologically "ethnocentric." That is, we "divide the human race into the people to whom one must justify one's beliefs and the others. The first group—one's *ethnos*—comprises those who share enough of one's beliefs to make fruitful conversation possible."[63] And the "others" (in principle) must also do the same.

Ethnos is the starting-point of all discourse, deciding what is important, meaningful, and justified according to particular, socially located criteria internal to its language-game.[64] To be "rational," then, means to hold certain beliefs confirmed within the interpretive horizons of one's own group, to hold justified beliefs—beliefs that are efficacious or useful in yielding some specific form of happiness.[65] So to stand for one's convictions means to identify with a community and to make use of the finite and provisional self-descriptive tools provided by its vocabulary.[66] This is why final vocabularies cannot be justified except by way of redescriptive circularity. Accordingly, instead of all languages converging ideally upon a single reality, a universal and objective nexus of validity, we have the opposite: a proliferation of languages spreading out in various directions into a polyphony of lived realities, a multiplicity of ethnocentrisms.[67]

Yet Rorty's polycentrism is not a bland homogeneity of equality among all ethnocentrisms, for some forms of ethnocentrism are better than others, in particular, the liberal form devoted to "enlargening itself, to creating an ever larger and more variegated *ethnos*."[68] Rorty's liberal utopia is, in a real sense, dedicated to the privileging of differences in a radical pluralism, "to the maximization of opportunities for individual variation, and group variation insofar as the latter facilitates the ability of individuals to recreate themselves," not to thwarting reflexive self-descriptions by becoming authoritarian—that is, insofar as it is "facilitated by a consensus that there is no source of authority other than the free agreement of human beings."[69] But precisely how is the alleged consensus of conversational solidarity to be achieved in an unrestrained proliferation of ethnocentrisms? Would such a system not spinter conversation into relativistic fragmentation and discord, or worse, give free reign to distortive and prejudicial forms of communication, tacitly underwriting even the most insidious, dangerous, and violent of perspectives?

On this point Rorty's position becomes a bit ambiguous, evoking charges of relativism and cultural chauvinism, even universalism. Though he seeks to evade the accusation of relativism and, based upon his liberal interpretation of "Socratic virtues," wants to uphold an ideal of conversation that is inclusive of the widest variety of participants, Rorty is ultimately able to offer neither a defense nor a positive estimation of what his vision entails, except by rhetorical re-assertion and redescription. This amounts to saying that his position is simply "what he happens (contingently) to think." His metacritique functions as a non-position, reducing his own final vocabulary to one among others, the veracity of which cannot be asserted. For as he claims, there is no noncircular way of defending one's final vocabulary, one's convictions, for any appeal made to some set of defining criteria is already referenced and constituted internally by the language-game in which one operates.[70] Legitimation means intralinguistic coherence and continued success, not representational closeness to reality.

Indebted to Donald Davidson, Rorty correctly asserts, however, that this does not dig an unbridgeable chasm of solipsistic incommensurability between interpretive schemes. For if there is no neutral ground, then we cannot intelligibly say that conceptual schemes are utterly different, that there is no such thing as an unlearnable or untranslatable language.[71] Rorty's position, then, is not kin to the self-refuting relativism that states that any belief is as good or true as another. There is no "objective" way to say this without a performative contradiction. Even if there is no commensurate "human nature" or "ideal culture," our linguistic horizons overlap enough so that another culture is always at least minimally understandable by the parochial lights of our own cultural perspective—for after all, we do in fact communicate.

This notwithstanding, Rorty's ethnocentric contextualism leaves him not in a benign but in a vicious circle, unable to state why conversation is better than closure, why the Socratic virtues are morally desirable—indeed, why "there is nothing in each of us, no common human nature, no built-in human solidarity, to use as a moral reference point"[72]—except by asserting that it happens to work better for "us." But according to this "ethnocentric" principle, there are numerous Platonists, Kantians, and Communitarians as well as Dictators and CEOs whose "us" might think otherwise. On what basis, then, should a pluralist conversation inclusive of maximally variegated voices proceed, if it should proceed at all? Indeed, how public or globally "useful" is a conversation that is only for and about "us"?

Rorty appears to soften his ethnocentrism by "going moralist." Slipping a crypto-universalism in through the back door, he suggests that the ironist "takes the morally relevant definition of a person, a moral subject, to be 'something that can be humiliated.'" He thus argues that there is a sense of (trans-regional and nonethnocentric?) human solidarity, "based on a sense of a common danger, not a common possession or a shared power."[73] According to Rorty, people want to be described in their own terms and treated kindly, to be self-defining and not marginalized or destroyed, and this "anthropology" creates the need for a liberal quasi-maxim: being cruel is the worst thing humans can do to one another. Thus, liberals must enlargen their acquaintance and become aware of, and sensitive to, the suffering of others, forging a solidarity "thought of as the ability to see more and more traditional differences (of tribe, religion, race, customs, and the like) as unimportant when compared with similarities with respect to pain and humiliation—the ability to think of people wildly different from ourselves as included in the range of 'us.' "[74]

As appealing as this sounds, however, Rorty, by virtue of his position, retracts its essentialist or transcendental-sounding character of this by showing how—in the mode of irony—cruelty and solidarity are primarily social constructs that can be made to look different in varied contexts.[75] In the end, "There is nothing to people except what has been socialized into them—their ability to use language, and thereby to exchange beliefs and desires with other people."[76] Rorty, at his best, wants to (and does) make universal claims about what is and is not the case, to initiate a program, to be cosmopolitan in his ethnocentrism, but he ends up a liberal ideologue. For what one culture (e.g., Rorty's) takes as cruelty, another may take as goodwill.[77] Thus, as Rorty claims, "the pragmatist, dominated by the desire for solidarity, can only be criticized for taking his own community *too* seriously. He can only be criticized for ethnocentrism, not relativism."[78] But as Anindita Niyogi Baslev perceptively queries, "If virtues, i.e., moral attitudes, were ethnocentric, rooted exclusively in the soil of particular cultures and traditions, how can one advocate (that is, consistent with this theory) spreading the same virtues beyond the boundary of a given tradition or culture?"[79] Simply sidestepping the charge of relativism will not do, for anything can be made to look good via redescription. Where is the "social hope" in this?

Thus, while on the surface a private and reflexive irony seems to be the best way of promoting publicly liberal behaviors, it slips all too easily into postures of indifference toward difference (e.g., bourgeois liberal "tolerance") or the co-opting inclusivism of assimilation (expanding the range of "us"). For the ironist, the "other" is either too unlike "us" to take seriously as a live option,[80] or it is enough like "us" to persuade, thereby extending "the reference of 'us' as far as *we* can" by socializing the other into our liberal language-game.[81] Far from maximizing and celebrating the play of differences, such a vision of conversation seems to be a bit facile and optimistic, as if "keeping it going" is all that it takes.

Rorty overlooks the severe constraints on mutuality that are implied by his ethnocentric sense of conversation, which can lead to pernicious cultural chauvinism and power play, all in the name of "solidarity." As Rorty himself admits, there is a fuzzy line between persuasion and force, for there is no neutral way to adjudicate between contingent vocabularies other than by playing those vocabularies off one another.[82] If the "us" of a "liberal utopia" is specified simply as whatever the prevailing upshot of conversational encounters turns out to be, then what prevents distortions of communication and manipulations of power from negating plurality?[83] There are indeed differences that corrupt, differences with the power to impose their own agenda; but Rorty seems unable to name them. And because of this, his anti-authoritarianism could easily become the rationale behind more subtle forms of authoritarian or elitist ideology and practice. We must be suspicious of collapsing the distinction between truth (rightness and justice) and consensus-driven utility, always asking the question: why and for whom is something useful and effective in producing happiness and well-being?[84] For as is often the case, one group's consensus can mean another's exclusion or oppression.[85]

Rorty's radically contextual perspectivism is loaded from the start, signifying a one-way assimilative process of incorporating what is alien into our (now expanded) vocabulary, of enlargening our interpretive horizon through an "inclusion" of otherness which, in effect, neutralizes it by rendering it "ours."[86] The other becomes instrumentalized, absorbed, and nullified in the process of the "persuasive" actualization of one's own world, one's own final vocabulary.[87] Ethnocentrism becomes egoism in social form, and tolerance is then just a nice word for a deeper and more insidious intolerance. Given the alleged self-doubting reflexivity of the ironist, this is truly ironic.

Rorty's recent discussion of religion exemplifies this problem. In *Achieving Our Country*, he goes so far as to promote the American utopian ideal of democracy as a kind of "religion," citing with favor both Dewey and Walt Whitman.

> They dreamed that Americans would break the traditional link between the religious impulse, the impulse to stand in awe of something greater than oneself, and the infantile need for security, the childish hope of escaping from time and chance. They wanted to preserve the former and discard the latter. They wanted to put hope for a casteless and classless America in the place traditionally occupied by knowledge of the will of God. They wanted that utopian America to replace God as the unconditional object of desire.[88]

It seems here that the benign ethnocentrism of Rorty's liberal utopia *is* America; it takes the place of God, functioning as a redescription of religion *as* democratic politics. One wonders, however, whether such optimism does not belie Rorty's own nonfoundationalism, reintroducing a new foundationalism into the discussion, one that looks and behaves just like America.[89]

Rorty tries to eschew the potential hazards of such a position by acknowledging that the ideal is not already real but is rather a contingent future, a "social hope for what might become real"—a future in which the life of individuals will "become unthinkably diverse and social life unthinkably free."[90] To this end, in "Pragmatism and Romantic Polytheism," Rorty suggests substituting religion with poetry.[91] Why poetry? Because it avoids the perils of institutionalized monotheism, offering instead inspiration in sacral visions that flower unavoidably into multiple strands: polytheism. Poets are priest-surrogates who can shape and consecrate a pluriform "us." Indeed, Rorty advocates a "religion" of literature.[92] Nonetheless, the cat gets let out of the bag when democracy itself—as the United States—becomes enshrined as the "greatest poem."[93] God is replaced with a pantheon, to be sure, but it is a deified "us." As Jason Boffetti quips, this kind of "quasi-religious zealotry" is disconcerting.[94] A new form of crypto-universalizing tantamount to proselytizing threatens to corrupt the very pluralism it seeks to maintain. Rorty's redescription of "religion" is ethnocentrism writ large.

For these reasons, Rorty's vision does not seem to be sufficiently critical and constructive for carrying forth the freedom-making and reflexive moments of the Enlightenment project. The end result is a fideism that winds up undermining the very ideas of freedom-from-domination and self-creativity that Rorty so admirably champions.[95] While Rorty is right to highlight human contingency and the fact that solidarity must be created through imaginative vision and ongoing conversation, the larger process of inculcating hope and the "willingness to live with plurality"[96] requires a more empowering and creative strategy than simply evading the foundationalist question of universal validity and letting the resulting plurality go free, keeping the conversation going in American form.[97] The best of Rorty's subversive rhetoric against those he disagrees with (foundationalists and/or nonliberals) loses its sting if it is simply a redescription that reflexively works better for "us" now than "them" in the past, across the sea, or in the slums of Calcutta. Whereas the later Heidegger waited expectantly for a god to save, Rorty must simply wait and see where the winds of the poets blow—and his ship seems to have no rudder, except perhaps as an ethnocentric, Americanized "polytheist religion." In this, however, Rorty ends up echoing Rudyard Kipling's famous quip: "All nice people like Us are We / And everybody else is they."[98]

The Critique of Totality

Whereas Rorty might be criticized for his lack of the sense of tragedy in human life and for failing to capture adequately the systemic dangers that all discursive practices present to human solidarity,[99] another trajectory of postmodernity dramatizes the tragic consequences of the corruptive power of language and rationality. That is, rather than celebrating the *jouissance* of polycentrism engendered by an affirmation of contingency, it seeks, in a more negative mode, to expose, name, contest, and dismantle human forms of theory and action that claim a totalizing hold on reality. Any system of communication that feigns neutrality and universality is suspect, for it works in subtle ways to homogenize, regulate, distort, suffocate, marginalize, and/or enslave differences. The end product is domination. Hence, as was stated earlier, this postmodern trajectory entails an ethos of protest against modernity's penchant for rational metanarratives, in particular against the disembedding universalizing rationality of the Enlightenment project's third moment. Taking my cue from Lyotard's phrase, "war on totality,"[100] which draws upon Emmanuel Levinas's use of the word *totality*, I shall call the postmodern resistance against universal reason a "critique of totality."[101] Totality here means the enclosing embrace of the same, a vision of reality that reduces all difference to its own logic, absorbing plurality into its sway. There is nothing outside totality; it is a closed immanence. Therefore, the aspiration of the critique of totality, through its critical unmasking of the repressive assimilationist logic behind metanarratives, is the emancipation of the other from the grip of totalizing discursive practices. This opens up the play of differences.

The critique of totality has its genesis in the freedom-making and self-critical components of the Enlightenment project, but is a product of the loss of faith in the normative limit-function of abstract reason to carry through the intention of the Enlightenment's first two moments. Whereas in Herder and Dilthey we see a turning away from Enlightenment reason through an increasingly historicist focus on sociocultural particularity, the left-wing Hegelianism of Marx, mediated through Ludwig Feuerbach, produces a different strategy of critique, one equally historically conscious—that is, an immanent materialist critique of ideology.[102] Focused on the concrete praxis-oriented foundations of theory, Marx set his sight on uncovering and overcoming false universals used to mask the exploitation of human beings. For him, all ideas are informed by, and are a product of, specific material socioeconomic conditions, reflecting the existing order of a society.[103] Insofar as those prevailing thought-forms in a society exhibit and serve to legitimate the self-interest of the dominant class, ideas are "ideological," comprising a "false consciousness" that either consciously or unconsciously claims to name reality, to be universal, self-evident, and axiomatic, but serves instead to mask inequity and rationalizes the status quo of the established order, "alienating" thought from the genuine social being of persons.

Human thought and culture, being historical, is conditioned by socioeconomic structures of power, related intrinsically to a field of action. Thus, as Marx bluntly put it, "The ruling ideas of each age have ever been the ideas of its ruling class."[104] Contextualism then, in Marx's case, hinges on material productive practices, adding a new critical twist to historical consciousness and its affirmation that there is no such thing as decontextualized or disembedded reason. By highlighting the "this-sidedness" of all knowledge, its social and material position and aim, Marx sought to expose the structural evils of capitalist bourgeois elitism—with its fiction of a free market based on private ownership—and to propose an alternative system designed to liberate and ensure the well-being of the wider human race. His concept of critique—principally of political economy, but secondarily of the cultural, religious, and philosophical discourses that serve it—is motivated by an understanding of ideology as an unhistorical and systematic distortion of reality, an illusion, a false construction that can and should be challenged, removed, and replaced. Social theory, therefore, functions as an ethical gesture. It clears the field of ideological distortions and, in so doing, participates in the dialectical and world-historical inevitability of a progressive (teleological) emancipation. Marx portrayed this emancipation as the self-actualization of the proletariat in a classless society. For in the final analysis, the point of theory is not just to interpret, but to change the world.[105]

Developing in the shadow of Marx, yet chastened by the failed project of communism and by the horrors of fascism and world war, certain twentieth-century figures and movements expanded Marx's critique of ideology into a broader critique of totalitalizing reason. The crucial contributing factor was the collapse of the notion of emancipatory progress and a growing suspicion of reason as its means, causing many to drop Marx's teleological optimism and to replace it with a more pessimistic vision. Weber, for instance, saw the technocratic rationality spawned by the Enlightenment—represented in the exchange system of capitalism, in the positivism of the natural sciences, and in the mechanization of modern industrialization—as progressively dominating the social world, trapping human beings in an "iron cage" that measures and so instrumentalizes human life according to objective laws. The lived world is thereby "disenchanted," subject to a single logic of formal, calculable, and abstract rationality. Such a rationality seeks to master and dominate all in its path, the human dimension of which is exemplified in the rise of bureaucratic systems of social organization whose focus is efficiency and productivity at the price of genuine community. This endangers the very freedom and democracy upon which modern society is built.[106] Human history does not automatically advance with the onset of rational autonomy; it becomes retrogressive.

Picking up on Weber's critique, the "critical theory" of Frankfurt School authors, from Theodor Adorno, Max Horkheimer, Herbert Marcuse, and Walter Benjamin to Jürgen Habermas, pressed the point that Enlightenment rationality in the shape of science and technology, which holds out the shining promise of achievable well-being and freedom from domination (both by natural and historical forces), has actually served to foster heteronomy, becoming a vehicle for oppression and suffering. The fundamental claim of the Frankfurt School is that, in purporting to be "universal" and "objective," scientific and technological rationality uncritically appropriates an ideological distortion whose hidden logic is violent, repressive, and totalitarian, legitimating a societal and economic system built on the calculability, abstract equivalence, and exchangability of things and persons.[107]

Because of this, argue the critical theorists, reason becomes irrational barbarism and loses its emancipatory and self-critical edge, reduced to a technique of productivity and standardization in the service of control and domination. One result is what Horkheimer and Adorno called the "culture industry," where individual things and persons are commodified and have value only insofar as they have a generalized, functional purpose in facilitating, reproducing, and administering the ideology of the status quo. This can only be the product of material forces, for "the basis on which technology acquires power over society is the power of those whose economic hold over society is greatest."[108] Technology is thus a reifying and totalizing ideology, repressing heterogeneity as an agent of identity by turning thought into an instrument that "objectifies itself to become an automatic, self-activating process; an impersonation of the machine that it produces itself so that ultimately the machine can replace it."[109] Progress thus spawns its reverse, dehumanizing through manipulation and mastery in the name of scientific "objectivity."

Here, the Enlightenment's third moment forgets and abrogates the positive achievements of its first and second moments, becoming an ideologically comprised concept of instrumental reason. Reason loses its power to distinguish between reality and ideology-illusion and becomes servant to the status quo.[110] Reason still retains a power to resist, only now it is a resistance to anything that does not conform to calculability and resists reduction to the interests of an administered totality.[111] This is indeed what motivated Adorno to state, contra Hegel, that "the whole is the false."[112] For "the whole" leads to a systematic denial of difference, to the banishment of the particular—to imperialism, to repression, to violence, to war: to Auschwitz, the Gulag, and Hiroshima. Critical theory, then, seeks to preserve space for critical thought within and against the identitarian and totalizing logic of instrumental rationality. Its aim: to free human relations from the repressive (even annihilating) effect of homogenizing reifications.

In this way, the critical theory of the Frankfurt School foreshadows the more recent poststructuralist work of Foucault, who represents a dramatic continuation of the postmodern critique of totality.[113] While repristinating many of their more salient themes, Foucault moves beyond the critical theorists by radicalizing Marx's critique of ideology in an overtly Nietzschean direction.

Though he shuns being branded a "postmodern" thinker, Foucault's work illustrates the impulse toward "resistance" perhaps more poignantly than that of any other in his generation. He does this through a rigorous employment and constant reworking of the fundamental principle that human knowledge is a "discursive formation," a malleable construction or fabrication that we have need of but that is ideological to the core, produced via a will-to-power (or in Foucault's words, a "will to knowledge") related intrinsically to material practices and sociohistorical matrices of power.[114] Reason's alleged show of order, continuity, and universality must therefore be exposed for what it is: one local discursive practice among many particular and heterogeneous practices whose productive force has gained hegemonic sway and become "normalized" through a series of strategic alignments, struggles, and clashes that constrict the play of alternative discursive practices.

Accordingly, modalities and mechanisms of exercised power shape human relations by determining "the forms and possible domains of knowledge."[115] Notions like truth, the self, or justice are not objects out there in the world, waiting to be discovered or otherwise corroborated by a benign logic of consensus; rather, they are human inventions that play out in complex power relations, put to work in the service of specific historical configurations and their techniques of production and repression.[116] There is neither value-free neutrality nor universality in human knowledge, for all objects are in a sense creations of specific fields of knowledge, coming into existence with the discourse formations that identify and display them.[117] Power designates a certain space that produces "acceptable" knowledge, and knowledge produces human reality, self-formation, and social commerce. Lineages of "truth" thus arise with the privileging of certain discursive practices in the ongoing interplay of power structures.[118] Or in Foucault's words, truth is "a system of ordered procedures for the production, regulation, distribution, circulation, and operation of statements . . . linked in a circular relation with systems of power which produce and sustain it, and to effects of power which it induces and which extends it."[119] There is no "outside" of power, no disinterested discourse. Power, in a way, functions for Foucault as an historicized transcendental—a condition that makes truth possible.[120]

As a result, the very notion of rational order itself becomes suspect. For "reason" is a sociopolitical reign of conformity which, in claiming to bear universal value, actually works for and administers to the interests of the powerful. Reason, then, is inherently hegemonic, linking truth with technologies of domination. Knowledge is not only constructed; it is also a specific violence, a pernicious mechanism of repression and exclusion.[121] This is precisely why Foucault links the humanism of the Enlightenment not with liberation but with coercion and terror. For "humanity" is defined by the Enlightenment as a common "rational subjectivity," and this yields specific practices that systematically cut away, marginalize, regulate, or manipulate alternate discourses as "irrational." Foucault produces a litany of examples to illustrate his point, from psychiatric treatments, penal systems, educational programs, to social welfare.

Foucault, therefore, is not as interested in discerning truth from falsity in any particular knowledge claim as he is in bringing to light *how* certain discursive formations have functioned historically to subjugate alternative and heterogeneous knowledges. His aim—like that of Derrida—is to historicize and uncover the contingent status of all human ideas and institutions, thus removing their false air of necessity or inevitability. But more specifically, working as a critical and self-reflexive historian, Foucault tells the story of the past as a "history of the present," seeking to shake lose the plurality of histories that constitute ourselves (the heterogeneous and discontinuous heritages and power-events that lurk behind our own identities) from what has been presented to us as univocal, continuous, and normative—that is, totalizing. He hopes, through this, to open up new vistas of possibility and freedom for the play of multiple discursive practices.[122] Consequently, critique is fueled not by the third moment of the Enlightenment project, as "the search for formal structures with universal value, but rather as a historical investigation into the events that have led us to constitute ourselves and to recognize ourselves as subjects of what we are doing, thinking, saying."[123]

Foucault's point is this: we are not the products of innocuous conversations, benign ethnocentricities, or innocent traditions. *Contra* the historicism of authors like Gadamer and Rorty, the "history which bears and determines us has the form of a war rather than that of a language: relations of power, not relations of meaning."[124] This leads Foucault to claim that history is a polyvalent and disseminating drama of an "endlessly repeated play of dominations."[125] The history of who "we" are is itself produced and governed by regimes of power that strategically impose direction and order, obfuscate their own locality and contingency, and thereby become insidious. Thus, an "historical ontology of ourselves" entails a (freedom-making and self-reflexive) critical labor directed at disrupting totalizing macroefforts toward closure by exposing their origins in material power relations at the microlevel. History is a subversive or "curative" science whose goal is to "disclose dispersions and differences" and name the "instinctive violence" perpetrated by the will to knowledge in regimes of power, opposing subtle injustices particularly as they constitute the present.[126]

Owing a debt to Nietzsche, Foucault's sense of critical history is not hermeneutical; rather it "is genealogical in its design and archaeological in its method."[127] It is genealogical in that it strives to show how taken for granted forms of teleology—including the search for origins or any metahistorical ideal—are really the play of power and chance woven artificially together in a broken and discontinuous line of historical effects.[128] And it carries this out archaeologically by excavating to unearth hidden discontinuities, all in an effort to establish "that we are difference, that our reason is the difference of discourses."[129] There is no organic and contextual holism of meaning and continuity, as "traditional history" would have it, but only the ambiguity, disparity, and strife of "effective history" (*wirkliche Historie*); history, as it actually is, is "a profusion of entangled events," for a "true historical sense confirms our existence among countless lost events, without a landmark or a point of reference."[130] There is neither a single point of origin nor an identical meaning that displays itself in successive configurations. There are only heterogeneous fragments that occasionally come together with varying results, splaying in indiscriminate directions, substitutions, inclusions, reversals, displacements, and conquests. This shatters "the unity of man's being through which it was thought that he could extend his sovereignty to the events of his past."[131]

Unlike Rorty, Foucault maintains that cultures and traditions (and selves) are not internally coherent wholes, unified ethnocentric fields of continuity, but rather are multivalent and ever-shifting webs of conflicting and disseminating power relations, having more the character of dissensus than consensus, of difference than identity. For Foucault, however, the waters of this historical sense become even murkier and more pluralized as the historian takes account of his or her own historicity. Since there can be no objective or universal history, genealogy must become explicitly self-reflexive as "the vertical projection of its own position," caught up in the movement of its own descent and emergence, wherein the past becomes self-consciously "fictioned" in order to expose, recast, even remake, the present.[132] And it is precisely at this "murky and pluralized" point that the liberative moment of Foucault's critical historical project stands out with bold clarity.

There is a pervasive ethical thrust to Foucault's work, a thrust that constantly beckons even in his most starkly pessimistic moments. As he suggests in the revealing essay, "What Is Enlightenment?" written just before his untimely death, a critical ontology of ourselves via "historico-critical reflection" is the positive legacy bequeathed by the Enlightenment, ushering in a philosophical ethos or attitude "in which the critique of what we are is at one and the same time the historical analysis of the limits that are imposed on us and an experiment with the possibility of going beyond them," an ethos that involves "a patient labor giving form to our impatience for liberty."[133] Foucault does not stand as an aloof observer, but offers a diagnosis and critique of our current situation, not from an outside objective perspective, but from within the field of normalizing power relations. This of course assumes that such power relations have not succeeded yet in totalizing all practices, in closing off the possibility for critique, for envisioning "the limits which we may go beyond . . . as free beings."[134] Foucault, thus, does not lock us in an "iron cage" of totalizing power relations from which there is no escape. Yet the task, according to Foucault, is not to free truth from power, to look "behind" or "underneath" power in order to get to some original "truth" or system of justice that has been corrupted and ideologically distorted. Rather, the task is "to give new impetus, as far and wide as possible, to the undefined work of freedom."[135] And this means unmasking and breaking the hold of totality through rigorous genealogical and archaeological tactics of dispersion, dissemination, displacement, and disruption—ultimately revealing discontinuity within continuity, difference within identity, and heterogeneity within homogeneity.

In this way, critique unleashes what might be called a "truth-effect." A space is opened up for resistance and change, for power relations to be altered and heretofore repressed discursive practices to be recovered in their differences and granted the freedom to act and exercise power in unrestrained and novel ways.[136] Indeed, as Foucault acknowledges, freedom is the condition of power.[137] And freedom-making self-definition (in the lineage of the Enlightenment) is the goal of critique, even if we have "to give up hope of our ever acceding to any complete and definitive knowledge of what may constitute our historical limits . . . [and are] always in the position of beginning again."[138] What is at stake is the question: "How can the growth of capabilities be disconnected from the intensification of power relations?"[139] And the goal is liberty. Yet Foucault's vision is not "utopian," for it is primarily deconstructive, rather than constructive. Instead, he advocates a "heterotopia," one designated by the free-space of discontinuity in which the disintegration of heterogeneity blossoms in an ever fluid and open-ended shape.[140] This is why Foucault's harsh denunciation of totalizing discursive practices, in its Nietzschean mode of hyper-reflexivity, makes a valuable contribution to postmodernity. It dissolves false continuities and singular histories, paying attention instead to ruptures and disparities, to the difference that "we" are.

Despite the ethical nature of Foucault's resistance to totalizing normalization, however, this more deconstructive program leaves us in the dark about redemptive hope, giving us only the faintest glimpses of what it might entail in a more positive sense—that is, the value-claims it proposes and the ideals toward which it aspires. Of course, his own Nietzschean disposition preempts any normative vision, any overt talk about, for example, the Enlightenment ideals of dignity and equality (because of a suspicion of "humanism"). Nonetheless, some productive vision, some explicit retrieval of rationality in the form of validity claims seems necessary if Foucault's critique is to have sharp and coherent focus and not finally concede to indifference and/or pessimism. Simply uncovering and letting-be heterogeneity is not sufficient to carry forth the freedom-making promise of Foucault's critique. As Habermas puts it, "A hermeneutics of unveiling always still connects a promise with its critique."[141] Salient constructive resources are required not only to unmask illusion and discern *that* change is necessary, but also to *determine* the shapes that alternatives should take. Such resources allow claims to be made about the desirability of a particular possibility as good, as warranted, as right.[142] Yet this is precisely what Foucault denies us, preferring instead to let the freshness and novelty of disparity, dissemination, and fragmentation run their due course—as if this were a panacea somehow flowering automatically (teleologically?) into a "more" ethical historical configuration. In the end, all that Foucault's position allows him to affirm is the rather positivistic view that change happens—that is, that new forms and strategies of power/knowledge are produced, hold momentary sway, and then disappear in an "endlessly repeated play of dominations."

This kind of hyper-reflexivity undermines the liberative component of Foucault's critique. Freedom-from is always a freedom-for, a release toward something which, though negatively defined, bears positive value and meaning; toward recognizing the beauty of the other as a subject with its own unique voice; toward just and right relations with others, toward nondistorted forms of communicative praxis; and toward dialogical solidarity among differences. Foucault indeed hints at such a productive vision in an interview with Paul Rabinow just before his death. Here, he contrasts "polemics" with "dialogue." Whereas the polemicist privileges in advance of dialogue a position that he or she will never question, and thus refuses to acknowledge the interlocutor as having the right to speak, genuine dialogue assumes that the "rights of each person are in some sense immanent in the discussion," depending "only on the dialogue situation" and its "reciprocal elucidation."[143] In contrast to the stable and repressive monological character of polemics, dialogue then presupposes the ethical conditions of openness toward the other, of intersubjective symmetry, of holding open the ideal possibility of agreement and consensus but letting-be the unstable difference of dissensus if the logic of conversation dictates otherwise.

Foucault's project as a whole seems to grant these preconditions. Elsewhere he even begins to admit that consensus may be a kind of "critical principle" guiding dialogue, but then immediately turns it into a negative position: "The farthest I would go is to say that perhaps one must not be for consensuality, but one must be against nonconsensuality."[144] The idea of dialogical reconciliation or consensus among differences is a priori ruled out because of its implicit totalizing connotations. We must ask, however: *why* be opposed to nonconsensuality? What is it about human beings that makes them irreducible to, and resistant of, totalizing forms of nonconsensual discourse? Why should this be a common concern for all human beings? What, after all, is the positive value of difference, of dissemination, of disparity?

Such questions Foucault cannot answer without a performative contradiction, rendering his critique of totality, I suggest, ineffective, and without productive focus in engendering the very ethical conditions it seems to presume as ideal. By denying us the resources for warranted claims, Foucault's diagnostic critique becomes groundless, a fact he would happily acknowledge. But, as Habermas rightly contends, this is most unfortunate because it renders his genealogical historiography "presentistic" (the historiographer remaining hermeneutically stuck in his or her starting situation), "relativistic" (the historian's understanding itself being context-dependent), and "cryptonormative" (unable to account for itself except as a deliberately rhetorical and fictive disruptive device, all the while feigning to be more).[145]

This gets to the heart of the "murkiness" described earlier. Foucault, with one hand, wants to claim that genealogy is dealing with facts, with real historical events that disclose genuine heterogeneity, and yet with the other, he purports to be doing fiction in order to open up the present from inside itself, the validity of which is reduced to the power-altering effects it sets in motion. This produces an inescapable incoherence. The Nietzschean genealogical critique is a "totalizing critique."[146] For all of its salutary benefits, it cannot help but thereby blunt the force of its own critique. It becomes merely a local rhetoric of disruption needing to hide its normative agenda, hence becoming yet another ideological technique of the will-to-power.

Foucault, as with Rorty, cannot escape the self-negating and provincializing consequences of radical contextualism, which in the final analysis function to undermine his (presupposed) ethical rationale for privileging disruption and discontinuity over stability and continuity in the "undefined work of freedom." Critical historical writing in the Nietzschean vein of Foucault, as Craig Calhoun suggests, serves a purpose tantamount to a kind of "Orientalism of the past," the unique voices of historical differences assimilated into the voice of the present for purposes that violate their integrity and uniqueness.[147] Ironically, this induces an inverted process of totalization, a perverted mirror image of the suppression of difference that it claims to repudiate. The emancipatory critique of totality, in becoming a totalizing critique, demonstrates its own need for a universalizing moment of self-authentication, the kind it outrightly rejects, if it is not to appear capricious and arbitrary. Indeed, if totality is a repressive illusion, then what criteria constitute freedom-making truth as an openness toward the other? Passing over this question means the loss of the ability to distinguish legitimate and enabling forms of power relations from those that are illegitimate and repressive. The fundamental lesson is this: by totalizing its critique, the postmodern critique of totality inevitably consumes its own liberative thrust.

This problem is omnipresent in all ideology critiques that are counter-Enlightenment and that operate in a postmodern and hyper-reflexive historicist modality. The critical theory of Max Horkheimer and Theodor Adorno finds itself in a similar quandary. Habermas notes: "If they do not want to renounce the effect of a final unmasking and still want to *continue with critique*, they will have to leave at least one rational criterion intact for their explanation of the corruption of *all* rational criteria."[148] In the end, seeking to purge reason of all reifying ideology seems to leave no way out other than an all-consuming pessimistic historicism. Insofar as it preserves critical thought and resists conformism by perpetually citing the depredations of reason, it offers no constructive or restorative alternative other than a "negative dialectics" that breaks the spell of identitarian totality and keeps the incongruous nonidentity of difference in play.[149]

In waging a totalized "war on totality," Lyotard's postmodern incredulity toward metanarratives falls into a similar predicament: it is able to recognize differences but unable to account for which differences make a difference, denying any basis for critical evaluation or even moral culpability that is not itself already caught up in an incommensurate language-game. Even Caputo's "ethics of dissemination," allowing for the free-play of differences as it does, cannot defend its moral adequacy and efficacy except by employing a kind of reverse logic: since totality breeds terror, its negation should breed liberty. A statement by one of postmodernity's most renowned exponents, Jacques Derrida, gets to heart of this reverse logic: "The absence of a transcendental signified extends the domain and the play of significations infinitely."[150] But how is the free play of difference an ethical configuration? Caputo suggests, à la Derrida, that it should not be an ethical configuration at all, for "the premises invoked in ethical theory always come too late." They are accidents of the play of differences that do not give themselves in advance.[151] Yet, in the words of Calhoun, this induces a "particularism so extreme . . . [that it] cannot justify even the very value of difference with which it starts."[152]

Historicist metacritiques, in their mode of hyper-reflexivity, deprive us of the analytic tools by which we might take the positive value differences seriously and construct a viable vision of pluralism. They are diagnostic without offering a viable prescription. By placing an absolute priority on difference and dissemination, the critique of totality winds up undercutting the emancipative praxis that it seeks to foster. What we have here is the overdramatization of an essentially good point. As Terry Eagleton contends, "It is not a question of denouncing closure as such . . . but of discriminating between its more enabling and more disabling varieties."[153] It is one thing to say, as does Adorno, that a "liberated mankind would by no means be a totality,"[154] but it is another to make concrete proposals based on a productive envisagement of what this might entail.

Perhaps the best intent of the critique of totality might be taken up in a liberative and restorative "critical hermeneutics of recovery," one which, while aware of its own historicity, employs a dialectical conception of the third moment of the Enlightenment project, not only to preserve the capacity to resist and expose corruptions and distortions, but also to retrieve the full capacities of human beings as productive agents of their own mutual flourishing in webs of dialogical solidarity.

CONCLUSION: RECONSIDERING THE POSTMODERN

Through a twin focus on radical contingency and the critique of totality, this discussion has centered on the hyper-reflexive privileging of difference that characterizes postmodern discourse. I wish now to highlight the threat to pluralism that lurks here, even amidst postmodernity's more felicitous moments. To oversimplify: it is the trivialization of difference. On the one hand, it is true that an objectivist and universalizing rationality violates the historically contingent character of human life, all too easily yielding the repressive homogenization of differences by turning genuine polyphony into the illusion of monophonic totality. Here, the other is reduced to the same, flattened out and measured only by its instrumental value in a larger system of exchange, a system of identity. This is indeed a kind of *loaded universalism* that invokes damaging consequences—that is, the xenophobic logic of exclusion, domination, or assimilationist inclusion.

But on the other hand, trained on fomenting the proliferation of difference without closure in an infinite field of unrestrained discursive play, postmodern particularism often yields the equally problematic inverse image of what it so adamantly rejects—becoming instead an *empty universalism*, a kind of polymorphous centerlessness that harkens back to Bruno. In this empty universalism, gravity does not exist, for no center can hold weight, and the sheer heterogeneity of sociocultural differences scatters all into what might be best described as a "pluralism of dispersion." Whereas a thinker like Nietzsche sees this as a boon that releases human beings toward the creation of new values, it should more appropriately cause us alarm. For such a pluralism unleashes an inadvertent homogenizing effect, stimulating a relativistic reduction of difference to depthless equivalence, to banal artifacts carrying the same weight and having an identical stake in the democratized "free-play" of a plurality without substance. As Terry

Eagleton sums up, "In *over*historicizing, postmodernism also underhistoricizes, flattening out the variety and complexity of history in a flagrant violation of its own pluralistic tenets," thus "becoming a kind of inverted mirror-image of the universalism it repudiates."[155]

This occurs in two ways. First, postmodernity fails to take historical specificity seriously, diminishing the uniqueness of cultures and histories in a presentism that is tantamount to the rationalistic decontextualization it so harshly criticizes, proving itself equally incapable of placing the particular in relation to its own context or to any other phenomenon.[156] Second, postmodernity precludes judgment by granting a priori equal status to all standards and perspectives, invoking (surprisingly enough) a posture of spectator-like neutrality that amounts to belittling the positive value of differences.[157] Radical particularism, with its corresponding contextualism, becomes simply what Habermas calls the "flipside of logocentrism,"[158] a species of objectivism's loaded universalism turned upside down into an empty universalism. The performative contradiction in this is evident: to say there is no center is to invoke a universalizing rhetoric that claims to speak from the center. Pure polycentrism is incoherent.

Furthermore, reacting nobly against imperialist claims of cultural superiority, polycentrism can rather quickly conjure, even vindicate, rhetorics of disintegration and fragmentation—whether in the form of parochialist cultural narcissism and tribalistic self-enclosure (i.e., the presentism of Foucault or the ethnocentrism of Rorty); traditionalist conservatism (i.e., fundamentalisms); separatist exclusion; or ironist indifference. At its worst, it may even justify forms of "sovereignty" that marginalize, manipulate, and/or dominate, rendering them immune to external critique simply because they play out their own inner logic.[159] In granting a carnivalesque profusion of dissonant voices, postmodern "tolerance" can be just as insidious and repressive of difference as the rationalist-assimilationist liberal version. Lyotard's characterization of the postmodern as an "ability to tolerate the incommensurable"[160] might then be seen as a paraphrase of "anything goes." Depth is replaced by multiple surfaces behind which there is nothing—differences being disconnected mirror surfaces that have no intrinsic meaning other than as artifacts throwing back the image of their beholder. The result is the trivialization of difference, the reduction of plurality to a monistic centerlessness that is polycentric in name but not in substance.

Postmodernity, it seems, needs the constructive resources of modernity to carry forth its own program of reflexivity and critique; its negation of the latter cannot be absolute. For indeed, not all difference is of equal value, a fact that such thinkers as Rorty and Foucault want to acknowledge but lack the productive capacity to develop in any way other than through a pluralism of dispersion. Genuine pluralism, however, is not sheer numerical plurality, but the recognition that many distinct, localized centers of meaning are in a certain sense unobjectifiable and irreducible to each other or to one specific way of thinking. Such a recognition is not trivializing but salient, dependent upon substantive evaluations and judgments about the plural character of human reality. A normative moment of advocacy is required, one that cannot help but invoke the third moment of the Enlightenment project, albeit in a self-reflexive form that takes critical account of its own historicity as a view "from somewhere." The Enlightenment project stands or falls as a piece; its three moments (freedom-making critique, self-reflexivity, and universalizing normativity) are joined inseparably. This is why the relativism of a hyper-reflexivity that absolutely privileges difference is the empty flip side of the loaded universalism it repudiates. Postmodernity exhausts itself without appeal to the Enlightenment project.

The task at hand, then, is to reenvision postmodern "reason" so as to steer between the extremes of an incapacitating *pluralism of dispersion* (with its empty universalism) and a *pluralism of identity* (with its loaded universalism). For a pluralistic vision of humanity can be achieved only by resolute opposition to its extremist detractors. True pluralism must take the middle road. Even if provisional and not absolute, discourse about what is real and what is illusion is important. As theologian Langdon Gilkey suggests and as Rorty would admit, while no inviolable vision of the center is possible, some "centered vision" seems necessary, some form of "relative absolute" that guides one's convictions and renders them public and arguable.[161]

But what grants this? Whereas Rorty's ironist-liberal hermeneutic of conversation rightly compels us toward forging solidarity, it lacks the capacity for critique and rational adjudication between competing alternatives, preferring to let a qualified but problematic ethnocentrism run its due course. And whereas Foucault's disparity-producing hermeneutic of disruption rightly unmasks the play of power relations in all discursive practices, it lacks the productive capacity for acknowledging and celebrating the positive value of differences. Hence, while nodding toward the postmodern privileging of difference, we must not abrogate the need for some form of provisional, nondistortive, and nondominative universalizing discourse about terms of shared relevance and hopefulness. This seems necessary in order to champion a liberating sense of solidarity amidst differences. Therefore, we must modify Rorty's sense of conversational solidarity and Foucault's ideological critique in the direction of a dialectical pluralism of solidarity, seeking to resist radical historicism by rethinking rationality in a way that is historically conscious and reflexive, yet able to sustain the palpable need for dialogically based truth claims.

We live in a planetary age, one graphically depicted by the picture of the earth sent back by Apollo 8 in 1968. The planet might be a metaphor for "sharing," as something we all belong to, a "big blue marble" that fills our entire horizon yet relativizes all local identities.[162] But of course, from the ground it is our particularities and differences that strike us as fundamental. From the ground, then, perhaps planetary sharing is something forged together in our differences, a pragmatic and open-ended "universal" that is constructed in a dialogical and reconciliatory praxis of solidarity and that blossoms out of a provisional yet productive vision of human dwelling together in the world, one that enables us to consider differences valuable and beautiful while allowing us the leverage of critique against those differences that preempt sharing. Even if provisional, some vision of commensurability is required, some anticipation of the whole as difference-bearing and enlivening in its connective power. Without a relatively absolute starting point, dwelling in a mode of hospitality is impossible. And hospitality is the root of sharing.

In the end, sharing is a nonviolent and nondominative dwelling together in communion. In a word, it is peace. But this is not the peace of stasis, of sheer identity; rather, it is the freedom-making power of human hospitality toward the other, played out in a communicative "fusion of horizons" that is self-reflexive and dialogical and thus is open-ended and unstable, neither self-enclosed and unable to acknowledge the other in an attitude of presentist ethnocentrism or separatist indifference nor bound by an assimilative logic that falsifies and subsumes the other for its own preservation or gain. Here, the strangeness of difference is not only a postmodern fact; it is an other to be welcomed. As Ricoeur counsels, by engaging others in "a dramatic relation in which I affirm myself in my origins and give myself to another's imagination in accordance with his different civilization," human truth as a sharing ideal can emerge, history itself progressively becoming "a vast explanation in which each civilization will work out its perception of the world by confronting all others."[163] This is what I shall call "dialectical pluralism," a pluralism of mutual recognition and shared solidarity: a robust pluralism of peace. Adorno captures the fundamental character of this in stating, "Peace is the state of distinctness without domination, with the distinct participating in each other."[164] But this process is not intrinsic to pluralistic consciousness, already present, waiting to be unpacked. It is an ongoing task to be carried out together; as Ricoeur speculates, "It is probably the great task of generations to come."[165]

CHAPTER 3

DWELLING TOGETHER: IDENTITY, DIFFERENCE, AND RELATION

Difference exists within identity. Otherwise identity would not be identity. Thought contains deferral and distance. Otherwise, thought would not be thought.[1]

As chapters 1 and 2 have shown, our postmodern context requires a normative picture of pluralism. Thus far, however, I have sought to attend to the felt reality of sociocultural plurality, exploring its implications. The portrayal of "pluralistic consciousness" is not, in itself, a prescriptive proposal about how human beings ought to live in the world. It is a reflective portrait: an attempt to describe a predominant way that human diversity has been experienced and accounted for during the past fifty years or so—that is, in the mode of a hyper-reflexive historical consciousness, dramatized by the postmodern celebration of difference and critique of totality. Of course, this is sharpened within a globalizing social, economic, and political context. In my view, this concept helps to uncover and make sense of an operative (even while unnoticed) cognitive filter that shapes how we perceive differences, thus motivating behaviors and thoughts. Through pluralistic consciousness, we experience ourselves as belonging simultaneously to multiple worlds, an "other" placed on the margins among equally placed others without a shared sense of place. The other is not far off, but is immediately at hand, "in here," "with us." Such proximity intensifies the experience of differences.

Plurality is, in this sense, a sociocultural *fact* conditioning how we understand ourselves and others. In today's postindustrial, postcolonial situation, it is an unavoidable given. And it calls for response. Thus plurality is also a *challenge* forcing us to reconsider our place in the world. Indeed, today's globalizing context makes it impossible to avoid taking a position toward difference, whether seen as a threat or as a promise. The question that besets us then is this: how should we address the pluralistic situation in which we live, resisting what denigrates or trivializes diversity and finding new ways to cultivate a more humane planet for all, not in spite of but amidst and through our differences? This is not an abstract philosophical question regarding the relation of the One and the many; it is an unavoidable praxis. For we cannot help but live out "answers" in the various ways we dwell together. We must, then, distinguish between *plurality* and *pluralism*, the former being a sociohistorical given and the latter being an ethical vision of differences in relationship.

This chapter develops the line of critique presented in chapter 2, pushing further toward outlining the *possibility* of a distinct way of sharing amidst genuine heterogeneity. This possibility is pluralism; and it is rooted in the already plural nature of human dwelling-together. Toward this end, my overall aim is now prescriptive, focused on building a theoretical framework that both acknowledges differences and gives access to their positive value. Such a framework seeks to engender solidarity and foster reciprocity among localized differences over and against forces that would fragment, trivialize, suppress, or nullify those differences. Whether as bigoted xenophobia, relativistic indifference, separatist ethnocentrism, or homogenizing universalism, distortions of genuine plurality involve dangerous fallacies against which correctives must be offered in order to promote a wider peace. Recall, however, that true peace is not the tension-free state of stasis, but rather, as Theodor Adorno aptly characterizes it, "the state of distinctness without domination, with the distinct participating in each other."[2] It is pluralism.

To be sure, pluralism forces an encounter with the "other" that is decentering. It ruptures taken-for-granted and stable senses of what it means to dwell and to be at home in the world. It signifies a broken whole. Yet this broken whole is not finally destructive to all meaning and value. For in it also lies the promise of new possibilities that call us (1) into affirming the concrete, difference-bearing, and relational character of human life in the world; and (2) into the drama of mutuality, the result of a praxis of reconciliatory dialogue between differences that *brings out* as well as *brings together* what is vital and most creative in each participant. I suggest—with a certain nod to Rorty—that this constructive possibility is nothing more than a praxis of *solidarity*, an open-ended and vigorously conversational dwelling together amidst differences, one that creates a shared space of relational attunement. However, neither reducing diversity to repressive homogeneity nor dispersing it into sheer heterogeneity, the vision of pluralism I put forth eschews both the loaded and the empty universalisms described in chapter 2. It embodies and carries forth the essential gains of historicism and hyper-reflexivity while at the same time retrieving the emancipatory and critical thrust of the Enlightenment project. That is to say, it offers a positive estimation of the intrinsic value and vitalizing character of human difference. This is the challenge and the responsibility of today's world. And it boils down to an imperative: each culture, nation, ethnicity, and religion must learn to live *with* the other (and the "with" shall become key) in creative and peaceful tension.

The task of this chapter will be to explore the groundwork for such a global imperative. In broad terms, I offer here an interpretation of human sociality or, more specifically, an analysis of human dwelling together as fundamentally plural. The analysis will echo some of what we saw in Rorty and Foucault, but it moves beyond them—conversing with thinkers like Ludwig Wittgenstein, Charles Taylor, Gabriel Marcel, Paul Ricoeur, and Hans-Georg Gadamer—to form a descriptive basis for the normative claims regarding pluralism that follow in chapter 4. Understanding how human communities *actually* are pluralized dwelling places of solidarity, their boundaries inherently opened up from within and permeable to the influx of difference (even through acts of bigotry and xenophobic violence), puts us in a position to make certain prescriptive claims about how those communities *ought* then to dispose themselves to difference. *Pluralism is an incipient ideal latent in the way in which humans actually do live together.* For all communities are hybrid forms of solidarity that are predisposed toward the possibility of openness. Let us explore how so.

COMMUNAL BELONGING: LANGUAGE AND FIELDS OF SEMANTIC POWER

Community emerges in human life as an inescapable reality. Not only are we born into an intersubjective network of kinship relations, but our survival often depends upon extending this network into a broader field of exchange relations with others—clan, tribe, city, nation, or globe. Bound together by a shared situation or "lifeworld" and its particular exigencies, local economies of various sorts take shape and circulate values and goods in distinct interactive patterns.[3] This context is the crucible in which determinate social frameworks arise and gain sway. And over time, patterns of interactive continuity become ensconced and outline the contours of a way of life, a corporate gestalt: a culture. As unstable and provisional as these patterns are, they mark a kind of social grammar that elicits the possibility of dwelling together, summoning commitments and allegiances that endow the relationships and events of ordinary life, past and future, with purpose and significance. Accordingly, we grow to identify with this grammar and orient ourselves to the world through the way in which it measures value and supports a collective sense of being together, insuring stability and longevity against elements that would cause disarray. Communities, like organisms, require some measure of integrated focus as they encounter novel circumstances. Without such focus they would dissolve into the babel of fragmentation and indefiniteness.

This raises a question: from where does such an integrative focus come into being? A public medium of communication is required—that is, a language. As those figures associated with the so-called linguistic turn in philosophy have repeatedly stressed, it is language that houses the meanings of practices that comprise a life together. Let us then begin by discussing the oft-quoted progenitor of the linguistic turn, Ludwig Wittgenstein, whose later writing is particularly important here because of the way in which it traces the connection between language and social conditions.

For Wittgenstein, language is neither strictly referential nor a free-floating means of expression, but rather functions within the limits of certain practices that regulate its use. In this regard, language behaves much like a game in which certain rules specify the properties and coordinate the activities of the pieces in play—hence the appropriate metaphor of "language games."[4] As in learning a game, humans learn to think about the world in a particular language that is rule-governed, has a grammar of its own, and that constitutes the meaning of particular thoughts and actions. Accordingly, what counts for "meaningful" depends on a context- and purpose-specific situation that generates distinct agendas and criteria of adjudication. There is, then, no such thing as a "private" language independent of language games, for the situation that determines a language's use is indelibly marked by sociality and tied to an economy of public conventions.[5] We are trained to understand the meaning of things via an integrated, self-regulating community of discourse. The meaning of something is never an isolated event. It conforms to its circumstance and position with reference to other meanings in the overall fabric of an interlocutionary matrix.

Meaning, therefore, is not simply the product of a disembodied head-game. The grammar of every language is tied to the praxis-oriented peculiarities of its lived context, to what Wittgenstein calls a "form of life." Languages are intractably local and contain unique meanings finely tuned to their own social and cultural circumstances. For instance, the sense of the word *doctor*—as someone who heals—will vary quite dramatically from a North American urban context to a traditional sub-Saharan African context, a function of how each group lives together and draws upon their reservoir of taken-for-granted allegiances and convictions. It is the lived context of relevance that gives language its capacity to mediate meaning.[6] The shared praxis of a lifeworld and its collective focus lays down the possible forms of a language game. Conversely, to speak a language is to participate in the form of life that gives meaning to language.[7] Forms of life and language games are inextricably intertwined, making language a storehouse of cultural content and valuation. Language not only communicates, but also legitimates and preserves the corporate sway of a certain social world. The process is circular: in reflecting a cultural tradition, language also continues it.

In Wittgenstein's view, human beings are linguistically engulfed creatures. We find ourselves always already in the middle of things along with others, in the public space of a linguistic matrix or what philosopher Charles Taylor calls a "web of interlocution." Indebted to Wittgenstein, Taylor notes how such webs function in terms of what he calls "frameworks."[8] Frameworks are interpretive background pictures or horizons by which we think, feel, and make judgments about what matters to us. Functioning as an overarching composite of language games, a framework draw various meanings and values together into a coherent (implicit or explicit) vision that enables us to spell out what makes sense to us. As such, it composes an "us" out of disparate elements and interests. In this, we become oriented to a certain kind of world. Human beings never simply occupy a position in time and space, represented by some objective, uniform and interchangeable quantity; rather, humans co-inhabit and dwell in a world.[9] By "world" in this latter sense I mean not just an external physical environment, but rather an integrative temporal-spacial horizon of meaningful orientation, a concrete whole.[10] Indeed, language is the communicative process of sharing a world (one among others), the resource by which we dwell with others and carve out a place in the scheme of things.[11]

Because we find ourselves in a framework-bound world with others, we are, in the words of Taylor, caught up in an "original situation" of interdependence.[12] We develop and relate to one another in a conversational space that precedes and circumscribes us, functioning as a kind of "transcendental condition" of human thought and meaning, an intractable necessity.[13] This emphasis on interdependence departs from the Cartesian emphasis on the isolated thinking thing (the monadic self) as the foundational condition for any and all thinking about the world. The "discovery" of what is meaningful is never "my own" performance, acted out in solitude; it arises by being conversationally "initiated into a language." For example, Taylor muses, "I can only learn what anger, lover, anxiety, the aspiration to wholeness, etc., are through my and others' experience of these being objects for *us*, in some common space."[14] The very possibility of being "placed" in relation to what is worthwhile is enframed socially, worked out within the pre-given and shared accord of a community of discourse.

This leads to a further point. As it is embedded in a framework's web of interlocution, the self is primarily relational, an intersubjective act of communal belonging. The "I" *is* insofar as "we" *are*. And following Hans-Georg Gadamer's lead, we might expand this to "define the idea of belonging on the basis of the linguistically constituted experience of world."[15] As a part becomes intelligible by being in relation to the whole, so too does the self. One cannot be a self alone. For as Taylor puts it, "I am a self only in relation to certain interlocutors."[16] We develop the capacity to be authors of our actions not as separate and autonomous beings, detached from all boundedness and concrete modes of dwelling, but as intersubjectively constituted within a shared conversational framework.[17] Granted, we act as individuals, as physical bodies with certain biological needs and propensities; yet the *meaning* of those actions for us, the way in which we come to interpret their intention and effect, arises in the linguistically circumscribed presence of others. In such a way, I become a particular person capable of calling this physical body "mine."

Gabriel Marcel's writings complement Taylor's in this regard, except that he, like Martin Buber, stresses the face-to-face or interhuman context of relation as the fulcrum of dwelling together rather than the larger social-linguistic context. Marcel states: "In its own intrinsic structure subjectivity is already, and in the most profound sense, genuinely intersubjective."[18] We might say, then, that the activity of finding orientation in the world—rather, in *a* world—is a participative act mediated by *specific* others (i.e., family, friends, and local community) in a network of social relationships (i.e., traditions, cultures, and nations). The self and its social world become what they are insofar as they are meaningfully connected and empowered within a more primary sphere of relations: an intersubjective situation.[19] We are not monadic, independent selves who happen to be joined with others along the way. Nor are we simply inscribed by societal forces. Marcel contests both of these ideas. For others are not secondary additions to an already constituted self, and neither are interpretive frameworks and their values simply internalized through impersonal mechanisms of power. Frameworks become what they are because human being is primarily a *being-with* (Mitsein), a *coesse*.[20] The self is a subject insofar as it dwells-with-others. And such dwelling comes meaningfully to the fore in the linguistic event of sharing a world: namely, conversation.

Hence, subjectivity—as self-awareness—is not an inner discovery but a dialogically bound construction, inseparable from the presence of others. It emerges as a socially embedded internalized dialogue, an inner self-relation that is simultaneously a relation toward, and a playing out of, public interlocutionary relations. Consciousness is never a self-enclosed interiority. It is itself dialogical—a kind of mediated immediacy. The subjective site of an appropriation of meaning, the "I" is personal and aware of itself only through a recollection that is dependent on an intersubjective scene of conversation. For thinking, as language-bound, is itself dialogical, a kind of conversation with one's self. One comes to oneself from the outside in. Selfhood, as an inner relation with oneself, already reflects outward relations with others.

This is why Paul Ricoeur, indebted to Marcel, can assert that "the selfhood of oneself implies otherness to such an intimate degree that one cannot be thought of without the other."[21] We grasp our lives, come to self-understanding, only in the localized matrix of an extended dialogue with others, most explicitly in face-to-face relations but also indirectly with the cultures, traditions, and societal structures that become instantiated in those face-to-face relations. In this, the drama of conversation is primary. Selfhood presupposes what Ricoeur calls a "dialectic of *self* and the *other than self*."[22] This is also why Ricoeur insists that self-understanding emerges via a hermeneutical "detour" through signs, symbols, and cultural works (i.e., texts).[23] Communities of discourse and their frameworks provide the symbolic matrix for intelligible action. Hence, any interpretive event involves an invocation of others.

In sum, meaning is not an introspective but an intersubjective event, happening in the dialogical space of community. And communal dwelling places are not just an amalgamation of isolated meanings subsequently put together by autonomous selves. They are, through the primacy of intersubjective relations, the condition by which we put things together and become selves. Frameworks join together, composing a shared, relational space.

Pushing further, then, I propose that we describe the generative and integrative force of frameworks as a *field of semantic power*. This description is a helpful addition because it highlights the dynamic and relational character of frameworks. Like energy *fields*, frameworks are not rigid or static, but hybridic, fluid, and constantly evolving. Why? Because they are mediated by a lifeworld that is fundamentally intersubjective in character, shifting and changing accordingly as novelty is introduced to and catalyzes localized conversations. Productive *power* is involved because such novelty is always encountered in terms of an interpretive apparatus that patterns the flow of information exchange, circumscribing the boundaries of a field of linguistic play and regulating the meanings that arise therein. The larger sway of social structures and cultural inheritances can and do affect intersubjective relations, for good and ill.[24] *Semantic* power, then, designates a certain meaningful social space, a world, a communal center with the capacity to invoke a certain measure of self-attributing accord.

Further still, this accord often takes on a "narrative" form, whereby history's discord is brought into communally instantiated concordance, exhibiting a kind of directedness or teleological intentionality. Experience is always construed in emplotted shapes, as disparate circumstance and events are brought together and configured narratively, drawn into an intelligible and unbroken temporal line of succession.[25] Indeed, my actions have character only insofar as they perform in narrative form.[26] For, as Taylor suggests, communities are structured in terms of a broad vision of where "we" come from and where "we" are going, connecting multiple voices into a coherent story-formed field of semantic power.[27] As many such stories converge and become writ large against the backdrop of a shared lifeworld, the character of a *tradition* unfolds. Traditions are communal formations of temporal depth, arising from the past and extending into an anticipated future.[28]

Understanding this helps us to see how fields of semantic power are products of conventions always already caught up in social practices and relations that are contingent and finite in their reach. There is, then, no objective or neutral field of semantic power, for there is no universally shared form of life that generates a univocal interpretive space. Beliefs about things are not based upon some pristine epistemological access to the world or upon an apodictic rational foundation. They are framework-bound, arising within a particular semantic context that shapes how the world is interpreted and sets up criteria for what counts for knowledge.[29] Knowledge about the world, indeed rationality itself, must therefore be seen as historically situated, for the world cannot be grasped independently of the language frameworks that render it understandable and meaningful for a particular circumstance.[30] There is no uninterpreted and non-linguistic world. For as Wittgenstein notes, "The limits of my language mean the limits of my world."[31]

Let us now make some summary claims. First, language is the empowering medium of inhabiting a shared world. Second, language signals an original situation of interdependence. The self is constituted intersubjectively; it is dialogical and conversational in character. Third, because of this, language plays a dual role: (a) it bestows meaning and orientation to persons within a field of semantic power, drawing them together into a community; and accordingly, (b) it fosters and mediates the reflective "I-ness" of human agency. Hence the close link between sociocultural and personal identity.

At base, fields of semantic power originate in the human need to inhabit a meaningful world—to dwell with others by way of a shared background horizon that provides discriminating perspective to questions of what is true, worthwhile, and good. As Taylor argues, humans "have a craving for being in contact with or being rightly placed in relation to the good."[32] It is this craving that makes the issue of frameworks inescapable, for they orient us toward a certain kind of world—one that displays the possibility of meaning and value. In fact, as Taylor notes, such frameworks are constitutive of human identity, for to know who I am is related to the issue of where and with whom I stand.[33] *Without frameworks there can neither be the recognition of belonging nor the recognition of what is foreign and "other" and in some sense does not belong (as "strange"), neither a sense of the continuity of the same nor of the discontinuity of difference.*

COMMUNITY BEYOND CLOSURE: THE OPENNESS OF DIFFERENCES IN RELATION

In order to advance this argument, we must supplement the more communitarian approach that was just discussed in the previous section by taking a reverse tack. In a more poststructuralist and postcolonialist vein, I now wish to underscore the point that fields of semantic power are neither selfsame nor fixed but rather unsteady and fallible products of sharing company with the strange and novel. Mediated by the contrapuntal play of ongoing conversations, a community or culture is not an identitarian field of enmeshment, but rather a dialogical composition. It is hybridic and pluralized from within.[34] This leads to the proposal that *communal identities—refracted in conversational fields of semantic power—are not monolithic and enclosed circles, but are differentiating, transgressive, and opened from within, infused with a vibrant and vital element of heterogeneity.*

Communities are always internally displaced, containing an irrepressible indeterminacy. Why? Because "we" *are* our differences, an identity-in-difference that illustrates the primacy of the intersubjective sphere of relation. This is not merely a retrieval of Hegel's unity-in-difference, which functions to gather together differences by sublimating them and incorporating them into a larger totality. For dwelling together entails a unity unable to fully gather together its participants into a collective sum. To borrow language from Jacques Derrida, communal identity is always already "different from itself," not identical with itself, ever deferring.[35] At base, this is because the adrenaline of conversation lies not merely in the convergence created, but in the contrast between differences. Like the creative energy field of a jazz combo trades upon the interaction of distinct musical voices, conversation is a dynamic interplay between voices in which something always escapes standardization.

Accordingly, within the centering, inward pull of any field of semantic power there circulates an interruptive, decentering thrust created by the tensional counterpoint of differences. And, pace Foucault, this haunts any and all self-protective maneuvering that would domesticate differences in terms of communal reification and closure. To the contrary, it facilitates a belonging that cannot help but erupt from the inside. From intimate face-to-face to the broader sociopolitical levels of human relations, conversation between differences simultaneously generates *and* interrupts fields of semantic power, rendering their boundaries porous and open to novelty, capable of being otherwise.

No appeal to some "pure" identity can be made. No community of discourse is its own fulfillment; it is always more than itself.

Again, a tack through the later thought of Wittgenstein can help demonstrate how this is so. As we saw earlier, the boundaries of a communal discourse produce its semantic world—as enframed or framework-bound. These delimiting boundaries, however, like the rules of language games themselves, are never secured wholes that are utterly centripetal and self-enclosed. As there can be no private language, neither can there be a language that is shut in on itself and solipsistic. For, as Wittgenstein suggests, there are many languages—or rather, many uses of language—and each is porous and crisscrosses with others, its horizon shading off into other horizons. Indeed, participating in a language game involves openness to other possible language games. For the very idea of a language "game" is itself unsystematic, uncircumscribed, and fluid. We know what a game is only by knowing other similar and dissimilar games, which often are overlapping subsections of each other.[36] No language is complete in itself, a uniform holism that is, as Wittgenstein puts it, "closed by a frontier. For how is the concept of a game bounded? What still counts as a game and what no longer does? Can you give the boundary? No."[37]

The very conversational character of language entails, therefore, that it involve multiple intersecting threads, each ever changing and adaptive. We make use of semantic rules for all sorts of domain-like situations (i.e., music, poetry, science, religion, politics, and mathematics), but none of these are necessarily mutually exclusive or utterly incommensurate.[38] To illustrate the point, Wittgenstein likens language to a city, a complex maze of intersecting streets and houses surrounded by newer streets and houses.[39] A language is thus not some clearly defined whole that can be designated clearly and distinctly—"how many houses or streets does it take before a town becomes a town?"[40] We share a city in which there are always deferred meanings and "blurred edges."[41]

But this does not necessitate the dispersal of language games into the sheer chaos of indeterminacy. There is no linguistic practice that is not in principle speakable, as long as we "find our feet" in a certain place of conversation. The *possibility* of intersubjective corrigibility is the basic hinge upon which language swings as a communicative praxis. Linguistic frameworks do not hold us captive in an epistemic circularity, imprisoning "us" in our own vocabularies, our own already constituted world.[42] While there is no neutral and univocal language to translate the multiple ways in which particular fields of semantic power shape our perception of things, there are in fact ad hoc points of intersection and convergence that open up our linguistic horizons to the possibility of interlinguistic exchange.[43] Without these implicit convergence points the recognition of, and conversation between, differences would be impossible.[44] There is no way from within language to enclose language; it is open-ended because of its differential and dialogical character. There is no absolute starting point in language. Relation lies at the core.

In summary, because languages are intersubjective performances, they are never single unitary threads, fixed and total. There is no metalanguage game that includes all other such games, a language in which all people speak univocally. As people in a community differ, so language itself displays multiplicity and diversity. Accordingly, language is a tensional and intertextual affair that cannot be fully stabilized. It is polysemous and open from the inside out. This renders a field of semantic power different from itself, displaying an *enframing openness* that both empowers and interrupts meaningful orientation in a world.

Such a vision has radical implications for thinking about the status of communal identity. It moves us beyond the perils of ethnocentrism without causing a complete diffusion of differences. Wherever there emerges a shared sense of being together, the other is already there in its midst, interrupting it and bursting it outward.

SHARING DIFFERENCES: GADAMER AND CONVERSATION

Bringing the first two sections of this chapter together, I wish now to employ the work of Hans-Georg Gadamer to take a further tack in the argument. *Precisely as differences interrupt established patterns of meaning, they are the creative font of the ongoing and fallible process of forging what it means to belong together.* The contrast of the other does not preclude but in fact *is* the empowering condition of linguistic practice and, in turn, of community. In this sense, contrast does not mean separation and isolation; it means dialectical coordination with another term. And such coordination occurs self-consciously in conversation. Hence, exploring the character of conversation will provide an excellent window into understanding how fields of semantic power are complex and dynamic horizons of *sharing differences*.[45]

The initial point is this: we share differences insofar as we share a conversation. More than a singular "commonality" among differences, "sharing"—as I mean to use the term—indicates a hybridic and holistic bonding, a togetherness of differences that is more than their collective sum, more than a unifying act of appropriation or conformity to some putative common ground. It is an ad hoc and open-ended exposure of others to others in a relation of mutual participation and engendering. Selves are related through their otherness. Like the counterpoint of jazz musicians caught up in improvisation, conversation creates an ever-shifting resonance in and through distinct tones playing off other such tones. A kind of composition is created. Resonating voices sound together in their diversity and collectively fashion a public and mutual space of sharing. Voices become attuned to one another. And this distributes singular beings, placing them differently among one another. The upshot is that a common being-together is sounded in the multiplication of voices.[46] Sharing differences in conversation is then both the process and product of communal dwelling. Such intersubjective corrigibility and attunement is the stuff of language, of conversation, indeed of worlds.

What, however, is conversation? Ideally conceived, conversation is a being-with in which one deliberately gives over something of oneself and also receives a gift from another. Voices participate in one another, joined creatively in an enlarged and inherently unfinished circle of mutuality. This circle designates neither a content nor an essence; it is an occasion of reciprocity. The work of Gadamer, particularly its way of highlighting the universality of the hermeneutical problem, now comes into play. For sharing is a conversation-bound event of understanding (Verstehen) between differences. And, as such, it entails what Gadamer calls a fusion of horizons (Horizontverschmelzung).[47] The experience of understanding "between" persons—which occurs in any and all linguistic interactions—offers a way of thinking about communities of discourse as a contrapuntal convergence, a sharing of differences. Seen in this light, Gadamer's work proves strikingly apropos to our postmodern and pluralist situation.[48]

Like Wittgenstein and Taylor, Gadamer asserts that human beings find themselves already immersed in social-linguistic practices. There is no presuppositionless access to the world. For, in his terms, our "prejudices" or prejudgments (i.e., pre-understandings or interpretive forestructures) *are* our historical being. Informed by an inherited tradition of discourse, they empower our ability to understand anything at all.[49] Prejudices, then, need not be taken as obstacles to genuine understanding, as the Enlightenment "prejudice against prejudice" would suggest. Rather, they are hermeneutically productive, allowing us to perceive things and texts and to anticipate their meaning for us.[50] Only on the basis of prejudices—formed within a field of semantic power and embedded in a tradition—can we come to understand something as it stands in relation to us. We read the world conditioned by a perspective.

Because of this, interpretation must involve something like an application process, wherein one encounters the strangeness of an other (a text) as it relates to the familiarity of one's own localized hermeneutical situation.[51] We do not first understand something in the mode of cognitive neutrality and subsequently apply it to "us." Rather, we encounter what is foreign only from within the interpretive horizon of a home-world, in terms of what it says to and for "us."[52] And only on the basis of a perception of likeness or affinity can such a process commence.[53] Only through the lens of a hermeneutical perspective can something come into focus. Consequently, there is no disembedded and unequivocal getting at the other qua other.

In Gadamer's view, this does not mean that the prejudices that comprise our world are self-enclosing or assimilative of differences. Acknowledging that we encounter the novelty of difference through operative pre-understandings does not give license to unchecked ideologizing and erroneous distortions of the other. For Gadamer, there is no necessary logic of absorption here. While it is true that we interpret from within a certain horizon, it does not follow that there is nothing other than this horizon. The following passage illustrates the point:

> [Prejudices] constitute the initial directedness of our whole ability to experience. Prejudices are biases of our openness to the world. They are simply conditions whereby we experience something—whereby what we encounter says something to us. This formulation certainly does not mean that we are enclosed within a wall of prejudices and only let through the narrow portals those things that produce a pass saying, "Nothing new will be said here." Instead we welcome just that guest who promises something new to our curiosity. . . . The nature of the hermeneutical experience is not that something is outside and desires admission. Rather, we are possessed by something and precisely by means of it we are opened up for the new, the different, the true.[54]

Understanding begins with something new—something *outside* our world—enticing outward *from* the vantage point of our world into something more than what we already are.

Thus, prejudices are built structurally ready for the new and different, tilted toward the other. Just as Wittgenstein asserts that language games are open-ended, so too does Gadamer assert that the linguistic horizons of a particular perspective are not constrictive and centripetal, but productive and centrifugal, "opened into the infinite realm of possible expression." For while we "live wholly within a language," we are not held captive by language and enclosed in dispersed and incommensurable worlds.[55] Linguistic horizons and the traditions of which they are a part comprise ranges of vision that potentially include everything that can be seen from a particular situation or vantage point. They do not, however, thereby exhaust meaning; rather, they are intrinsically opened up toward their own expansion, "not being limited to what is nearby but being able to see beyond it."[56] Prejudices are not necessarily blind or constrictive but rather constitute a window into the new, empowering the capacity to be surprised by the different.

By being given full play, our prejudice—and so our world—is rendered capable of experiencing the force of the other's claim to truth. This is because, in turn, our own prejudices make it possible for the other's prejudices to have full play. It is precisely through the unfamiliarity and contrast of the other that our own operative prejudices, embedded in fields of semantic power, are put at risk and opened up to further possibilities.[57] Indeed, it is only by first encountering the different that we discover self-reflexively which prejudices are blind and which are productive.[58] Prejudices become exposed for what they are not by being suspended in advance, but by being given full play. Coming to know the other, therefore, does not require stepping outside our skins into a mode of cognitive neutrality. For it is through ingression of difference that our horizons become self-reflexive and augmented from within.

But how does such augmentation occur? The answer: in the form of a question. Questions result from the eruptive and distancing force of the other's strangeness. The unfamiliar inscribes itself into our world and throws the familiar into question, inducing an adjustment. Consequently, we ask about it, guided by anticipations of meaning based upon the familiar, the historically effected world "we" inherit. The claim of the other is thus a kind of call that provokes us to question further in its direction. As Gadamer suggests, "every understanding begins with the fact that something *calls out* to us" and calls us into question.[59] Indeed, what is other is experienced as other in the form of a question, propelling thought into motion.[60] It is here, in the question-producing tension between the familiar and the foreign, that the hermeneutical task is engendered. For any interpretive act simultaneously hovers between *belonging* to a tradition and the *distancing* effect of the other, which displaces that belonging.[61]

Understanding is thus a liminal event happening on the margins—between identity and difference. The tensional betweenness created by the play of familiarity and strangeness is the true locus of hermeneutics.[62] In order to understand what is encountered as alien, the process of application must relate it to and bring it within the context of what is familiar, and this process itself is guided by "the constant transcendent expectations of meaning," which proceed from the encounter itself. From *within* there is a fundamental anticipation of the meaningfulness and coherence—the possibility of likeness and familiarity—of what the other is saying, presupposing that its call really has something to say to "us," some truth to tell from the *outside*.[63] It is the anticipatory expectation of likeness and resemblance that renders the different meaningful, able to resonate with us. Indeed we ask questions of the other on this perspectival basis, bringing certain things to light, leaving other things in the dark.

This is why Gadamer claims that when we understand, we understand ever differently. For application is never a universal but a situated, limited, and therefore ongoing event.[64] This also is why a field of semantic power is never caught in a unified circle of enclosed immanence. The difference of the strange beckons us (from the inside) outward with its call; we ask questions because "we" have been unsettled and called into question, propelled into the dynamism of anticipating (from inside our hermeneutical situation) a resolution in the form of an answer. Why? Because the claim of the other sets a tension into play, invoking a sense of distance that inspires efforts toward understanding in the form of an anticipatory stretch toward something shared, concordance.[65] Concordance, however, is always only partial: a *discordant concordance.*

This discordance results from the fact that the other is not the object of an impartial gaze, but a living force that interrupts our prejudices and throws us open. And by bending our ear to listen to its voice, we become different, transposed, alerted to new possibilities that render our world strange and other. In the structure of questioning, we tacitly affirm that we are not selfsame and complete, but in truth alienated from ourselves, thrust outward from the inside. For, as George Steiner puts it, "The 'otherness' which enters into us makes us other."[66] Through the encounter with the different, we become exposed, aware of ourselves by way of the other, taking account of the otherwise unnoticed assumptions, prejudices, and prevailing anticipations we inherit and that operate from behind us—that is, from the historicity of our hermeneutical situatedness in a field of semantic power.[67] By recognizing the call of the other, we dialectically come to recognize "us" and the ways in which we belong to our own history.

In sum, self-understanding is an other understanding. And because understanding the other is an ongoing and never finished event, the knowledge of oneself can never be complete.[68] "Only through others do we gain true knowledge of ourselves."[69] We can see this in Gadamer's further commentary on the openness of horizons:

> Just as the individual is never simply an individual because he is always in understanding with others, so too the closed horizon that is supposed to enclose a culture is an abstraction. The historical movement of human life consists in the fact that it is never absolutely bound to any one standpoint, and hence can never have a truly closed horizon. The horizon is rather, something into which we move and that moves with us. Horizons change for a person who is moving. Thus the horizon of the past, out of which all human life lives and which exists in the form of tradition, is always in motion. The surrounding motion is not set in motion by historical consciousness. But in it this motion becomes aware of itself.[70]

And by recognizing ourselves—our own historicity—we are in turn further opened up toward the authentically different in its own horizon. Horizons are centrifugal in that they are centripetal, and vice versa.

Gadamer's position cannot, therefore, be considered an ethnocentric conservatism. The tensional play of the hermeneutical circle—in this case, the back-and-forth movement between one who understands and that which is understood—keeps our interpretations from becoming arbitrary and succumbing to a logic of absorption by throwing "us" into the between space of questioning, anticipating, and listening. Interpretive horizons are thus perpetually expanded in a dialectical play *between* identity and difference. Gadamer's position is instructive in that it helps us see how a field of semantic power is an open frontier, an outward-oriented receptivity that is constantly surpassed, supplemented, and hence enlarged by the call of the other. Linguistic horizons are essentially contingent, porous, and self-transcendently opened outward from within—ready and available for the other.[71] There is, in the hermeneutical circle, a double beginning point that has the character of a betweenness. Something strange is encountered, as related to us.[72] But what, then, is the character of this relation?

At this point, Gadamer's notion of understanding as a conversational "fusion of horizons" becomes of critical importance. In confronting the other and finding it intelligible, there is a collision of worlds, not as monadic billiard balls bouncing off one another, but as a dialectical and transformative relation. In heeding the call of the other and opening ourselves to its claim, there is a fusion of horizons whereby our own field of semantic power is enriched and expanded. Just as an historical horizon is always already projected via its anticipatory pre-understandings, so "it is simultaneously superseded" when it confronts that which is strange.[73] The event of understanding thus entails a praxis, a transpositioning of ourselves into the interstices of an encounter between horizons.

But this is neither a passing into an alien world unconnected with our own ("going native") nor a totalizing subordination of its claim to our own standards ("imperialism"). Rather "it always involves rising to a higher universality that overcomes not only our own particularity but also that of the other."[74] The world of the other is thus only relatively other, not absolutely other, for it offers something to us that invokes a relationship.[75] The relation itself is what Gadamer means by "higher universality," not a static monism or equilibrium in which both are "fused" into a totality. An in-between zone is created as horizons overlap and as their energies charge the formation of a larger shared horizon, not as some thing or object, but as a zone of relatedness in which we become attuned to the other. This is understanding: the dialectic of familiarity and strangeness, a logic of "both-and," not "either-or." Universality, in this way, is an intensification of particularity that at the same time signifies relationship. It is a participatory attunement between differences, an intersubjective convergence rather than a foundation. And there is no stopping the momentum created.

Glancing back to the Platonic-Socratic tradition, Gadamer depicts this as the ongoing to-and-fro play of dialogue, of question and answer between I and Thou. Dialogue is discursive speaking (*logos*) in-between (*dia*) differences. He suggests that the Thou is not an object, but rather a fundamental relation of the other to the self in the play of a "constant struggle for mutual recognition."[76] When we confront the other, I and Thou are already intertwined, belonging in a sense together. Each is thus constituted by an openness to the other, able to be surprised, to listen, and more, to respond and question.[77]

Dialogue, then, presumes a type of knowledge that concedes to not knowing, an admission of ignorance that grants the strangeness and distance of the other. This is the very structure of openness.[78] But openness is not a traumatic recoil created by an utterly alien and uncanny other. The fact that the other is announced, that we perceive its call, implies an affinity that makes it accessible as other. This does not, however, mean that otherness is thereby annulled or diluted in a melting pot of commonality. Rather, the other comes and leaves its trace as an interruption, inscribed into a field of semantic power as a dissonance, a contrast, a known unknown, something at a distance, triggering and energizing real engagement and questioning. We hearken to the other, bending our ear, turning toward it in an attention-giving posture that suggests, insofar as its call has become audible, that we now already belong with it.

Seen in this light, moving outside the orbit of Gadamer for a moment, I suggest that what we seek through engaged questioning is to *draw near* something that announces itself as alterior. And this event takes us into the interstices of encounter in the form of *interest*, which is fundamentally a coexistence or being-with (*inter-esse*).[79] The very praxis of questioning presupposes that the other exerts a provocation that is "interesting," a voice with semantic power of its own that calls us to draw near, directing our ears, through its novel claim, toward itself as of possible value, as something worthy of being given a hearing. A question carries us forward, then, not into the other qua other, but rather into the between space of dialogue, into an ongoing interplay of likeness and difference. Through such dialectical tension—a Heraclitus-like "strife" or struggle—we become attuned to the new, open to its similar dissimilarity. We recognize the other as similar only through the surprise of its difference, which calls us into the give-and-take play of questioning.[80]

This presumes a fundamental *availability* to the other's call. "Availability," a term I am borrowing from Gabriel Marcel, means to be disposed toward the other. It marks a willingness to participate in the other's difference, to be vulnerable to change, to risk being open to clash and conflict.[81] Placed in the context of our discussion of Gadamer—who does not draw from Marcel—availability is manifested in the interested "drawing near" of a question, which both signals and preserves an "orientation toward openness" that pushes us into the "both-and" of dialectical thinking—a fusion of horizons.[82] Availability is a posture presupposed by the event of understanding. It means being exposed to the exteriority of the other's call, being drawn out into the margin-dwelling openness of the "with" in being-with. It means sharing differences.

For Gadamer, this comes to pass in the linguistic context of conversation. Dialogue itself is the art of speaking, of conducting a conversation, of thinking, of question and answer; it is the happening of language.[83] In the tensional reciprocity of dialogue with an other (the new, the strange, and the known unknown) we learn to recognize and revise our biases and prejudices. This need not entail agreement or consensus, but it does signify a transpositioning into a common linguistic space, or shared subject matter, even as the other remains other, something at a distance. And this transpositioning fuels the fusion of horizons, rendering the other meaningful *for us* while at the same creating space to acknowledge that the other has its own standpoint and horizon, which is itself elusive and cannot be reached, an inexhaustible alterity receding as we query further.[84] Thus, there is no perfect understanding, no complete fusion of horizons, no universal or univocally shared world.[85] What Wittgenstein notes of language, Gadamer notes of worlds: worlds—precisely as linguistic—are not enclosed but perpetually deferring conversational events open to further explication and supplementation.[86]

In the end, there is the finite betweenness of ongoing conversation, wherein players participate in one another and are taken up into a dialectical back-and-forth movement, willing to be vulnerable and thrown into questioning. "To enter in conversation with another," says Alphonso Lingis, "is to lay down one's arms and one's defenses; to throw open the gates of one's own positions; to expose oneself to the other, the outsider; and to open oneself to surprises, contestation, and inculpation. It is to risk what one found or produced in common."[87] This is what makes all understanding only relatively adequate, unstable, requiring the ongoing art of interpretive attention in a plurivocal community of discourse. For understanding happens, as Paul Ricoeur notes, "in front" of the other (the text), neither behind it as its private possession, nor within us as ours.[88] It is the common and noncontrollable *between* of dialogical mutuality. Gadamer sums up the discussion richly:

> Every conversation presupposes a common language, or better, creates a common language. Something is placed in the center . . . which the partners in dialogue both share, and concerning which they can exchange ideas with one another. . . . To reach an under-

> standing in a dialogue is not merely a matter of putting oneself forward and successfully asserting one's own point of view, but being *transformed into a communion in which we do not remain what we were.*[89]

No one thinks alone. For to think is to understand; to understand is to converse; and to converse is to be exposed to the other and carried into a momentum through which we become different, an other to ourselves. "To be in a conversation," suggests Gadamer, "means to be beyond oneself, to think with the other and to come back to oneself as if to another."[90] Understanding is then a sharing that releases us from self-enclosure out into the open. Let us now draw out some implications from our analysis of Gadamer.

COMMUNITY AS HYBRIDIC SOLIDARITY

It is clear from the discussion so far that the sharing of a common language is no uniform Tower of Babel. There is no one single idiom of communicative relation.[91] Conversation is more than the collective sum of opinions in consensual convergence. For human beings, especially in our current postcolonial and globalizing context, often simultaneously inhabit multiple and internally differentiated social worlds, such that consensus, while important, is neither a helpful way of describing the actual process of communal dwelling-together nor a practical overall ideal.[92] Empirically speaking, it is improbable that a person's horizon of experience will be determined by a single dwelling place or narrative framework. Differentiation, instead of integration, has become paramount as contexts are deterritorialized and cross-fertilized into hybrid identities. No longer is it possible to speak of an internally cohesive linguistic whole, for such an ideal is ruptured and opened up by the ineluctable presence of difference. Frameworks are composed of a multilinguisticality that demonstrates crisscrossing and hyphenated identities.[93] Differences are not only confronted daily within local spaces, they also become integral to those spaces, introducing dispersion into taken-for-granted discursive practices and breaking open fields of semantic power in the between space of cross-cultural horizons.[94] Pluralistic consciousness suggests this much.

Furthermore, rather than mandating that differences and disagreements be foreclosed by consensus or baseline agreement, conversation seeks the give-and-take of mutual understanding between differences. It is through tensional juxtaposition that each player becomes something more. This requires that the contrast of differences be attended to and indeed preserved, not canceled to foment unity—the anonymity of unanimity. The creative tension of dialogue cannot be reduced to the singularity of some collective unification, for it is the irreducible dialectic of multiple voices in relation to one another. It means, as Gadamer states, "to participate with the other and be a part of the other," requiring that we "learn to stop and respect the other as an other."[95]

A conversational matrix does not require agreement to be put into motion, for it is the collaborative and dialectical coordination of a plurality of voices.[96] It is sharing differences. And such sharing is an ad hoc process that is never finished or fixed. In conversation, persons forge what they share in common; they don't demarcate, in advance, what they share, for such a process would already involve conversation.[97]

Indeed, the process of gaining understanding cannot begin with the condition of consensus in mind, for the desire for consensus sets up a polemical attitude of argumentation wherein a nonparticipative asymmetry exists from the start. In such a conversation, the other is seen as an object to be overcome, a vehicle for semantic triumph, rather than as an interlocutor worthy of respect. This tacitly excludes those who disagree, or whose disagreement is not considered potentially conquerable. It either ignores contrast or treats the other as an adversary rather than as a partner. The immanent danger of this stance is a totalizing logic, for the underlying assumption of polemics is that one side possesses, in advance, the prerequisites for proper judgment: principles and prejudices that are not open to question. This stance negates the possibility of any real dialogical reciprocity.[98]

In the course of conversation, genuine argument and contestation may ensue, but only by being brought first into the broader dialectic of understanding, which hearkens continually to the individuality and concrete identity of the call of the other. When a particular understanding is challenged or when a validity claim is at stake, argument may occur as clarification or defense, but only within a presupposed partnership of conversational understanding. Understanding assumes a more fundamental form of mutual correlation than argument, marking a fusion of horizons—not as an annulment of difference or its assimilation to an "us" but as a relation of differences dialectically woven together. Even more, it is a transformative being-with, a tensional living between self and other that implies a continual willingness to enter into the open frontier of relation and to subject oneself to being an other for the other, to being displaced, to following the question wherever it may lead. There is neither a first nor a last word, but a dialogue that is in principle unfinished.

This is why Gadamer is careful to show how dialogical understanding is not simply a technical affair (*techne*), nor a theoretical musing (*theoria*), but a *phroneis*—an ethical know-how—which involves a praxis orientation and effect.[99] Echoing Gadamer, David Tracy puts it succinctly:

> Conversation is a game with some hard rules: say only what you mean; say it accurately as you can; listen to and respect what the other says, however different or other; be willing to correct or defend your opinions if challenged by the conversation partner; be willing to argue if necessary, to confront if demanded, to endure necessary conflict, to change your mind if the evidence suggests it.[100]

And the goal is not something outside of conversation, some truth-in-itself, some foundational ground point of stasis, but rather the partnership generated in the dialogical game of sharing understanding, which continually calls a differentiated "us" forward into new possibilities of convergence, community, and even solidarity. If it is based on understanding, consensus *may* then be forged in the between space of dialogical partnership, but never as something posited in advance. Indeed, the accord of compromise may be the best form of consensus we can hope for in some situations, for a compromise agrees to disagree but remain in conversation. This is precisely why understanding is primary.[101]

In a practical sense, human friendship provides a good example. The mutual understanding and trust achieved simply by talking together about various things joins two persons together in a way that builds a relational context in which real disagreements can subsist creatively without destroying the relationship. In fact, conflict resolution is often about cultivating understanding so that mutual agreement might eventually be reached.

Conversation, therefore, is reconciling but never fully reconciliatory; there is belonging but not the stasis of the same. Always suspicious of any talk of reconciliation, Adorno puts it carefully: "If speculation on the state of reconciliation were permitted, neither the undistinguished unity of subject and object nor their antithetical hostility would be conceivable in it; rather, the communication of what was distinguished."[102] The stuff of reciprocity is not tension-free commonality or full reconciliation, but sharing—the creative communicative relation between mutually distinguishing differences. Reciprocity is a mutually participative attunement of one to another.

Communication presupposes not consensus but rather the willingness to risk being-with the difference of the other. This means being critically self-reflexive, open for questioning and open to critique. For the "common" communal boundaries of an identifiable "us" are not so much composed by stable consensus as by the unstable sharing of differences and disagreements, making such boundaries fluid and permeable, ever opened outward. In such an economy, we exist by multiplying voices, not by diminishing them.[103] The togetherness of genuine community understanding is not a common substance but an activity.[104] And this activity, which trades upon understanding, engenders what we might call a "hybridic solidarity," an explicit and vital mutuality with prescriptive ethical implications.[105] Through the give-and-take of conversation, linguistic worlds are disclosed and broadened, drawn and redrawn, transcending themselves in the between zone of relation. In coming to understanding, one *receives what the other says*, seeking commonality but respecting differences in a *willingness to let the other's call prevail.* One thinks with the other, a thinking that extends beyond oneself to undergo the claim of the other, joining self and other—us and them—in a unique hybridic bond that belongs to neither alone but to both together. And through this something genuinely new is born.

Conversation is interlocutional action oriented unpredictably, and indeed improvisationally, toward the unstable convergence of mutual understanding. In the sharing event of understanding we belong together to an opening world. In fact, the "we" is an open-ended dialogical praxis of solidarity, one that is living and breathing, not the imposition of order on chaos, but a dialectical coordination of contrasts with its own quasi-reconciling momentum of reciprocity. This is why Gadamer's approach, I believe, upholds the best of Rorty's vision without succumbing to the dangers of pragmatic instrumentalism and ethnocentric enclosure. It also provides possibilities for affirming real heterogeneity and discontinuity, as in Foucault, without dispersing differences into isolated fragments, islands unto themselves.

Conclusion: Toward a Normative Vision of Pluralism

Insofar as we risk the openness of conversation, hybridic solidarity happens. And such relational differentiation—as a creative harmony of contrasts sounding together—is not only a hermeneutically productive fact; it should be seen as an achievement worthy of being desired and sought together. There is a moral character to the dialogical event. What this suggests is not the posture of neutrality or mere "tolerance" toward the other, but an attentiveness to otherness from the vantage point of one's own horizonal perspective. Including the other in a conversation is not an act of absorption, but an act of creating space for the other to dwell with "us" while remaining unique. *It is then a welcoming act of hospitality that actualizes our availability to, and readiness for, the call of the other.* This inclusion is not mediated by a monological discourse, which sees the other merely as an extension of us, but by the force-field of conversation itself, which opens up pre-understandings and carries us into new and unpredictable places. Why? Because the dialogical praxis of solidarity is an activity that can never be a content or substance. For, as Gadamer suggests, "who we are is something unfulfillable, an ever new undertaking and an ever new defeat."[106]

There can be no simple selfsameness of identity unmarked by the tension-filled nonidentity of difference. For a shared framework of identity—precisely as a conversational matrix—is not some preestablished system defined outright for all who inhabit a particular dwelling place. It is elusive and has no identifiable center, never able to be straightforwardly signified and converted into an object. Its center, if it is to have one at all, lies in the interstices, in the margins of its own resonance-generating differences, marking a determinate yet undetermined and fluid hybridic bond larger than the mere combination of individuals. In this way, conversational matrixes and their fields of semantic power are more like misty horizons or halos that surround engaged interlocutors, always in excess of itself, present yet elusive and incapable of being clearly drawn. Stated differently, conversation generates overtones that always transgress the limits of its constituents—as a friendship or jazz duet transgresses the simple collection of two persons, calling out something shared between them, something more than each has to offer and more than each may be able to signify.

Thus, while an economy of limits and boundaries is necessary for communal functioning, these boundaries are inherently porous and never fixed, constantly ruptured, deferred, and redrawn as a field of semantic power shifts with the continual play of differences. Boundaries never contain internally consistent and sharply defined cultural "units," for they are always compromised by the differences within. Communal singularity is a vacuous illusion. As Jean-Luc Nancy suggests, the singular uniqueness of a "we" paradoxically consists in "pluriform multiplicity."[107] The conditions for discursive plurality lie within the play of the conversation itself. If dwelling together necessitates some kind of semantic center, it nonetheless can never possess a center. Centers lie on the margins, constituted not by the homogenizing domestication of differences but by the productive force of contrast, of real intersubjective heterogeneity. Wedged in a relational zone of betweenness, centers are best viewed as fields of semantic power fertilized by the crisscrossing of differences. It is this kind of interlaced crisscrossing that forges shared, but not uniform, matrixes of meaning and value. Frameworks, then, are sharing events passing *between us*.[108] Like Wittgenstein's city, a framework's semantic field is an open whole, the borders of which cannot be clearly drawn but are implied as the conditions of meaningful dwelling together.

As parts of a hermeneutical situation in which we are embedded, fields of semantic power contain an integral ambiguity, multivocity, and indeterminacy.[109] There exists a tensional quality to human co-inhabitance that can never be fully stabilized, can never be brought into the final unity of synthesis. Indeed, any move to ascribe to it a common and substantive center moves toward neutralizing the very differences that constitute conversation, evoking the dangerous potential for creating totalizing mechanisms of exclusion.[110] Communal consonance without the resistance of dissonance is the oppressive stasis of the same, of death. Everything living springs out of relational interaction in the to-and-fro tension of contrasts.

In the end, there lies embedded in the nature of community a transgressive openness that implies a potentially universal horizon of solidarity. Unpacking this implication will be the task of chapter 4.

CHAPTER 4

DIALECTICAL PLURALISM: TRUTH, THE OTHER, AND THE PRAXIS OF SOLIDARITY

To live with another, to live as the other of the other, this basic task of human beings applies in the smallest and in larger contexts.[1]

Reflecting on chapter 3, we must note an intrinsic double play between the necessity of a framework of orientation in dwelling together and the unavoidable presence of differences that crisscross within it and destablize it. To be sure, conversation is galvanized by the interaction of genuine differences; yet the contrast of difference is recognized as such only within the interpretive sway of a field of semantic power. Just as there is no identity that forms itself without reference to a commonly forged horizon of values, there is no difference not related to some background of common recognition.[2] For we must stand somewhere, and where we stand influences what we see as significant. We don't encounter what is alien in the mode of cognitive neutrality; we interpret it via the productive force of the traditions we inherit. Otherwise, difference becomes unintelligible and a matter of indifference. It is its sense of likeness and resemblance to what we already know, then, which renders difference meaningful. To know the other is to recognize similarity in it by way of a certain analogy to ourselves. As Aristotle points out, "knowledge is of the like by the like."[3] But, still, genuine discordance and dissimilarity must be there—in some original sense—if the other's difference is to affect us, grab our attention, and call for response. For utter similarity or likeness is a matter of triviality. Conversation is as equally neutralized by equivocated sameness as it is by sheer difference.

How, then, are we to understand the circularity here? It seems that we must steer a tenuous course between drawing-together and letting-be, between the one and the many, between identity/sameness and difference/contrast. The key to traversing such a middle path, I suggest, is continuing to think dialectically, holding the two sides in a fruitful tension. The previous discussion of Hans-Georg Gadamer was aimed at providing the raw material for such an endeavor. Now, however, we are faced with the task of developing this into a productive vision of pluralism, one that has both theoretical plausibility and ethical relevance. The overall task, then, is not merely to acknowledge the fact of difference, but to thematize and underscore the positive value of difference, cultivating communities that are opened toward greater and more inclusive shapes of conversation.

Building upon the analysis of chapter 3, this chapter argues that the self-other entwinement contains within itself a normative pulse pointing toward disclosure over closure. *For the very pulse of conversation engenders the possibility of a translocal space of pluralistic solidarity*. Such solidarity is what I shall call, drawing from Anselm Kyongsuk Min, "dialectical pluralism."[4] Dialectical pluralism is a form of dwelling together that is both an "always already" and a "not yet," on the one hand a fact, and on the other a task stretching indefinitely forward, intimating the ever-deferred possibility of a maximally inclusive horizon of conversational solidarity among differences. All localized dwelling is not only open to, but of its own accord calls for, further supplementation. No community is an island.

There is, however, an additional element to this process that grants it ethical heft. I shall uncover this element in several steps. First, the human concern for truth reflects a will-to-community that affirms existence as trustworthy and worthwhile. This, in turn, suggests that the character of being-with is an event radiating with surplus value. Relation is an invocation, an opening toward the promise of further possibility. From where does this possibility arise? From the singularity of the other's presence, which summons response. And from this arises a double imperative that lets-be and at the same time draws-near the other's difference. Accordingly, we can discern, embedded in conversation, certain anticipatory presumptions as ethical signposts. Precisely these presumptions offer the means by which we may retrieve critical reason in a dialogical modality—that is, as a *dialogical rationality* that can advance the cause of solidarity among differences, exposing and resisting deformations.

Dialectical pluralism must be informed by an analysis of the conditions of being-with if it is to promote a global form of sharing. This is my proposal for a path out of the disembedded and "loaded" universalism of Enlightenment rationalism that at the same time retrieves its positive, productive capacity to generate normative claims about the value of difference, and does so in a way that eschews the perils of postmodern historicism. What we end up with then is a nondogmatic, nonfoundationalist universalism. The upshot of the argument amounts to the following point: *immanent in the play of conversation lies the possibility of retrieving a provisional form of the third moment of the Enlightenment project, critical reason, which will allow us to make normative claims for the attunement of solidarity over and against the totalizing violence of homogenization and the anomie of dispersion*. Indeed, the centripetal force of localized dwelling together is itself a centrifugal force breaking open provincial boundaries, creating a potentially universal dialogical praxis of solidarity.

Therefore, the community that takes up and incarnates the ethical heft of this dynamic is humanizing and good. It is a community that willingly exposes itself to and welcomes the other as central to its own healthy functioning. Pluralism then ensues in an ethical responsibility, an idea well captured by Gabriel Marcel's term "availability," which—as we have already seen—means the capacity to dispose oneself to an "other."[5] Availability binds us together in an attunement to difference. It also has the critical weight to name dehumanizing principalities and powers. The task of this chapter is to give substance to such claims, building momentum toward developing our vision of human religiosity.

THE SHAPE OF A DIALECTICAL PLURALISM

I have argued that communities, as conversational, are never insular entities but rather are self-transcending and liminal, opened to more than themselves, existing in the interstices, on the margins. And margins, as boundary zones, are not barriers or lines of demarcation that separate; instead, they are crisscrossing spaces of interrelationship, of overlapping and mutually trespassing contents, windows whereby we are opened out beyond ourselves and onto the other. Shared identity is never simply a singular given, a conformity; it emerges as a pluralized sharing in the act of conversation itself. Yet far from dispersive, differences are relational and participate in each other so as to be productive of meaning.

Because of this, solidarity should not be thought of as some totalizing collective identity. For it is a dialectical achievement that always already and energetically transcends itself as a "not yet," a task stretching forward toward an ever-greater and differential inclusivity. The being-with of sharing at the same time implies a being-beyond one's own local horizon. Herein lies the productive possibility of solidarity. I am suggesting that the very pragmatics of localized conversations engender a potentially universal space of pluralistic solidarity. Here the postmodern privileging of difference is taken up into a productive vision, an affirmation of what and who "we" already are.

This potentially universal horizon, in its ideal form, takes the shape of a *dialectical pluralism*, a pluralism of differences in relation, of contrasts in connection. Ironically, it is not something different from what we are at the local level—that is, open-ended communities of sharing conversation. In its concrete form, I contend that dialectical pluralism is the incarnation of a globally operative availability and conversational solidarity. Because each particular community of dwellers already intimates such a translocal and universal horizon in its own meaningful sharing, it ideally is open to all other such horizons.

But contrary to what we might call a *pluralism of identity*, dialectical pluralism does not exclude the other by way of a monological and heteronomous logic of either-or, which denies outright the value and importance of difference, demanding that all genuine meaning be "ours," that diversity is perversity, and thereby validates (implicitly or explicitly) xenophobic violence and semantic colonialism. Neither does it seek to annul the other by absorbing it in an encompassing logic of disembedded rational discourse. Dialectical pluralism thus eschews the totalizing "loaded universalism" of both traditionalist ethnocentrism and objectivist Enlightenment reason, the latter of which, in its desire to escape the heteronomy of the former, winds up claiming for itself a neutral field of semantic power *for all*, ironically standardizing and flattening out all difference in its purview. By universalizing their local discourses, pluralisms of identity falsify their historicity and contingency, suppressing discontinuity and heterogeneity.

Yet contrary to a *pluralism of dispersion*, dialectical pluralism neither envisions communities as localized self-enclosed totalities, a stance which, despite benign intentions, validates (implicitly or explicitly) separatist indifference, nor sets loose differences in an ever-disseminating centerlessness comprised of free play, which—under the banner of liberating critique—undermines any and all identity formations as inauthentic closures or totalizing mechanisms of domination. In this way, it eschews three unproductive consequences of the "empty universalism" of hyper-reflexive relativism: (1) the tendency to trap discourses in their own incommensurable frontiers and frameworks (cf., Karl Popper's "myth of the framework"); (2) the tendency, as in Richard Rorty's putatively benign ethnocentrism, to advocate the consensual extension of a predetermined "us" (i.e., the "liberal utopia"), which nullifies the call of the other; and (3) the tendency, as in Michel Foucault's genealogical method, to espouse an extreme logic of "neither-nor," so dispersing all fields of semantic power that the relational force of difference becomes irreparably unraveled, disruption and deferral winning the day. The danger in all three cases is a loss of the capacity to estimate the positive value of some differences over others, for there is no criterion of adjudication between alternative claims. In Rorty's case, there is indeed conversation, but its solidarity is always ironic and fatally self-undermining, fueled not by the value of the call of the other, but simply by our ability to keep the conversation going and expand the "us" of a liberal utopia. For Foucault, on the other hand, there is simply conversation without solidarity, for the interpretative meaning-event itself is dangerously hegemonic, falsely masking a more primary discontinuity and dispersion that goes all the way down.

As I tried to show in chapter 2, Rorty and Foucault's hyper-reflexive approach are unable to productively envision pluralism as a constructive praxis. Where dialectical pluralism has the advantage is in its thrust toward a dialogical praxis of hybridic solidarity, envisioning a robust and dynamic sharing among differences. It neither begins with the concordance of universality nor stops with the discordance of particularity. Rather, it envisions the possibility of a discordant concordance, a vigorous solidarity among differences produced in the dynamism of historical life.[6] As pluralisms of identity universalize the local, pluralisms of dispersion so localize the universal that dwelling together itself becomes fragmented not only as a reality but as a possibility. While a critically hyper-reflexive and deconstructive moment always remains essential to the dialectical betweenness of sharing, if made central it leads to the anomie of *separation* rather than to the creative productivity of *contrast*, ironically negating the very dialogical character of the we-relation that makes critique possible as a linguistic event. The play of contrasts involves tensional correlation and the possibility of convergence, even though these points of convergence and their subsequent world-horizons are provisional projections of momentary and liminal acts of being-with.

Some discourse of sharing is essential for a constructive dwelling-together, especially discourse that seeks to preserve itself against the double threats of domination and diffusion. And yet such discourse must remain vigorously conscious of its own finitude, reflexive and willing to risk itself in meeting the call of the other—that is, if it is to remain authentically dialogical and evade falling into the nondialectical and totalizing logic of identity. In this way, normative judgments about which differences really make a difference, which are enabling and which are disabling, become an important part of the dialogical praxis of solidarity. Dialectical pluralism, as a pluralism of solidarity, does not therefore grant favorable status to every call of the other simply because of its otherness, for this would reduce all local positions to depthless equivalence. A genuinely mutual conversational solidarity, one that is *available* to difference, both presupposes and produces certain criteria for the critical comparison and evaluation of differences; not all differences are the "same," equally endowed with the capacity to make a difference. With this the question of truth arises, the need for productive claims that uphold pluralism against its ruinous collapse.

TOWARD A PRODUCTIVE PLURALISM: TRUTH, RELATION, AND THE OTHER

Two important and interrelated motifs call for our attention at this point, each of which has been present all along in our discussion but never directly or constructively addressed. The first motif points to the necessity of *advocacy*, of making productive truth-claims of one sort or another, naming and preserving the creative openness of conversational sharing and resisting forces that would abrogate its play. The second motif, implied by the first, points to the *corruptibility* of sharing, to the fact that conversation is capable of being, and often is, distorted. If sharing is a meaningful coparticipation in the projection of a world, a point of collective orientation playing out in a field of semantic power, then how are we to make sense of the fact that sharing is often caught up in ideological distortions and asymmetrical mechanisms of nonmutual power play that corrupt conversation? How should a dialectical pluralism fueled by a praxis of solidarity preserve the ability to expose and resist corruptions of dialogical relationality when they occur? If the vision I have proposed retrieves the full sense of human beings as agents who flourish in culturally specific webs of hybridic solidarity, where does it contain critical weight? Where does it pragmatically deliver? To answer these questions adequately we must develop a *hermeneutic of suspicion* that remains ever aware of rupture and discontinuity in the flow of conversation.[7]

But a hermeneutic of suspicion is not the whole story. It is only a part of a larger story. For it must be based on productive claims. It must be joined with a liberative ethic of advocacy, one that while remaining conscious of its own historicity still makes claims about what should and should not be the case in an ideal human community. In the most fundamental way, we must be able to distinguish between reality and illusion, between true or genuinely productive and false or unproductive forms of dialogical relationality. This distinction is crucial to any ethic of sharing over and against forces of exclusion or dominance. Otherwise we gain no leverage to name certain constructions as oppressive, damaging, or alienating. The hermeneutic of suspicion loses its power if ideological construction goes all the way down.[8] If dialogue simply weaves thread upon thread of mere projection, prejudices piled upon new prejudices, wherein lies its capacity to perceive the genuine possibility of value in the call of the other? Thus we are led straight to the heart of the question of the truth-bearing status of dialogue itself—that is, whether and how it discloses the real.[9]

Truth as Relational and the Will to Community

Human beings are creatures who cannot be indifferent toward existence; we take a stand somewhere in terms of what is experienced as worthwhile and meaningful.[10] Orientation is not an "optional extra." This is why, as Simone Weil pointedly puts it, "The need of truth is more sacred than any other need."[11] But truth is not mere closure; neither is it the property of one. Rather, it is a disclosure, an opening onto the being of being-with. That is, the search for truth is a will to community.

Perhaps one of the more obvious implications of a dialogical praxis of solidarity—as an event of sharing—is the view that truth is relational. Neither the correctness of a representation nor the dominance of a technique of power, truth is more like a picturing or mapping of the real, an interpretive rendering of experience. And the authority of such a picture lies not in its mimetic accuracy, its ability to access the logos of the real, but in its epistemic gain for a community of persons engaged in conversation. This point hearkens to the discussion of "mapping" in the introduction of this book, so I will not belabor it here. Suffice it to say that truth is an interpretive viability justified ongoingly in a process of mutual application.

In line with Gadamer, then, the "rightness" of a certain meaning is the product of a relational performance supplemented by other interlocutors in a process that extends indefinitely. Reality is neither simply found "out there" nor created subjectively "in here" by fiat; it is interpretively constituted between persons, composed conversationally.[12] Truth is not the private property of one; it is dialogical, a *dia-logos*. It is the way in which reality comes to pass in language, emerging in conversation as the meaning of things for an "us." Thus, no single voice can lay claim to truth, for it is not the dead weight of a substance to be grasped once and for all. Truth is a disclosive performance, not an excommunicative closure, but a communicative openness in which the meaning of who "we" are arises in the shifting force field of an evolving dialogue. The fact of dialogue assumes as much, moving in the space of a creative coordination of contrasts. And such a coordination does not rise in a vacuum; it is not an arbitrary or haphazard gathering of parts. It plays out in an economy of belonging. Whenever we engage in dialogue, truth is at stake *as the communicative meaning of an intersubjective world.*

This is certainly not to say that there is nothing beyond language. Only that what is outside language cannot be communicated as such. The "beyond language" is itself unthematizable, noncommunicable because, as Wittgenstein reminds us, language cannot cross its own frontiers, speaking without speaking. The objective existence of the world is assumed, perhaps trodden by all, but its meaning *for us* is ensconced in particular fields of semantic power. For what is taken as real becomes meaningfully so only in a language-map, and language itself is conversational.

Hence, truth is a disclosure—a nonclosure or opening—of the real insofar as it is an opening up of the being of being-with, which because of its ongoing tensional and dialogical character is ever deferred and can never be finally or completely signified. This fact makes verbally constituted "worlds" inexhaustible and open-ended, finite communicative wholes capable of augmentation and supplementation.[13] Truth is the protracted hermeneutical act of cultivating a shared world. In this sense, it is a will to community.

Ontological Weight

The will to community, however, hinges on a more originary impetus. Indeed, truth becomes an issue only in the throes of what Gabriel Marcel calls an ontological exigency (*L'exigence ontologique*)—that is, a need for an abiding connection to a meaningful and vital world.[14] After all, because human beings cannot be indifferent toward existence, we restlessly seek to mine the would-be significance and value-ladenness of our experiences. Consequently, we build dwelling places to "house" us in a way capable of carrying the weight of our questions, bearing forth truth. Thus, it is important to add another piece to the argument here: the need for truth is a passion for *ontological weight*, a passion for import, reality, and, dare I say, being.

Ontological weight, however, is not something the self can ever possess individually. For as a dimension of truth, its possibility cannot be occasioned outside of relation with others. Only in the dialogical relation does ontological weight become a concern. Human existence gathers ontological weight as it comes to share a meaningful world with others and participates in the disclosure of truth. And this comes to pass not as an achievement, but rather—following Marcel—as an exigency, an urge toward an affirmation.

This affirmation is found in the Augustinian dictum, *esse qua esse bonum est*. What do we mean by this? The character of being-with is such that within its sway arises an inescapable attestation to existence as trustworthy and good. Conversation is testimony to this attestation. Stirring the momentum of conversation is an affirmation that acts "as if" the real is capable of bearing and upholding our need for value, and more, is something that takes precedence over and against illusion. Put succinctly, *the need for truth is an ontological exigency that anticipates the possibility that existence is at base trustworthy and good.*

Lest too much be assumed here, we must stop momentarily to raise a possible objection. Have I not just slipped a metaphysical premise through the back-door, declaring existence good simply because of the anticipatory affirmation that it actually is good? Could not such an "affirmation" be a fictional projection based on fear and anxiety, a wish-fulfilling fantasy that goes against the grain of what is in fact value-neutral and without meaning? Could not a naturalistic worldview explain the need for truth as a function of the cerebral cortex conditioned by its own need for survival? I must admit, "yes." But this is not the whole story.

It is true that we cannot claim to "access" the objective world via some direct correspondence between word and reality. And there is no proof of the world's humanizing promise, no ready-made foundation we can appeal to that would guarantee such a promise. Yet this need not issue in a naturalistic subjectivism that denies the reality of meaning outside its human creation. For, as sociologist Peter Berger has argued, it is not impossible that the significance we ascribe to reality is in some sense actually there.[15] Perhaps the inescapability of the exigency for ontological weight signals more than an anonymous and indifferent world composed of static noise. Perhaps there is more at stake here than a merely negative gesture of willful defiance against the experience of lack or deprivation, something we have decided in advance that life cannot give us. Perhaps something positive is at work here. Perhaps humans participate in reality, such that, as Berger notes, "there is a fundamental affinity between the structures of consciousness and the structures of the empirical world." "Projection and reflection," then, may be interrelated movements situated within a basic reality that encompasses both.[16] Perhaps the cosmos elicits trust in the meaning of things, as if to say, "have trust in being."[17] The "perhaps" is key. It marks not a new foundationalism or transcendental logic of necessity, but a *possibility* based upon the way in which we actually live our lives.

Indeed, meaning and value cannot self-consciously be avowed as fictions created by fiat, forged out of nothing. We act together "as if" our conversations connect to something real. We build worlds upon such a premise, resisting illusion and meaninglessness in provisional acts of understanding. While this does not point to some necessary or metaphysical ground that secures truth over illusion, meaning over meaningless, it does suggest the possibility that we are preceded in the order of being.

I wish, then, to build a case on the premise—the audacious presumption—that the passion for ontological weight signals an *original realism*. For being-with overflows with the operative conviction that reality is itself full of import and consequence, reflexively affirming an elemental belief that the real has ontological weight. *The very character of conversation trades upon a fundamental decision in favor of meaning and value. How so? By being caught up in a momentum that requires suspending disbelief and indifference.* And this, I suggest, indicates an exposure to what Paul Ricoeur calls a "superabundance of sense over non-sense."[18] The ontological exigency is a response to something prior, a "being affected by" a field of excess that cannot be cognitively mastered but that exerts an intractable tug on human life.

Dialogue, therefore, can be seen as a response to an invocation. Rather than merely projecting value and meaning onto an empty screen, it rises from the presentiment of an abundance and fullness already there. Dialogue marks an exposure to a positive excess of reality. And it suggests that the locus of such an exposure is being-with, within which a surplus of value and meaning radiates with ontological power. In brief, an inexhaustible "more than" overflows into all communicative events, rendering them anticipations that circulate the possibility of ontological weight. Such a possibility tilts human beings in a certain direction: toward meaning rather than toward chaotic anomie; toward vitality rather than toward banal repetition.

We are led, then, to a major point: *at work in being-with is an exposure to the possibility of ontological weight that signifies the trace of a surplus of meaning in the other, the alterity of which is not dispersive but fundamentally value-laden in its contrast.* The experience of the other, in its difference from the same, contains the promise of ontological weight. Indeed, human endeavors to build dwelling places, worlds, are an effort to follow after and participate in this fundamental promise. We are always already saying, "Yes." But promise does not mark an accomplishment, something achieved or readily achievable as an object desired; rather it marks an eschatological "not-yet," a future horizon of possibility. And this has radical implications that spill out into a potentially unlimited matrix of conversational solidarity.

Thus, we come to a second major point: *the need for ontological weight arises as an anticipatory affirmation of the value of the whole of existence.* To be sure, the exigency for ontological weight is a local event, modified dialogically by a particular language. Yet it is also one which, in principle, reaches toward a translocal horizon of differences in relation, an open whole in which all beings are differentiating correlates. In such an ontological exigency the local extends toward and anticipates the universal, even if only provisionally and fallibly, opened out toward a "higher universality" (Gadamer) against the backdrop of an inexhaustible horizon of being-with. But inexhaustibility does not mean indeterminate. Conversation is not neutralized by a Derridian "undecidability" that hovers over a chasm of unknown potential. Rather, it trades upon an abundance that issues in two anticipatory presumptions: (1) the presumption of the singular worth of the other; and (2) the presumption of the complementarity of the other. These are what "tilts" us toward ontological weight, as just mentioned. But how we are to understand the character of such a dual "anticipation"? To answer this question our discussion must turn again to the character of relation. Only here we shall supplement chapter three's exploration of Gadamer with a kind of hermeneutical phenomenology of being-with.

The Presence of the Other in Being-with

Being-with entails an originary experience of orientation toward the other. This is, indeed, what makes the intersubjective or I-Thou sphere of relation primary.

In basic terms, such an orientation begins when the self responds to another who is otherwise than and alterior to it. But what is it that constitutes the other as "otherwise" than the self? It is that the other is not a calculable and exchangeable object among others, but a singular interruptive force. The other is not something I grasp; rather, it grasps and takes hold of me. In this regard, the other is that which grants or gives itself as an invocation. How so? As a *presence*, an invocative facticity that throws me into question and makes me answerable to it.[19] Accordingly, I address one who has announced itself not *for* me, as an object to consume, but in a certain sense *before* me, from an immemorial distance that is not reducible to my own project and its expectations. This distance is created by the fact that the other is not something I cannot produce; it is not a duplicate or mirror image of something I already am, an alter ego. Neither is it a being-present, an experience of something present. For this would render it capable of being subsumed into the same. Rather, the other gives itself as singular, something noncomprehensible and noninterchangeable, a transcendent being that comes from elsewhere and that designates from beyond myself.

In this regard, the facticity of the other—that is, its presence—is an excess that escapes totalization, an inexhaustible surplus otherwise than myself. Presence is an opacity that always means more than can be thematized.[20] It overflows my intuitive capacity and signifies without fulfillment.[21] While presence is always incarnate, an embodied gestalt, there is more signified than a machine-like body in relation to me. Something more remains left over. The trace of something irreducible to function and utility passes of its own singular potency—a person, one who is body yet is also more than objectification as body. Marked by an initiative of its own, the other gratuitously submits itself in its freedom and vitality and thus eludes overdetermination, happening without condition, before I have determined what or who the other is, whether is it beneficial to me, whether it has the right to be. But if the other is given without condition, and simply comes, how do I identify it as such?

Presence is recognizable not by a knowledge content, but by an affectedness in me. I am subverted and opened to response. A radical foreignness surprises me and interrupts my program, my expectations, displacing what is taken-for-granted in my own horizon. I stand back, traumatized or *astonished*, exposed to the more-than-myself.[22] A strangeness that can neither be foretold and occasioned nor reduced to the familiar and ordinary gives itself with dramatic suddenness. This event shocks opens up a gap between interior and exterior, between immanence and transcendence, between what is "mine" and what is not. The other takes place. How do I know this? Because I am thrown into question, dislocated, made strange to myself. A new space is carved out, creating a breach in me that beckons forth response. I become transposed, positioned anew. The epiphany of the other is an experience of the pressure of the exterior, a freedom and individuality external to me that not only resists becoming a mere echo of me, an alter ego, but also stakes a claim upon me. Presence is an invocation. The sovereignty of the ego is ruptured.

Such an invocation, however, need not, as it does for Emmanuel Levinas, introduce a relational asymmetry whereby I am utterly subjected to the other in passivity, held hostage by an undeclinable and unconditional responsibility.[23] For, if so, the other becomes so radically overpowering and incommensurate that it ruptures all categorical mediation, receding into an indiscernible and anonymous horizon, making me in principle responsible for all, even the one who would destroy me.[24] Such hyperbolic language rings of masochism, fashioning a subject helpless and humiliated in its abject poverty before the other, indeed "possessed" to the degree that it is a substitution for the other.[25] Here there can be no shared space of reciprocity. While it is true that Levinas does wish to retain the possibility of dialogue between an "I" and a "You," he introduces an "absolute distance" that effectively drives a nondialectic and asymmetrical wedge between the two terms. To insure the ethical transcendence of the *You*, which he thinks Buber and Marcel overlook, Levinas insists on a form of dialogue in which "the *other counts* above all else."[26] The end result, however, is a relation without relation, one in which *I* share the burden of the other alone. The dynamic is one-way, leaving no room for my own otherness for the other. There is no space for self-differentiation from the other. This leads us to a further point of criticism.

Levinas's way of depicting the ethical relation, as a one-way relation, empties the subject of any capacity to mediate the other. The other cannot be known as such. And this effectively surrenders my ability to recognize the other as other, as distinguishable from me.[27] We might ask, then, on what grounds is it possible for Levinas to claim, as he does, that the subject is constituted in response to the summons of another? Levinas would reply that responsibility has no ground in intentional consciousness; it is anarchic, signifying a nonintentional relationship with exteriority prior to any act of representation that would affect it.[28] But this strategy seems duplicitous. It claims responsibility without naming the other for which the subject is responsible. It removes the other into anonymity—a face without a face—in order to protect responsibility from being compromised by the violence of conscious representation. Why then "responsibility"? Why not, as Derrida suggests, an "undecidability" in which we do not know what to do, in which every decision requires the sacrifice of responsibility in some respect, for every innumerable other is totally other?[29]

I think it is possible to appreciate Levinas's way of giving ethical primacy to the other rather than to the self without going to such a hyperbolic extreme.

To say that the self is relational means to affirm that subjectivity is an exposure to the other's presence. Consciousness always already displays the trace of alterity. It is an affectedness that signals a constitutive openness to the other. For all genuine relation begins with the call of the other's presence. Such an invocation precedes dialogue and makes it possible. But while the call of the other *must* be privileged, it does not thereby attain to absolute privilege. To say "Here I am!" means to testify neither to an utterly unknowable other nor to every other as totally other, but rather to some particular other signifying itself before me and calling me unto it. There is a provocation, and this implies distance and discontinuity. Distance, however, is not curved into an inaccessible height, as Levinas would have it.[30] Why not? Because *provocation* is also an *invocation*.

The other is a presence who solicits my response by signaling a promise precisely in its distance. Its call is not anonymous, but signifies the trace of something that invites recognition and bids me to pay attention to it. I respond. My world is adjusted. I am transposed, tilted toward the exterior, not merely in some general sense, but in a certain direction. The surprise of the other not only astonishes, it delights as something precious in its own right, a gift that excites my interest and draws me beyond myself toward it. My response is the ecstasis of *wonderment*.

Wonderment, however, is not a possessive grasping that disqualifies or overcomes the gap created by the force of difference. It is a transposing of the self by way of an other who remains transcendent, exterior to me. Indeed, insofar as it is connected to astonishment, wonderment consents to and preserves the gap between self and other. I do not present the other; I am affected by the other's gratuitous summons, caught up in a momentum of surprised fascination with something—an embodied proximity—at once alluring yet strange and inexhaustible in character, something outside my power to master. Unable to "fit" the other neatly into my own program, I follow its trace without guardrails, without clutching to categorical leverage gained from my own familiar world. Such a following is a kind of migration into the liminality of being-with. I venture into the unknown, asking questions. For my world has been defamiliarized and put into question. Wonderment is a migration into the space between self and other carved out by astonishment.

Accordingly, wonderment is an ecstatic activity that celebrates the difference of the other in a kind of self-transcending reverential delight. Marcel describes this as "admiration."[31] But what is it about the other that draws out admiration? In one respect, we cannot say. For this would reduce the other's transcendence to a calculable object in the economy of the same, absorbing its freedom. But in another respect, because the other is an embodied proximity, we might say—with a nod to Levinas's idea of "the face" as a locus of the other's givenness—that it is the fragile and vulnerable preciousness of an unrepeatable singularity, a dimension of alterity that invokes response not merely out of its capacity to supplement and enrich my world, but out of its capacity to be ignored, even violated.[32] There is pathos to presence, for the other's freedom entails a call to be recognized and heeded. As presence gives itself as its own freedom, an agential quality emerges that outlines the shape of a person, one with possibilities of meaning and value that are distinct from mine and that emanate from its own center of being. Admiration, then, is not a superficial acknowledgment of something attractive, but rather it is reverence before something with dignity and power in its own right, something beyond my horizon and its expectations.

As a state of reverential delight or admiration, wonderment then radiates with connective power. It is a pressure erupting from the inside out, indicating exposure to a superabundance, a "too much." Wonderment marks the trace of presence as an invocation. It signals that a surplus of dignity has taken hold of me. An incalculable value-density has ruptured ego-absorption by singling me out and inviting interest. I undergo a summons to draw-near and accordingly am thrown outward in a gesture of participatory attunement to the other's difference. In this way, wonderment participates in the distinct preciousness of the other. Attuned to its contrast in a kind of *sympathy*, or feeling-along-with, I am brought into relation with the other's own way of being.[33] Wonderment, then, is, a being-with wherein I experience the other's invocation precisely in its distance and dispose myself to it in a posture of attentiveness.[34]

Accordingly, it would not be overstating the point to say that to wonder is to love, to hear in the presence of the other a certain call for admiration and care. It is as if the other says in a singular and unrepeatable sense, "love me."[35] Without appeal to some utilitarian economy of exchange or logic of equivalence, I respond, carried beyond myself toward an *alter ipse* that is real and not illusory, a gift that is immeasurably good and worthy of response.[36] A love-filled exertion of the self toward the surplus of reality contained in presence, wonderment is an "interested" aspiring to draw-near, attend-to, and be-with otherness for its own sake, as beloved. Hence, wonderment is a dynamic power of linkage with the other. It is what leads dialogue along the path toward understanding by being the impetus behind the asking of questions. For questions presume a prior invocation, something that excites the ecstasis of interest. To question is to care, to give oneself over to the potential meaning and value of the other. Ideally, it is to love. As Augustine knew, loving and knowing are intimately connected, the latter being an act of will delighting in its object.[37]

It is crucial, however, to stress here—pace Emmanuel Levinas—that there is a breach that prevents wonderment from deteriorating into a self-integrative and erotic appropriation of the other. For, again, the other is not an object merely "there for me," for my appetite, but a presence, an excessive "more than" I can contain. In this regard, the experience of presence is also an experience of *absence*, not as an empty nothing, but as a pressure—an excess—that surpasses me and thus is incapable of being enfolded into the same, of being totally congruous with me. In fact, this is why the other elicits a self-transcending response: I am made insufficient to myself, put into question, astonished, and opened up toward exteriority. Precisely because it is self-transcending, this response cannot be a self-preoccupied urge for fulfillment. It is a transposure in which I become oriented in a new key rather than the other becoming absorbed into the key of the same.

Wonderment, then, is not a libidinal desire that seeks its own satisfaction. It does not long for self-absorbed union with an estranged other out of its own lack. Rather, it migrates toward the other in reverential delight, and in this, consents to a goodness that is opaque and not capable of being owned. Hence, in this sense, love is not strictly self-interested; it is ecstatic, other-interested. Out of being exposed to a superabundance, I am brought to care for more than myself, as if to say, "Here I am." And this is the stuff of compassion and responsibility.[38] It is a summons into the moral life. Strangely, such love finds itself fulfilled not by seeking fulfillment, but by extending beyond itself to participate in the preciousness of the other.[39]

Presence thus elicits a response from me not in an objectifying and utilitarian modality, but in an exigency—an ever-deferring, migratory desire—to participate in an elusive abundance, a *mystery* larger than I can enclose. The other's presence is a mystery not because it is a problem capable of being solved, but because it surpasses objectification and its very character is that of singular incomprehensibility.[40] Not because it is unknowable and anonymous, but because it is acknowledged as beyond categorical expectation, beyond the totality of the same. Insofar as I have been caught up in wonderment, there is always more. Questions beget new questions; the further wonder advances, the deeper astonishment becomes, and vice versa. For in the end, I am brought to notice and pay attention to a good distinguishable and at a distance from my own project. *Connected with astonishment, wonder does not claim anything for itself; it is the harbinger for an acknowledgment of value and meaning in the other that always remains a future potential, never being present as such.*

Consequently, being-with is a relational coordination that hovers paradoxically between having and not-having. The other's presence is given in an absence, as a proximity that distances, a facticity too much to fully intuit or master. It is a mystery that both astonishes and evokes wonderment. There is no perfect coincidence or congruence between self and other, but rather a dialectic of distance and relation, a dynamic that is tensional to the core.[41] We come again to the hermeneutical circle, but in a much richer sense than portrayed in our earlier analysis of Hans-Georg Gadamer.

Let us now draw out several implications as they connect up with themes explored earlier. First, the other is never given as such, immediately known or directly signified as an essence. It is always mediated hermeneutically by its reception via a framework's field of semantic power. Yet, second, insofar as I have been called into question, the other is neither absorbed into the same nor rendered anonymous. Something happens that allows the other's call to be heard, distinct from both my world and the static noise outside it. Presence happens. I am exposed to a "more than" myself, not in some general sense but by a non-interchangeable singularity. As we saw in our previous discussion of Gadamer, such exposure yields questions, which manifest an aspiration to connect with the other, to understand it. Thus begins the dialectical back-and-forth of conversation. But more, there is created a disposal toward the other—in its distance—that has the character of a participative attunement, even love. Dialogue ensues, then, as a way of attending to the other, asking questions in fidelity to the other's presence before me. Finally, what is at stake in all of this is ontological weight, the being of being-with. Experienced as presence, the other modifies and thus expands consciousness in a gesture anticipating that the other's contrast and difference has a vitalizing meaning—not solely "for me" but for an inclusive "us." And the result is the "between" of genuine relation.

In this light, two anticipatory presumptions come to the fore. These presumptions, mentioned at the conclusion of the previous section, are elemental to being-with and are borne out in the praxis of conversation: (1) the presumption of the singular worth of the other; and (2) the presumption of its complementary. From these, two correlative ethical imperatives can be named: the need (1) for preserving the freedom and singular dignity of the other; and (2) for an inclusion of the other as a possible partner. Consequently, we shall see how these implicate a potentially universal horizon of sharing voices, an open whole.

Letting-be Differences: Reciprocity, Freedom, and the Presumption of Singular Worth

Opened up by the presence of the other, the self becomes a response to the other, caught up in the throes of being-with. One mode of the resulting self-transcendence is an anticipation of the singular worth of the other. And this issues in a fundamental orientation of responsibility for the other that acknowledges its distinguishable freedom from me and its potency for reciprocity with me. Hence, an imperative is implied—namely, that the other be recognized and attended to in posture that presumes its distance from me, its call respected *in principle* as of singular worth, precious in its own right.

At this point, again, we move beyond Gadamer, who neither feels obliged to stake out the criteriological conditions of possibility for the dialogue he advocates nor fully accounts for possible structural distortions in the dialogical encounter.[42] True, Gadamer does suggest that a pragmatic condition must be satisfied for dialogue to ensue: the call of the other's difference must first be hearkened to as interesting, drawing us out.[43] But this itself suggests something more fundamental. It involves a utopian thrust, a *fidelity toward the other in which the singular worth of its difference is let-be.* I employ Gabriel Marcel's term, "fidelity," because of its moral connotations as an ongoing event projected toward a future. Marcel notes that "fidelity is the active perpetuation of presence," a way of continuing to undergo the summons of the other.[44] It means to exist toward the other in faithfulness to its uniqueness, preserving its value as otherwise than myself. Fidelity is not a stale, dispassionate perseverance conforming to some external duty, but rather bespeaks my involvement with the other. Insofar as presence happens, I am already caught up in being-with the other. I am made available for the other. And in this opening, I simultaneously become open to other others as well, able to hearken to their call and to engage them in conversational exchange.

An egalitarian ethos emerges. When I hearken to the call of the other in astonishment and wonderment, an "ideal" shape of power symmetry and reciprocity is anticipated—indeed actualized to a sufficient but never definitive degree—between myself and the other. This ideal shape, in principle, applies to all others universally.[45] It entails an acknowledgment of my limits, that I am finite and do not possess absolute meaning. I have been opened to the possibility of meaning and value in what is otherwise than myself, something that merits recognition on a par with me, equal in dignity and weight.

This does not mean that, in the final analysis, I owe respect to all voices as equally valuable and valid, only that they must initially be *presumed* to be so for the dialectical relationship of conversation to be set in motion. As conversation is oriented toward understanding, it incarnates a basic covenant between free partners, a fidelity that in essence spills over to include all possible participants without preemptory expectation. And more, without the imposition of demands and expectations. Why? Because being-with entails an exposure to a surplus value—namely, presence—that by its very character opens the self up to the *possibility of value* in the call of every other, not merely those selected prior to conversation. Indeed, an open receptivity toward the other's singular worth—and in principle, toward all others—is the condition of possibility for genuine conversation. This is why conversation is irreducible to the polemical logic of "either-or"; it aims at the broader telos of understanding with its "both-and," not at semantic conquest, manipulation, or exclusion.

There is here an axiomatic and originary responsibility: the other must not only be acknowledged in its alterity, as something beyond me, but also be noncoercively privileged and undistortively let-be in its difference and in its distance. The upshot is a liberative praxis of letting-be.[46] The letting-be of the other is the presupposed covenantal requirement of fidelity, a regulative imperative built into in the very fabric of dialogical relation. It is not a duty that pressures conversation from the outside. Rather, it is immanent in conversation itself, emanating from the distanciating effect of being astonished by the other's presence. To hear the other speak, to allow her to speak, grants her a certain freedom to present herself and not be reduced to my project. This means avoiding the kinds of preemptive closure that introduce hidden strategies and promulgate distortions in advance, falsifying and putting real differences out of play.[47]

Hence, a moment of unconditionality is unleashed. It issues from the presence of the singular other but spills out into all potential relations. Of course, this unconditional moment is never fully actualized, for unacknowledged prejudices and distortive strategies do in fact constrict communicative interaction. The point is not to suggest that conversation is ever "pure" and untainted by egocentric motives. Rather, that its very performance enacts, in provisional and fallible ways, an ideal that bears the trace of presence. In its communicative praxis, dialogue anticipates an ideal of symmetrical reciprocity and mutual recognition between differences. Horizons can never be totally fused, for the distance of the other is the condition for relation. In this sense, symmetry does not mean equilibrium. It means letting-be the tension between differences.

Furthermore, while this does not signify the de facto actuality of equal value among all differences, it is more than simply an abstract regulative ideal. For the presumption of singular worth trades on the *possibility* that such worth is actual and real, even as it is only through the interplay of conversation that qualitative judgments of worth are subsequently made.[48] As Charles Taylor states, "real judgments of worth suppose a fused horizon of standards," which assumes that we have already been exposed to the call of the particular other and have already been taken up into dialogue.[49] This, then, not only rules out any abstract and disembedded ethic of a generalized and anonymous other in which all differences are the same (i.e., a loaded universalism) but also eschews the strict sense of value relativism whereby all differences are trivialized as merely equal (i.e., an empty universalism).

We are now engaged in retrieving the universal and normative third moment of the Enlightenment project, critical reason, but are trying to do so in a way that upholds the dialogical praxis orientation of a pluralism of solidarity. The basic claim is this: *the difference that conversation assumes and requires, entails freedom, and this entails a fidelity to the other that lets-be the other as a person who has the capacity to bear forth her own singular—that is, noninterchangeable—value, which can be subsequently tested in the sphere of an intersubjective public.*[50] Though real judgments of worth are the determinative *result* of conversation, they are a possibility anticipated as the indeterminate *condition* of conversation. And in this, reciprocal freedom is both an implicit given and an explicit task that outstrips every given context.

The truth of dwelling together in conversation, thus, is not a frozen "objectivity" but a living and open whole, a disclosure in which the other is let-be. For truth's dialogicality is pluralizing and freedom-making, clearing space for the equal representation and mutual recognition of singular voices. Truth is neither merely theoretical nor simply the play of the will-to-power; it is a concrete and practical wisdom with ethical implications, a *phronesis* empowering a way of life marked by reciprocity and mutual acknowledgment.[51] It is, broadly speaking, a responsibility incarnate in our love for others.

Drawing-together Differences: Reconciliation, Accompaniment, and the Presumption of Relational Complementarity

I now introduce the word *reconciliation*, but do so only with strict qualifications, as a relative term of the act of *accompaniment* implied by fidelity. Always a fragile and fallible covenant between differences, reconciliation is the praxis of mutual participation and sharing, wherein "we" agree to be together—willing to listen, to speak, and to change if necessary—as an other for each other.

This possibility first emerges from the affirmation of value in the presence of the other, which in wonderment bids me to draw near it. *The gesture of fidelity thus not only seeks to preserve the singular worth of the other by letting it be, but seeks also to accompany it along the way, to be there with and for it.* Here the self is conjoined with the other as a term of relational correspondence and supplementation, a value coordinated with me in its contrast. There is an anticipation that the other's difference is not utterly different and distant but rather is constituted such that it is capable of being with me through extended time. I shall call this the "presumption of complementarity." Along with the presumption of the other's singular worth, this is an additional element presupposed by all local conversations. For in conversation I accompany a different other who not only has potential worth in itself, but also offers a gift of worth that potentially complements and enriches me. There is more at stake than simply letting-be the other.

If letting-be the other were the principal responsibility, as it seems to be in Foucault and Derrida, dispersion and discontinuity become the last words. Diversity becomes its own end. Here, a sheer indeterminacy is produced that lets loose a freedom so totalizing that it neutralizes the very relational character of dwelling together, undermining the viability of conversational sharing. While there is a measure of validity to such a view, its privileging of difference goes too far, fatally compromising its own capacity to make critical claims about what differences make a difference, undermining the ability to distinguish between reality and illusion, indeed between self and other.

Against this kind of reductionism, I suggest—drawing again from Taylor—that any relation of accompaniment between self and other assumes the working presumption of complementarity as its fundamental condition.[52] Indeed, the axiomatic presumption of value that lets-be the other cannot help but also involve the anticipation of complementarity, of parity between voices, without which conversation splinters apart into windowless monads. Fidelity to the other signals a fundamental affinity with the other. And this, in principle, implies all others.

Again, there is a moment of unconditionality at work. By the force of its own openness, an openness that is held out in a presumption of the singular worth of the other, the dynamism of a conversation implies, imagines, and seeks to actualize a potentially universal horizon of mutuality in which all differences are compatible and harmonically reconcilable in their contrasts. In a word, the presumption of complementarity is an anticipation of a global shape of accompaniment. It attests to the possibility of a maximally inclusive solidarity, a universal modality of interrelation that affirms that differences fundamentally co-inhere and are relationally intertwined as supplementing correlates. It is this utopian ideal—ensuing from the lure of the other's presence and radiating outward from the other's singularity to include potentially all others—that makes accompaniment possible.

Hence, a kind of *omega point* of conversation emerges, not merely as an abstract regulative ideal, but as a point that entices from ahead as a possibility. The fact that we actually do converse presupposes as much. As a localized and provisional event, conversation intrinsically strives toward mediating deeper and wider understanding. And in this fallible praxis it intimates an ever-larger and inclusive horizon of complementarity, anticipating an omega point of sharing solidarity, an unrestricted domain of relational inclusiveness. Through such a quasi-teleological stretch, the meaning of a universal modality of local sharing might accordingly be disclosed as the *truth of us all.*

I say "quasi-teleological" because while its anticipation is inherent in the very act of dialogical exchange, the omega point of conversation—the truth of us all—can never be hypostatized or realized in itself. For it is *the* dynamic correlation of all differences in relation and as such cannot be a totality. It remains an open, incomplete, and elusive whole. Every conversational understanding, as a fusion of horizons, is a de facto actualization of the dialectical reconciliation of differences, never a de jure achievement of it.[53] Complementarity remains ever-deferred, releasing new possibilities for accompaniment as it releases new possibilities for letting-be differences. Contra G. W. F. Hegel, there is no triumphant march toward the absolute.

Thus, all localized events of meaningful understanding—precisely in their particularity—are predisposed toward imagining a wider horizon of complementarity that outstrips all of their provisional achievements. In all genuine acts of conversation where understanding and reciprocity prevail against forces of misunderstanding and distortion, the anticipation of complementarity empowers us to risk further conversation, to step toward further possibilities of novelty.

This idea corroborates the presumption of worth in the call of the other and eschews the logic of polemics, which establishes the other as a threat to be overcome or excluded. Gadamer suggests as much with his idea that in attending to the call of the other we transcend ourselves in anticipating its coherence and meaningfulness, its resonance with "us."[54] Indeed, *to understand at all implies the telos of the broadest horizon of human solidarity, a universal horizon of mutuality within which all local horizons can be understood as valuable and against which they can ideally be measured.* This fuels the exigency for ontological weight.

Even more, this gives substance to the ideal of a dialectical pluralism. For any act of communication, as a relative approximation of intersubjective accord, takes its stand in reference to a universal horizon of sharing, not declaring that such a horizon presently exists nor guaranteeing that it will necessarily exist, but only presupposing it as a possibility, a task to be forged together. But such a possibility is not an utterly open-ended and indeterminate horizon. I use the words *telos* and *omega point* to indicate a directional thrust to conversation. Even amidst the most trenchant disagreement, complementarity is implied as both the condition and task of conversation. It is anticipated as a telos and, as such, is always pre-grasped as an already not-yet.

The ideal of complementarity is a relational drawing together that lets-be differences in their singularity and uniqueness. It anticipates a simultaneously interconnecting and freedom-making dialectical pluralism, a reconciliatory reciprocity that is always a relative consensus, an open whole. For the presumptions of singular worth and complementarity suggest the possibility of an undistorted and freedom-making horizon of mutuality among all voices. This possibility is latent in all dialogical exchanges, no matter how isolated.

Meaningful Vitality: The Fundamental Affirmation of Being-with

Two interrelated and elemental affirmations can be gleaned from the twin ideals of complementarity (in which differences are drawn together) and equal singular worth among free participants (in which differences are let-be). First, the anticipated ideal of complementarity implies a fundamental confidence that differences are not utterly dispersive and discontinuous, but *meaningful* and able to co-inhere as partners. The very need of human beings to belong to a shared world of orientation suggests a fundamental resistance to the anomie of sheer indeterminacy. And this resistance reflects a primary intuition of the relational determinacy of human dwelling, of the fact that value-producing frameworks are an inescapable requirement for self and communal formation. Frameworks are the products of a fundamental confidence in the coherence and order of things. Human beings dwell together "as if" differences are worthy of trust, "as if" they contain the promise of meaningful counterpoint and interrelation and are therefore hospitable to our deepest desires for recognition and validation. Within the space of this original affirmation of the meaningfulness of difference, human beings dwell together in fidelity by drawing together a world.

Second, there is implied in the ideal of the equal worth of the other a confidence that the singularity of its difference is not reducible to the monological mechanism of the same, an absorbing totality, but rather is a reservoir of creative invigoration, novelty, and individuality in its contrast. Human beings need more than to belong; we need to flourish and find vitality in dwelling together. And this suggests a fundamental resistance to the boredom of homogeneity, repetition, and stasis, and even more crucially, the oppression of being overdetermined by the ordering power of logos over dia-logos. The very need for recognition suggests an exigency toward differentiation, toward the freedom-bearing power of singularity and individuality.

This reflects a primary intuition of the living fecundity of differentiation, the fact that singular contrasts hold the creative power to unleash novelty, to animate and enrich our lives together. Without the uniqueness of uncoerced individuality, the call of the other has nothing to offer; and it is precisely the other's singularity that beckons to be recognized as having something of value to offer, quickening conversation. Hence, intrinsic to dialogue is a fundamental hope in the promise of *vitality* in mutual recognition. Vitality is the creative power of the other experienced in its freedom. And within the space of this original affirmation of vitality, frameworks become disposed to let-be differences in the act of drawing them together as meaningful. It is not merely the meaning, then, but also the vitality of mutuality among individual differences that we desire in dwelling together.

Together, these two affirmations, coupled with their corresponding modalities of resistance, comprise a dialectical affirmation of the *meaningful vitality* of differences in relation. Meaningful vitality is a product of the tension between relation and distance that occurs in the presence of the other. It hovers between (1) the connective power of meaning and (2) the distancing and individualizing potency of vitality. For vitality without meaning is fragmenting dispersal, and meaning without vitality is banal repetition. This twofold activity of confidence in the promise of difference, played out in both anticipation and resistance, is immanent in the praxis of all dialogue. Indeed, it adrenalizes dialogue. Based on the presence of the other, the promise of meaningful vitality is the empowering force animating intersubjectivity. Conversation itself is testimony to a basic confidence in the meaningful vitality of relational differentiation, following after its promise. And this promise is what I have described as ontological weight.

Accordingly, following after the promise of ontological weight might be characterized as a *praxis of hope*, a hope stubbornly resistant to both (1) chaotic dispersion and (2) oppressive overdetermination as it anticipates an ideal dwelling together. Human beings live together "as if" being-with is worthy of trust and hope, "as if" relation contains, despite its tragic conflicts, the promise of valuative enrichment, indeed love.[55] Thus, meaningful vitality is the constitutive affirmation of being-with, an affirmation that reflects a presentiment of surplus value intrinsic to the we-relation.

We shall have more to say about this in chapter 5. At this point, it is enough to conclude that the anticipatory drive toward ontological weight occurs in the affirmation of meaningful vitality. And this reflects an intersubjective ontology, the character of which outlines the human capacity for dwelling together in the widest, richest, and most complex matrix of differences. Being-with is a particular dialectic of the one and the many that stretches toward the possibility of a universal horizon of global solidarity, an open whole.

DWELLING TOGETHER IN THE UNIVERSAL OPENNESS OF SHARING DIFFERENCES

We now are in the position to draw out further claims regarding the "universal" implications of being-with. This amounts to a retrieval of the third moment of the Enlightenment project, critical reason, but in a dialogical modality. A drive toward universality is enacted in every concrete act of conversation, emerging from an anticipatory grasp of the meaningful vitality of the whole. Exploring such a drive can illuminate new possibilities for thinking about reason in a dialectical manner—that is, as a fallible and tension-filled play between the local and the universal. All communicative claims manifest this dialectic, and what is more, they do so in the dialogical space of differences engaging one another. Accordingly, reason is a solidarity-producing power because it traffics in plurality. This underscores the self-reflexive and emancipatory character of reason and its dual potential for deformation and restoration. Indeed, reason opposes reifications, totalities, and instrumentalizing abstractions because it is a fallible anticipatory stretch from the local toward the possible whole that we all share.

The Nature of Communicative Claims as Localized Universals

I submit a thesis: if truth is relational, it plays out formally in a gesture toward meaningful vitality, and does so pluralistically in the diverse content-shapes of what can be called "localized universals"—that is, localized anticipatory grasps of a difference-bearing whole, of one humanity and one history in a universal horizon of intersubjective corrigibility. Universal attestations are an inevitable part of communication. In conversation I make a claim *that* something is the case, that some difference is meaningful and vital. But I can do so only with and for others *within* that conversation, within a localized interlocutionary situation. There is no way to escape the relative adequacy of the dialogically local, no way for universals to become disembedded. Localized universals, then, are (1) local in that they are context-based construals of reality—of a world—*for* a particular community of discourse in order to instantiate the meaningful vitality of a certain way of dwelling together. They are based on disclosures of what is of shared value for that particular community. But they also operate in a way that (2) simultaneously extends beyond that community, making claims about the potential complementarity and individual worth of all differences. Despite being local and historically embedded, the intention of these construals is universal in scope, their meaning always in-front of itself, a projection applying explicitly to local frameworks but implicitly aspiring to an indefinite array of interlocutors. This carves space for all voices and affirms them as worth a listening.

If, as we saw in chapter 3, a local field of semantic power is opened outward toward the translocal, the localized universal is the concrete manifestation of this openness. And further, given the primacy of presence and the dynamism of the dialogical situation, a universal solidarity is tacitly affirmed in all linguistic utterances. Yet because this solidarity is never achieved in itself, only intimated as an already not-yet, it is always provisionally and fallibly staked out in particular frameworks, or fields of semantic power, which lay relative claim to what is and is not the case for an "us," orienting persons toward what is capable of meaningful vitality and embodying this in specific practices and institutions that mediate ontological weight. It is then in the dialectic of conversation with new and different voices that these claims are subjected to questioning, subjected to redemption, revision, and reconfiguration, perpetually augmented toward Gadamer's "higher universality." A potentially unlimited matrix of conversational understanding is the performative co-implication of all localized conversation. This makes all local claims universal in scope, though never in reality. The disclosure of truth, therefore, is a particular envisionment of the potentially universal and not a universal vision of the particular.[56]

Hence, *the issue of truth emerges as a localized event through which a given interpretation finds a particularized universal relevance as a disclosure-concealment of the whole of human solidarity*. All discourse is public and suggests a potentially global situation of sharing wherein perspectival claims become subject to, and augmented by, the greater human community. We are not then left with the aspiration to solidarity *within* the ethnocentric language community to which we happen to belong and from which we seek to extend an "us" (à la Rorty). We are instead caught up in a dynamic that passes beyond the privileged frontiers of every local community and moves in the direction of a potentially universal nonassimilative and liminal sharing of frontiers—a pluralistic solidarity. All validity claims are immanent to a particular field of semantic power and the lifeworld it presumes; but in addition, all validity claims are transcendent in that they aspire to the meaningful vitality of all differences in relation. The supposition of a transregional solidarity is intrinsic to all dialogue. A moment of excess, which issues in a claim of unconditionality, is built into the process of mutual understanding, bursting every provinciality asunder and opening to an infinite realm of possible expression.[57] No community or culture remains an enclosed insularity.

Dialogical Reason: Critical, Self-Reflexive, and Emancipatory

The notion of a localized universal allows us to retrieve the dialogical capacity of *reason* to yield critical, self-reflexive, and emancipatory results. Reason is indeed contingent, linguistically situated, and context-dependent. Yet all linguistic utterances, claims, and judgments are not enclosed in their own specificity. For the praxis of conversation points to the possibility that all truth-disclosures mutually co-inhere in their differences, each subject to the meaning and vitality of the other.[58]

Reason, in this sense, is the performance of truth, a dialectical identity-in-difference propelled conversationally forward by the creative tension of contrasts, not by the ideal stasis of homogeneity (i.e., *logocentrism*). For it belongs neither to "us" nor to "them," but "in between" both, emerging in the marginal space of the "with" of being-with. As such, "the rational" is not capable of being hypostatized and rendered determinate as universal, but only as a dynamic that is thrust beyond itself, anticipating the coalescent and open whole in which all differences are related. Though they are fallible and imaginative projections located in diverse languages, rational claims are not therefore illusory and empty of reality. Rather, they reflect a communicative openness oriented toward an ideal, a not-yet that is always grasped in finite ways as a possibility intrinsic to all particular conversational matrices. As Gadamer notes, "it is completely mistaken to infer that reason is fragmented because there are various languages. Just the opposite is the case. Precisely through our finitude, the particularity of our being, which is evident even in the variety of languages, the infinite dialogue is opened in the direction of the truth that we are."[59] The "truth that we are" is the sharing solidarity of mutual understanding in the broadest of possible contexts, a global Mitwelt wherein all exist liminally, exposed to the excess of the call of the other and hence alive as an other for the other.

Dialogical reason, therefore, is the source of its own transcendence in multiple voices, not in contradiction to some more fundamental unity, but in fulfillment of its own movement toward the truth of being-with. Though this is only intimated as a possibility, it nonetheless animates the intentionality of all discourse, opening all validity claims to questioning and possible redemption in a would-be global conversation. The appeal to reason is thus an appeal to the potentially universal solidarity inherent in all communicative praxis. Such an appeal, though anticipatory and contingent, is never ironic. For the hope of meaningful vitality is to share differences, and this is of ultimate consequence for the way in which we live our lives together. Reason refuses both totality (as the oppressive hegemony of rationalizing order) and illusion (as the dispersive fragmentation of chaos) in staking claims about what it means to dwell together.

Hence, in the final analysis, reason might be construed in anticipatory terms as the *possible* complementary between parochial grammars, each reaching out for the whole that none completely owns in itself but that promises the capacity for mutual recognition and sharing. *Universality lies in the local performance of an open and outward stretch, a readiness for the other.* It is not reducible to any kind of factual content, for such content must be subject to the potentially universal and inclusive sway of conversation itself, standing the test of intersubjective corrigibility. While we may be ever tempted to produce arguments that reduce interlocutors to silence, which stop the flow of conversation with claims for certainty, in the end, all truth-claims are only hypothetically universal, justified provisionally by their ability to induce and preserve a conversational togetherness that lets-be differences: a reconciliatory reciprocity.[60]

In this light, as Jürgen Habermas maintains, rational discourse can serve in a fallible manner to organize our communicative practices in ways that promote mutual understanding, eschewing and seeking to overturn those ideologically distorting and rationalizing practices that impede such understanding. A dialogical reason eschews the disembedded Enlightenment notion of universal reason while still upholding the possibility of normative claims that estimate the positive value of differences. For it seeks by nature to build dwelling spaces of freedom-making recognition and sharing. This is no mere semantic play, but a lived praxis of truth-disclosure that has dramatic consequences. As Habermas succinctly puts it: "Communicative reason makes itself felt in the binding force of intersubjective understanding and reciprocal recognition."[61] This entails neither absolute claims to certainty, which are conversation-stoppers, nor a kind of unidirectional historical teleology, as in Hegel. For reason marks a possibility: understanding as a sharing of differences, the inclusive complementarity of a pluralistic letting-be of differences.

Communicative Deformations and the Praxis of Restoration

Of course, rational discourse can and does go awry, collapsing into mere rhetoric or becoming subject to ideological distortions and reifications that undermine its freedom-making potential to let-be differences. Because universality is an openness that is never fully guaranteed, the localized universal, as an instantiation of the affirmative thrust toward meaningful vitality, involves an instability, a disequilibrium that demonstrates a "lack" even as it points toward the promise of the "fullness" of being-with. For we dwell together in the tensional space of having and not-having the truth. This is precisely what makes conversational practices dynamic and fluid, open to novelty.

Given the instability and vulnerability of this "lack," however, a conversational matrix can refuse its own contingency, its own finite locality and historicity, and fixate on a particular way of thinking and doing "as if" this offered final relief from its contingency, guaranteeing a secure or fixed framework of identity. Hence, while it is true that identity-forming boundaries are essential for intersubjective orientation toward what is deemed worthwhile, it is also the case that the need for orientation contains the germ of its own illness. The affirmation of meaningful vitality, which resists nonrelational anomie, can become disposed neurotically in a fear of diffusion, a fear that magnifies the perception of its own vulnerability. Reacting out of such fear, communities can become deformed and be compelled to master and control the other.

Communicative sharing, thus, is a fallible praxis that can nurture its own deformation. Its variously actualized conversations can obscure either (1) their *local* origin and conditionedness by feigning completeness, artificially closing themselves off from their own open-endedness and difference-bearing character, thus becoming exclusive and oppressive; or (2) their own *universalizing* thrust by denying their own individuality and creative power, letting themselves be overdetermined in a relation of inferiority and/or dependence.

In the former posture, what might be called *overextension*, a dominating and objectifying power over others is asserted that strategically serves the interests of those voices able to control the sway of conversation. Differences are defused or intrumentalized, managed by a calculative reason oriented toward preserving the totalizing identity of the same.[62] This kind of objectification occurs even in acts of disengagement from, or indifference toward, others.[63] For differences become neutralized and rendered effectively voiceless, deprived of unique value. As Max Horkheimer and Theodor Adorno maintain, this is precisely where the dialectic of the Enlightenment becomes fatally self-subversive and totalitarian, the emancipatory power of critical reason inadvertently totalizing itself as an instrumental reason that treats all individual differences as if they were the same reified, interchangeable, and anonymous individual in a vast system of exchange equivalency.[64] This is exemplified in the culture industries of capitalist societies, where the quest for freedom ironically becomes the worst form of enslavement, a pseudo-freedom based upon mechanisms of consumption, production, and capital accumulation, ironically labeled "growth."

The latter posture, *underextension*, displays an opposite tendency, an overdeterminedness or lack of empowerment. Here, one party takes refuge in, and gains identity from, the power of another as if it guaranteed security, thereby gaining legitimacy by "losing" itself in the other.[65] Often, however, this is a symptom of a learned dependence based on derision, repudiation, marginalization, or exclusion. For a discourse of domination can so affect the self-perception of the dominated that it "forgets" itself and sees itself as the reverse underdetermined image of that which feigns to have the power of determination and thus legitimation. This logic has functioned prominently in colonialist expansion, slavery, and gender relations.[66] Because the need for identity-forming orientation is so strong, one can come to recognize oneself as inferior and dependent in the eyes of another who claims putative superiority and self-sufficiency.

In both of these postures, however, differences are seen as threats to be overcome or avoided. Thus, if it is to remain reflective of the primary we-relation, dialogical reason must not only construct communicative dwelling places of mutuality (resisting underextension) but also preserve the deconstructive power to name, counter, and transform those distortions of relationality that inhibit conversation by systematically seeking to alienate certain voices (resisting overextension). A truly dialogical reason must continually act reflexively to expose the suppression of genuine heterogeneity, resisting those systems of closure which, in the name of security or identity, falsify the availability of being-with and administer relations instead of sharing them. This is where the critical component of dialogical reason shines. It resists the reification of differences, anticipating their unique worth and relational complementarity. In the words of Adorno, "it refuses to affirm individual things in their isolation and separateness: it designates isolation as precisely a product of the universal," which totalizes.[67]

Dialogical reason must therefore guard against both disinterestedness—a forgetfulness of the other tantamount to a refusal to engage the other, assuming a position of superiority—and xenophobic hostility—the perception of the heterogeneity of the other as a threat to semantic stability. For both seek to constrict discourse and cut off its open-universality in favor of a closed-universality, which remains strictly parochial and thus disingenuous.

Furthermore, a dialogical rationality must eschew both ethnocentric and polemical logics that demand an outcome of agreement as the prior condition of conversation, a process that tacitly justifies or outrightly leads to semantic assimilation—wherein the other is an object to be neutralized in order to eliminate disagreement—or semantic exclusion—wherein the other is rejected in advance as unworthy of communicative engagement, its difference signifying its inferiority and incapability of becoming properly rendered like "us."[68] We do not have to look far to find violent examples of this: colonialization, ethnic cleansing, segregation, anti-Semitism, and so forth. In whatever form, assimilation and exclusion both amount to self-contradictory refusals of the universal thrust of dialogical intersubjectivity, corrupting the meaningful vitality of a community's own sharing by turning it into an object to be possessed and managed. Any conversation that seeks to guarantee its own modality of orientation inadvertently falsifies its relational contingency. Genuine dialogue inevitably accents differences and so aids in exposing false closures and corrupt universalisms.

More than fostering critical acts of exposure and resistance, however, dialogical reason must *advocate* the material inclusion of potentially all others into the conversation. It must invoke the praxis of partnership over exclusion and competition. This involves working in constructive solidarity with and for those voices that are systematically, and by coercive power mechanisms, excluded from the meaningful vitality of sharing in particular communities.[69] By giving voice to those with no voice, remembering also those voices and histories tragically marginalized in the past, conversation can become a liberative force of reconciliatory reciprocity, transforming and redeeming the very praxis of its sharing. *Dialogical reason in this way directs us toward a universal accountability for particularity, an availability that is no mere receptivity but an emancipatory and freedom-making momentum oriented toward mutual fecundity and flourishing.* An *ethic of conversational solidarity* thus comes to the fore: to be responsive to, and responsible for, the call of the other. This is availability: the praxis—the *phronesis*—of being lovingly disposed to the exteriority of the other, affirming the other in its difference.

Thus, while dialogical reason can become tragically deformed, this is not cause for defeatist pessimism, for an eschatological hope is built into its very performance. Because any communicative action always already anticipates the creative possibility of a universal solidarity, the power of sharing renews itself and rises here and there to transform communities of discourse into further and greater moments of the universal openness intimated by their very intersubjective constitution, by their hope in the promise of meaningful vitality. We can, suggests Habermas, "locate a gentle but obstinate, a never silent although seldom redeemed claim to reason" operative in conversational mutuality.[70] Reason understood this way is a "stubbornly transcending power, because it is renewed with each act of unconstrained understanding, with each moment of living together in solidarity, of successful individuation, and of saving emancipation."[71] As I see it, however, this claim to reason is not one of consensus but of the potentially universal solidarity implied in mutual understanding. In this way, I go with, but go differently than, Habermas. There is a telos immanent in the communicative praxis of all conversation, a kind of "tilt," one leaning toward the freedom-making mutuality of differences in solidarity, thereby directing us both to approximate the ideal of a reconciling reciprocity and to identify and overcome those practices undermining its possibility.[72]

In this light, misunderstanding has the implications of an ethical failure, an irresponsible and unresponsive breach of intersubjectivity. But even in such tragedy, hope is ever-dawning. And this hope is the desire for reciprocity and inclusivity in dwelling together. The telos of dialogue as mutual understanding is a fragile task but one set before us all in the public space of the planet. In this way, conversational solidarity has a world-historical effect. In solidarity, particularity is included more than overcome, opening up universality rather than imposing it.

Conclusion: Pluralism, Universality, and Hospitality

In being-with the other through hope, we become an other to the other, held out into the openness of dialogue in the absence of any final reconciliation but in the tenacious affirmation of an ever wider scope of meaningful vitality. The ideal community that fully incarnates such a hope would be itself universally true, actualizing the liberative sharing praxis of being disposed to the other. But this universality and this liberation, as Adorno would hasten to point out, would by no means constitute the conformity of totality.[73] Rather, it would enact the anticipatory thrust of conversation itself as an implicit solidarity—the unity of differences in relation. Genuine universality is not a closure, not a designated content, but an openness (a disclosure) that is a readiness for the other, for difference. It exists more as the harmonic overtones generated contrapuntally by interacting voices sounding together in their differences than as one privileged tone ringing above all. Only in this sense can communal discourses be seen as open circles of "identity in difference" instead of closed circles of homogenizing identity.

This brings an "us" into the liminal between-zone of encounter where we are available for the other in the mode of neither hostility nor mere tolerance, but welcoming hospitality.[74] Hospitality is an invocation to let borders be crossed, to dwell-together, to render fluid and permeable the boundaries of one's home so that the stranger might co-inhabit and share it. Such an activity pays attention to the call of the other and so marks a willingness to be brought into the between of genuine relation. Fostering not a relation of asymmetrical condescension but of democratic solidarity, hospitality is a fruitful metaphor for the being-with of relational differentiation. Differences here are not swallowed into the home-dwelling, but rather preserved in their uniqueness as they are welcomed and taken in, thus enlargening and enriching the scope of the resonance created by the "us" now dwelling together more inclusively, extending the frontiers of that dwelling's field of semantic power and becoming more complex and beautiful because of it.

Thus, as an availability for the other that simultaneously welcomes and lets-be, hospitality shows its worth as a moral imperative in an increasingly global and interconnected human dwelling space. The ethic of hospitality is the praxis of sharing; it is what pluralism is about. It is a willingness to let-go of oneself in order to let-be the other in being-with it. If boundaries are essential for centered dwelling-together, hospitality names the liminal and open character that is already implied by these boundaries. For dwelling together *is such* only as because of its capacity to be decentered and transformed into a place of pluralistic solidarity that welcomes the stranger, enriched by the gift of its difference. Human beings need to be placed somewhere, but the power of the truth that "places us" is disclosed only on the margins of being-with. Here, between similarity and strangeness, and through conversational sharing, we are summoned always into a potentially universal and transregional community of difference in relation, a liberative yet inclusive "us" in which no particular manner of dwelling enjoys special privilege.[75] From this betweenness we begin again and again to negotiate the meaning of the plurality that we are, each of us an other *for* the other in the dynamism of sharing and remembering that cultivates a larger, more differentiated—but ideally better—"us." A new global form of parochialism emerges, a precarious configuration of interdependence steering between totalizing identity and diffusive repulsion. For we dwell together in the widest diversity.

There is much potential in such a dialectical pluralism for engendering cross-cultural conversation. The power of dialectical pluralism lies in the productive hope that conversation itself assumes and already begins to enact: to foster social agents not irredeemably self-enclosed but capable of creating, shaping, and sustaining the kind of intersubjective climate in which mutual recognition and reconciliation thrive, capable of invoking a dynamic justice and peace in dwelling together. This is an imperative in our increasingly interconnected planetary situation.

To be sure, pluralism signifies a being-with the "other" that is decentering, rupturing taken-for-granted and stable senses of what it means to dwell and be at home in the world. Communities are decentering centers, themselves broken wholes. Giordano Bruno's polycentric centerlessness finally does seem to win the day; there can be no central metanarrative in which all humanity must be wrapped. Yet I have maintained that in this also lies the promise of new possibilities that are not finally destructive to all meaning and value, but rather call us into affirming the concrete, difference-bearing, and relational character of human life in the world, and more, into the drama of reciprocity, as a praxis of cooperative dialogue between differences that both "brings out" and "brings together" what is vital and most creative in each. We are all related. Any denial of this is a breach of what we are. Yet, precisely as intersubjective beings, we are all margin dwellers, exiles living in a liminal zone between worlds, caught up in conversations that make us all heterogeneous sharers.[76]

In seeking a meaningful orientation toward what is worthwhile, human being is a world-openness—a boundary transgressive openness toward being-with and being-for others. Perhaps the possibility of solidarity among all differences hints at a universal center that is revealed yet concealed in the concrete performance of all our finite conversations, never achieved but always already hoped for, its unpresentable presence anticipated as a kind of *decentering center* that calls us ever outward in partnership. It is here that the possibility of the "religious" emerges and gains coherence. For there exist traces of an unconditional horizon at work within all localized events of understanding.

CHAPTER 5

THE TRANSCENDENT GRAMMAR OF PRESENCE AND THE RELIGIOUS SENSIBILITY

At bottom, the ordinary is not ordinary; it is extra-ordinary.[1]

I now wish to supplement and broaden the scope of our discussion of pluralism by exploring a set of issues anticipated by the argument in chapters 3 and 4. The purpose of this chapter is to bring into focus the possibility of a discourse about God—that is, the unconditioned and infinite—that does not merely acknowledge plurality but is itself pluralistic. Briefly, my proposal is this: insofar as the human exigency for ontological weight marks an exposure to the other's presence, it designates the infinite. For it opens up what I have called "the between," employing Martin Buber's category, a zone of relation in distance between self and other that overflows with surplus possibility. While the other is always particular, neither anonymous nor general, it invokes an anticipatory momentum that extends to a horizon of unconditioned potentiality. This not only inaugurates the imaginative projection of worlds, but also swings outward the conversational matrices of those projections toward being-with *all* differences.

The *religious sensibility*, I shall then argue, is a poetic enactment of this process. Put in a phrase, it issues in a *faith that anticipates the unconditioned power of being-with by thematizing meaningful vitality in the explicit limit-terms of an image of transcendence.* Talk of a universal "God" takes rise from this. Religion, then, does not disqualify but rather is commensurate with dialogical reason. It is a possibility built-into the fabric of being-with, emerging within the sway of conversation. Furthermore, the religious sensibility not only supports but also serves positively to inculcate a pluralistic and dialogical praxis of solidarity. Indeed, if love—as a drawing-near that lets-be difference—is our highest human hope, then religion is a particularly poignant way of emboldening this hope.

Hence, whereas the last several chapters function as a philosophical anthropology, this chapter and chapter 6 take steps to develop the hitherto articulated argument into a philosophy of religion, or more specifically, a philosophical interpretation of religious pluralism. The argument of the present chapter unfolds in four main steps. First, I set the stage for the constructive proposal by forging a path beyond what I consider to be methodological "dead ends" in approaching the problem of religious pluralism. Second, I argue that "the between" of being-with overflows with an abundance incapable of being circumscribed, an openness that designates not an indeterminate and vacuous space but an infinite space, a horizon of "Presence." Connected to the prescence of the other, "Presence" is the ultimate term of relation. Its impact is traced in the passion of trust, not as an ordinary passion happening here and there, but as elemental—as an "absolute affectedness." Third, I examine the character of trust as a passion fraught with anxiety, but that affirms the trustworthiness of life even amidst its ambiguities and imperilments. Finally, I offer a detailed analysis of the religious sensibility, arguing that Presence is the *Whither* of the religious affirmation. Religion is faith in a transcendent source of meaningful vitality that concretizes and modifies trust's anticipation of Presence. Chapter 6 will flush this out more completely as a lived praxis with the potential to promote love and hospitality in a global situation of diversity.

"RELIGION" BEYOND POLEMICAL, MONISTIC, AND HISTORICIST PLURALISMS

While it is true that the "universal" nature of religious convictions can breed absolutism and promulgate conversational closures, often even fostering violence, I wish to argue that the initial universalizing impetus from which religious claims emerge is not inherently hostile toward difference. To the contrary, human religiosity at its best implies not closure but the openness of availability, a performance luring us out of self-enclosure and encouraging us to greet differences with hospitality and love. The overall slant of my proposal makes three general claims: that the religious sensibility is (1) a modification of the affirmation of trust in the direction of an appeal to transcendence that is (2) fundamentally intersubjective and communal and (3) in its authentic form invites the praxis of an extensional availability toward differences that cannot help but suggest a potentially universal community of solidarity. This chapter will focus upon the first point, outlining its features so that the second and third points can be better grasped in chapter 6.

But we must tread carefully. It is obvious that, in the vein of pioneering thinkers such as Friedrich Schleiermacher and Ernst Troeltsch, I am intentionally distancing the term "religion" from normative ethnocentric association with one faith tradition as definitively superior to all others.[2] I shall call such a view *polemic* because it sets up a binary logic of elemental incompatibility between differences.[3] Here, truth is not only one—that is, factually singular—but also is assumed to be the possession of one group against or over all others. Where there are conflicting claims, others are naturally in error.[4] While it does acknowledge the empirical fact of diversity, a polemical pluralism projects diversity and weighs it substantially in its own image, judging others accordingly by wielding a special claim to uniqueness, revelatory or otherwise. Difference is construed as somehow "outside" the closed circle of truth, as evil, deluded, or ignorant, either a competitive threat or superfluous and altogether lacking significance. Despite the sense of assuredness it brings to its adherents in a decentered world, this approach is fraught with serious difficulties. It promulgates a tribal absolutism that blunts its capacity for self-criticism and masks its own fallible texture as a localized field of semantic power. It distorts the dialogical character of rationality by taking the standpoint of the universal and identifying with the ultimate itself.

For these reasons, polemical communication preempts the posture of availability integral to a dialogical praxis of solidarity, so privileging a particular community of discourse that all others are either (1) semantically excluded and denounced outright as empty of value, at best well-intended errors; or (2) semantically assimilated by being neutralized, expropriated, and colonized by the home world as partial truths in need of a truth already fully granted. Whereas the former tends toward a demeanor of hostility and coercive domination, the latter moves, albeit in a less overtly coercive direction, toward legitimating the "voluntary" cooption of others via efforts at evangelization (as in "missionary" endeavors). Either case betrays a polemical posture toward other possibilities of authentic religious truth, operating out of an ideological system of totalizing closure and constrictive universality that cloaks its own dialogical embeddedness and vulnerability.

There is, however, a more subtle version of the second, assimilative, option just mentioned, one that brandies a softer and less outright absolutism. It acknowledges that other faith-stances, while they do not fully grasp the truth, are nevertheless approximations of a final truth that only it possesses. It admits that there is some kind of basic continuity among faith traditions, a common horizon unifying them. But this continuity is polemically "loaded," having its ultimate location only in a single consummate faith tradition. This logic is exemplified in classic Christian apologetics (e.g., Justin Martyr), which neutralizes the religiously other in order to expropriate its wisdom for Christian purposes, incorporating it within the purview of God's revelation and salvation in Christ.

Other faith traditions seek the salvation that only the Christian truth grants through the work of God in Christ. Such an apologetic polemic also comes out, though in a more refined and nondoctrinaire shape, in modern Protestant notions of a "superior" or "absolute" religion. Here, Christianity, as the authentic revelation of God, sums up or most adequately concretizes everything that other traditions exemplify and desire on the basis of some kind of "original" or "general" revelation available to all persons.[5]

This apologetic posture takes an even more subtle shape in the work of Catholic theologian Karl Rahner, who goes so far as to positively appraise the salvific efficacy of non-Christian religions. Yet, for Rahner, it is the Christian revelation that "includes" all other revelations and renders them ultimately salvific as the explicit manifestation of a universally present implicit grace. God is revealed and saves within non-Christian traditions, but definitively only through Christ, thereby enabling Rahner to call other faith traditions "anonymous" expressions of Christianity.[6] For this reason, Rahner's position is often called "inclusivism." David J. Krieger more appropriately calls it "apologetic universalism."[7] For it interprets all truth, even when found outside the purview of Christian faith, as its own.

But as there can be no single, universal culture, there can neither be a single "inclusive" tradition in the world's religious beliefs and practices. Inclusivism contains an imperialistic impulse toward semantic colonization. One might argue that this is only natural, for religious claims have an unavoidably universal and comprehensive sweep.[8] But as we saw in chapter 4, because no field of semantic power is truly universal, it is a falsification of historicity to universalize the local. Embedded in traditions, religious claims are localized universals, and are therefore opened up to the dialectical force of differences. Even in its more benign versions, apologetic polemics obscures this basic fact, and in so doing, artificially removes itself from historical life. Thereby, and ironically, it cuts itself off from the source of its own nourishment. The basic point: there is no one, true religion for all people.[9] There are many religious possibilities, each distinct from the other.[10]

Yet by employing the term "religious" I do not mean to fall into the equally problematic posture of a *monistic* view of plurality, suggesting that there is indeed, abstractly speaking, one truth behind all religious forms, a truth that is brought into focus and given voice differently according to different historical horizons. Such a view holds that all religious traditions express essentially the same pristine reality: some univocal core experience or content that is described in various culturally formatted ways but is possessed by no one tradition absolutely.[11] Though interreligious monism seeks to avoid kinship with the Enlightenment goal of a "natural" or rational religion for all people and should be applauded for taking us beyond the parochial absolutism of polemics and for advocating mutual respect and tolerance, in the end it proves curiously defective. The fault lies in an overt essentializing which, in sweeping all into one, nullifies any resulting gain. Despite its attention to history, monistic pluralism amounts to a denial of genuine historicity and the novelty of particularity. It ignores the uniquely embedded sociocultural character of religious differences by reducing all to a homogeneous totality, a loaded universalism.

Furthermore, monist pluralism grossly underestimates the productive world-making import of community. It tends to place the seat of religion in the individual's prethematic yet immediate access to *the* transcendent, regardless of what community one happens to be in. The inevitable upshot, then, is that community and plurality itself becomes nonessential or at best peripheral to the main event. Here the problem of religious plurality is solved by being dissolved, blending differences into a similarity comprised of what religious traditions are "really" saying behind the surfaces of symbols, rituals, and doctrines. But history is no mere secondary accretion that finds its way into the flavor of the pudding, an accidental quality added on to a prior and transhistorical essence that is everywhere and always the same. Rather, experience, and thus understanding, is always conversationally inscribed and tradition-bound, the "cultural-linguistic" event of sharing a world.[12] And because there can be no neutral experience not already informed by location, there can be no religion in general, prethematic or otherwise. After all, genuine dialogue assumes real plurality. It occurs efficaciously between genuine—not artificial or happenstance—differences.

Building on this, a final and more devastating criticism can be launched against a monist version of pluralism. Though it has the advantage of disavowing parochialisms, it is deficient in that it surreptitiously introduces a more abstract but equally problematic claim to absoluteness, feigning disembedded descriptive neutrality while actually presupposing particular tradition-bound (theological?) criteria of adjudication for what counts as normative. The danger of a subtler but equally pernicious semantic colonialism looms large. For to deny one's own local "prejudices" is to give them unbridled authority, effectively reintroducing polemics into the game. Second-order theory is itself embedded; no one can claim a suprahistorical freedom from the sway of localized perspective. If it is supposed that the shared "truth" of religion—its core experience or content—is prethematically universal, we must ask precisely which second-order language has the privilege of gaining immediate thematic access? The answer is none. History circumscribes both knower and known. The postmodern pluralistic consciousness, therefore, weighs heavily against both polemic and monist pluralisms. Each approach distorts differences.

If no one tradition can claim absolute sway, and yet all are not equal manifestations of some originative event, have we not then abrogated the grounds on which we aim to speak? Why bother with the term "religion" at all? Perhaps it is inherently reductive, distortive, and/or ahistoricizing?[13] Despite the prospect of serious problems associated with its tendency to be employed in ways that gravitate toward the monistic view of pluralism,[14] I contend that the category "religion" still warrants use as a second-order abstractive and genericizing device.[15] It helps us avoid the shortcomings of worse alternatives—namely, polemical pluralism and its opposite, the relativizing pluralism of *historicism*. Thus, we come to a third way of conceiving religious pluralism—that is, the historicist way. It holds that particular traditions are equivocal and relative to their historical context, the epiphenomena of culturally produced fields of semantic power and therefore reducible to the local environments in which they occur. While employed in many contemporary approaches to religious studies, this kind of view is tantamount to an empty universalism. If historicism is granted, not only (1) does the content orientation and unique first-order reality claims of religious convictions evaporate as nonessential, thus (2) undermining the comparative capacity to identify and distinguish between their real differences, but (3) the door is opened for unrestrained ideologizing and isolationism.[16]

There is danger here. For the sheer discontinuity of historical differences is not only incoherent or unintelligible, worse, it gets us nowhere beyond ourselves. It leaves us self-enclosed, unable to access real difference, for we can do nothing other than "project" the other in our own image. And this is effectively the same as claiming that the reality of the other makes no "reflective" claim upon us, exercises no control over the way we envision it. Historicism tends to legitimate a sectarian impulse tantamount to tribalism. Such is hardly the stuff of a vibrant and coherent dialectical pluralism. Indeed, it is tantamount to a pluralism of dispersion.

This is why I am skeptical of theological writers who, on the nonfoundationalist supposition that all thought is locally conditioned, too quickly assert the narrative consensus of Christian community as a given, normative "for us."[17] We are led to an historicist polemicism against what lies "outside" the presumed authority of "our" way of reading the world.[18] Though this position need not entail absolutism, it tends to relegate the question of universal relevance and truth to criteria already inscribed within each faith tradition.[19] The logic is self-congratulating and circular: Christians are Christians because they are Christians, informed by the Christian story. Intracommunal conformity to the Christian tradition—and indeed often a very selective reading of "the" Christian tradition—becomes the key to being Christian.

While it *can* be viewed as the basis for a religious pluralism, I vigorously oppose this kind of conclusion on the moral and epistemological grounds staked out in chapters 3 and 4. By refusing to let the openness of dialogue have full sway, such a view is plagued by a myopic vision that obscures the multiple texts and traditions that constitute Christianity. Furthermore, this position overlooks the character of all discourse as a localized *universalizing*, the hermeneutical fact that conversation implies a potential sharing among the widest differences. Finally, and perhaps most troubling, it can preempt the capacity for genuine self-criticism and the openness of availability. Yes, we always speak "from" a local situation, so there is no such thing as disembedded reason, but we must be circumspect about retrieving pre-Enlightenment theological visions on the basis of postmodern precepts.[20]

Dialogical reason offers some corrective possibilities. The inquirer, insofar as he or she is caught up in conversation, hovers between worlds. Along with Charles Taylor and in the spirit of Hans-Georg Gadamer, we must remember that any encounter between self and the other involves an ambiguous composite of generality and particularity, of comparison and contrast.[21] Differences thus emerge dialectically vis-à-vis a horizon of comparative reference. In the throes of conversation, and as horizons are coordinated in their contrasts (or "fused"), a palpable set of qualities emerges that exert a certain differential force, making a claim upon the "home-world" of the inquirer. Contrasts are then configured and rendered discernible in a constellation of possible complementarities. In this way, contrast is not absolute, but opens up interpretative possibilities that lend themselves to investigative questioning. And this is only possible because there are, indeed, potential shared points of contact and relation amidst differences. How do we then name these potential points of contact? We name them in terms of continuity and resemblance.

A kind of qualified, hypothetical, and open-ended "essentialist" model—a hermeneutic that grants the capacity to designate certain differences as similar to other differences—seems required for the comparative task. We do this all the time when we designate music in comparison to noise, marriage rituals in comparison to courting, human beings in comparison to birds. The point is that the purified difference and contrast of sheer historical particularity is finally unintelligible. And regarding "religion," something similar is at stake. One cannot investigate the particular histories of the world's faith traditions and decipher any kind of intelligibility to the language without a comparative context for reading those histories and making connections. But conversely, without taking into account real incongruity and difference, comparisons and commonalities themselves become either vacuous or filled with the ethnocentric biases of the inquirer. Taylor acknowledges this by stating that through comparison we develop a "language of contrasts" that makes understanding possible, a language that cannot help but make "general" claims about what is "really" going on among a state of affairs.[22] In our case, then, second-order comparative reflections cannot help but involve making judgments about first-order affirmations and the reality-status of religious claims in general, invoking question of whether and how religion holds ontological weight. Assumptions about the character of reality are always already involved in a "language of contrasts." The point is to be rigorously explicit about what it is we are up to when investigating religion, critically acknowledging and arguing for an interpretive position rather than taking it for granted.

Thus, I advocate a hermeneutic of religion, a heuristic point of departure that goes beyond the "said" meanings of first-order discourse to interpret those meanings as ingredients representing a unique way of being related to the cosmos. This will allow us to develop a cross-cultural vocabulary or language of contrasts that (1) makes meaningful sense of the peculiarity of the subject matter by diagnosing it as religious and placing it on the broader map of human experience. Furthermore, it will (2) allow us to access the diverse meanings of various first-order languages. To be sure, such a vocabulary will (3) function only as a localized interpretive rendering, the universal plausibility of which is never immediately given as some foundation but remains to be legitimated as one possibility among many competing constructively for viability. A hermeneutic of religion therefore will never be exhaustive. The richness and complexity of the historical detail exceed any comprehensive grasp.[23]

But even while remaining pluralistically conscious and open to critical supplementation and the possibility of falsification, a cross-cultural language must nonetheless self-consciously and in the rigorous spirit of critical inquiry (4) put forth substantive—and universalizing—claims about the character of human life in the world.[24] Hence, I affirm a critical realism that acknowledges that while "reality" is always already overdetermined and theory-laden, it is not a deliberate fiction, but an interpretable horizon of patterning events, displaying an array of formations that invoke response, which invite curiosity and investigative inquiry, and which make a claim upon the imagination. Reality is the other-than myself to which I am summoned to pay attention and of which I am compelled to take account. Indeed the arguments that I have put forth throughout the book thus far assume such a viewpoint.

Perhaps we can champion the integrity and cross-cultural applicability of the religious sensibility as a generic feature of human existence without doing injustice to its historical embeddedness and without becoming closed off to real historical difference. I wager so. It is with experimental tentativeness, then, that I seek to risk an exploration of the religious sensibility, offering an interpretation of those anthropological conditions of possibility that account for its ubiquity and power as a motivating force in human life. Of course the assertions that result are not neutral descriptions merely read off history. They are hermeneutical constructions that cannot help but import certain assumptions and prejudices, implicating myself as a first-person participant in history and not merely an idealized and neutral observer. Yet despite their unavoidable provisionality and uncertainty, the claims put forth do aim to invite heuristic sway regarding something real and efficacious in human life across cultural dividing lines, their productive efficacy potentially corroborated in the crucible of conversation with other such accounts.

Thus, I advocate a dialectical version of religious pluralism. I am not interested in right answers but rather in a kind of epistemic profit, the movement away from problematic viewpoints and toward more adequate ones amidst dialogue between a variety of alternatives. In the final analysis, the advantages of such an approach most creatively surface as they resist closure and keep the conversation going, supporting relations of hospitality between differences. I wish to present an alternative to the polemical, monistic, and historicist approaches by steering a tenuous course around them into affirming substantive religious value in a pluralist modality.

ON THE INFINITE

To set up the argument, we must regroup to note how availability has a double intentionality. As a disposal of self toward the other, availability is a passion that both draws near the other and at the same time lets the other be in its inexhaustible difference. This is because availability, as we saw in chapter 4, is a posture characterized by the tensional coordination of astonishment and wonderment, standing-back and drawing-near. It signals a reverential delight in the proximity of a reality too saturated with meaning and vitality to be an object or acquisition. There is then a gap, a noncoincidence in the performance of being-with that can never be mediated and traversed. No simple and conclusive one-to-one correspondence exists between self and the other. An unclosable breach exists deep in the heart of relation.

It is this breach that has the character of the infinite, not as an "otherworldly" foundation, but as a region of inexhaustibility opened up by the tension *between* distance and relation. As it reflects this, then, availability opens up to the infinite, a passion that can never become sufficient to itself. And this makes the exigency for ontological weight incapable of being resolved or fulfilled.

Accordingly, I wish to suggest that the dialectic of distance and relation exposes the possibility of a postmetaphysical affirmation of God, a God beyond ascriptive discourse yet immanent in all discourse as a boundless leftover, a pleroma or overabundance traced by the anticipatory stretch toward ontological weight. It is crucial to note, however, that "the infinite" here does not mean the God of onto-theology, a being above all others or being in general. Though, in the end, it is not unrelated to the way in which certain religious traditions speak of God, by "infinite" I mean to indicate a formal designation or placeholder marking a region of unconditioned openness, a space of transcendent fullness that is beyond closure. Never given in itself, such a region or space functions as a context of recognition, an ultimate horizon by which religious images and conceptions become meaningful and relevant possibilities. Put in somewhat different terms, specific revelations (Offenbarung) always occur within a context of revealability (Offenbarkeit), manifesting a more originary possibility. And this possibility is wider than the concrete "revelations" of particular traditions. Indeed, *God* is a word rich with polyphonic narrative and historical resonances, a localized way of existing toward the infinite. Religious traditions, in various ways, trade on the anticipation of the infinite, their languages and practices riding the arc of its hyperbolic surplus. For this reason, it would be presumptuous to assume at the outset the particular Abrahamic formulation of God as *the* infinite.

Abundant Openness as the Infinite

The reality—that is, the being of being-with—opened up by the presence of the other bears the mark of the *infinite*, hollowing out interiority and exploding it outward in the shape of an abundant openness that can never be resolved or totalized.[25] In astonishment, the presence of the other is experienced as a limit-event designating infinity in its excess. Astonishment indicates something inexhaustibly exterior, something that transgresses adequation as an interruptive mystery surpassing our powers of appropriation. Hence, it signifies an absence. And such absence evokes a corresponding nonadequation in the heart of subjectivity, summoning a passion that cannot be satisfied or fulfilled in the same.[26]

A boundless openness is created, one that has an infinite stretch. The other's presence interrupts and creates disjunction, its exteriority rupturing any and all closures. In this way, exposure to the other is at the same time an exposure to the infinite. But the infinite is not a feature of the other. *Rather it is the open space between self and other brought on by the other's presence, an irreducible site of distance-in-relation into which the subject is summoned by the other.* The "between" outstrips all contexts, exposing an infinite horizon, an incalculable sweep of transcendence that passes the limit of all closures.

Yet, contra John D. Caputo and Jacques Derrida, we are not talking about a desert-like emptiness or abyssal chasm (*khora*).[27] Recall that the presence of the other is not an utterly anonymous interruption. Within the sway of presence there lies a positive invocation, an enchantment that signals the affinity of a relation and summons interest rather than disinterest, inspiring wonderment. The "lack" generated by being exposed to the infinite openness of the between does not then denote the final absence of relation, only the impossibility of a relation of synthesis, of closure. It confirms a capacity for being-with beyond totality, a relation of openness that actually comes from distance, remoteness, and separation.[28]

A paradoxical disequilibrium is produced: the presence of the other distances while it simultaneously allures. Its provocation not only sets apart difference as other, but also draws out and implies relation. *And this disequilibrium sets in motion a dynamism that spills over into a potentially unconditioned matrix of relations, an infinite horizon of being-with.* There is a nonconclusive dialectic charged with an excessive pulse that runs aground any attempt to stop its play at some determinate end. It is beyond adequation, not as an empty nihil, but as a surplus goodness, a superabundance of sense over nonsense, the inexhaustibility of which conditions the relational liminality of being-with.[29] The infinite, then, suggests not "too little," but "too much"; it tastes like nothing because it escapes any resolution.

In this light, we can say that availability gestures toward an infinite possibility. For an *omega point* is implied, a possible but ever-deferred universal horizon of complementarity that lets-be differences. This is why the term "infinite" rather than "indefinite" is a more apt characterization of the openness of the between. As the other is a finite freedom that bears a promise anticipated in certain shapes—and not simply an anonymous or vacuous indeterminacy—so too does the inexhaustibility of the between. That is, there is at work a plentitude that suggests a promise, an excess that tilts us toward the utopian possibility of being-with all possible others. This "tilt" is manifest in availability.

True, the experience of the other initiates a constant momentum of deferral, not a stable union of correlates. But this is not tantamount to an utter dispersion in which all possible others are utterly other. For deferral can only happen in the dialectical context of relation. It comes to pass as a vibrant being-with, a coincidence of opposites in constant suspension. Accordingly, infinity is more than an attribute of the other's presence (i.e., its nonadequation to the self) and more than the response that is summoned by it (i.e., the self's nonadequation to presence). It is most properly a quality of the abundant surplus and self-surpassing openness of the between. Infinity floods the entire landscape of being-with.

Dwelling with the other is a performance in which there always remains an uncircumscribable excess. We are not talking about a necessary ground here, something that makes being-with possible, but rather a horizon of possibility that is ever-deferred even as it is simultaneously embedded in concrete relations. The infinite is not realized, grasped as a possession, for it escapes achievement. In this regard, the infinite is *impossible* in finite terms. And yet it is a limit that passes through all finite experience, as being-with is an exposure to something more. Put in Derridian terms, it is the quasi-transcendental status of this impossibility that unhinges us and opens up further possibilities.[30] Yet, unlike Derrida, I maintain that the impossible does not mark the desert-like chaos of *differánce* or *khora*, but rather the pulse of an overabundance, the infinite possibility of differences-in-relation.

For this reason the infinite does not signify a first cause, but an anticipated future possibility, of which the other's presence is a kind of foretaste. This is why I have used the eschatological language of *promise* in place of "arche" or "ground."[31] The other's presence is the advent of a promise, an infinite and indeed impossible possibility that is announced as "already not-yet," experienced as a beyond in the midst of things. Here, built into the local experience of presence, there arises the possibility of an unrestricted horizon of meaningful vitality. And availability is the response, a forward momentum tilted toward this promise in the shape of an ontological exigency, an urge toward an affirmation. Availability bears testimony to the possibility that the whole of existence is trustworthy and good, a place hospitable to our need to dwell together in a world.

Moreover, such testimony gains sway in an enduring disposition of *trust*. Trust is an anticipatory affirmation of the goodness of being-with that plays out in openness toward the infinite. It is not based upon the certainty of knowledge, on the claim to possess some determinate idea or content, because it is nonconclusive, a gesture always affirming *beyond* itself. Trust, then, is a modality of availability. It trades on the possibility of a promise received in the presence of the other and, as such, affirms every possible other as meaningful and vitalizing. In this way, human dwelling together bespeaks the plentitude of an infinite and unconditioned horizon of relation. *The disposition of trust signals an absolute affectedness that gives witness to the infinite.* This notion, however, requires further unpacking.

The Infinite as the Presence of the Open Whole

Because it is an absolute affectedness, trust is not merely one isolated feeling among others. It is an enduring disposition that implies a fundamental orientation to the *whole of reality* as itself a mystery full of promise, as trustworthy, capable of carrying ontological weight. By "whole" I mean to speak neither of a part—that is, one field of objects among others—nor of a totality composed of such parts—that is, a collection of all such fields as the mere entirety of things quantifiable. To be sure, the whole is bodied forth as the event of all things taken together in their collective power. But this need not suggest closure. For as a totality, the whole is broken. Indeed, it does not exist as such. Precisely as broken and interrupted, however, the whole—anticipated by trust—is a dynamic surplus more than itself, an *ecstasis*.

The whole is the disclosure or openness of the infinite, the limit-horizon of existence as an ever-extensive possibility radiating with promise. By this I seek to designate not an ideal concept or regulative idea, but rather the toward-which of the anticipatory affirmation of trust: the dynamically difference-bearing and complex complementarity of all things authentically possible in being-with. Itself a living mystery, this whole might aptly be characterized as the Other of the other's presence. And in keeping with this line of thinking, stressing its living and vibrant surplus value, I shall refer to the open, infinite whole as *Presence*. But what does "Presence" mean and how is it distinguishable from "presence"?

A correlate of the infinite, Presence is the extensive and universalizing dimension of local presences. For the happening of a local presence opens to the beyond of a dynamic whole, ushering us infinitely outward from the surplus of a finite event into a between that indicates participation in a transcendent horizon of difference-bearing plentitude. The unconditioned context of relation itself, Presence is not a totalizing foundation that we comprehend, but rather an excessive power of relational differentiation that comprehends us. It gives itself. It comes to pass *before* us. But it does not already exist as such, merely an object—the totality of things together. It is rather the infinite possibility of being-with, a horizon of excess that is such because it is yet to be, its superabundance a potentiality that lures us, as it were, from ahead.

Thus, like presence is the "more than" of the other, Presence is the "more than" of the whole, a surplus that remains left over. And like presence, Presence designates from beyond, experienced as having an initiative that gives itself precisely as it eludes determinative calculation. But unlike presence, what comes to pass is not the noninterchangeable singularity of this or that other, but the excessive singular potency of an infinite being-with—that is, the whole as the possibility of all things related in their difference. A vibrant surplus without a context, the infinity of the between radiates outward in a way that absolutely affects, invoking trust's anticipation of a relational whole that is always creatively self-transcending but that is also trustworthy and not finally abyssal and dispersive. Presence is the limit of this "absolute affectedness."

Engendering and sustaining the fidelity and hope of availability, trust is an existential refusal of both the chaos of dispersion and the homogenizing oppressiveness of totality. It affirms and follows after the trace of an originary promise deep in the heart of reality.[32] And as such, *trust indicates the trace of Presence as the potentia, the possibilizing power, of the trustworthiness and sheer gratuity of what is real.* Meaningful vitality is then no mere capricious wish-fulfillment; it is a reflection of the actualizing potential of reality disclosed in being-with.[33]

In brief, Presence is the dynamic potency of the open and infinite whole. It not an essence, but a transcendence that escapes closure and yet inscribes itself into all relations as their omega point, their ultimate possibility. While I have stressed that it is not utterly indeterminate or anonymous, I do not wish to suggest that this omega point of possibility guarantees some specific outcome, unfolding in a logic of triumph. There is teleology, to be sure, but it is nonconclusive, tilting toward open-ended possibilities rather than toward a predetermined end. Teleology is not a developmental necessity but more a "power to become" that is itself infused with relational meaning and vitality. It is not oriented to a predictable and historically achievable goal. For the infinite is an open surplus that always remains out in front, an impossible possibility.

In this way, we might say that Presence is ultimate Reality, a beyond than which nothing greater can be conceived (to employ Anselm of Canterbury's classic phrase). But we are not talking about an absolute being or even being-itself. For this would imply pure actuality. Rather, Presence is an already not-yet, an ever actualizing eschatological possibility traced in the dialectical performance of being-with. A utopian dynamism breaks through all provisional acts of being-with, pushing them forward toward Presence. This is why I have stressed that Presence, as an infinite event of being-with, is more than being. Indeed, it does not exist as such, but is ecstatic, the dynamic power of the between, the potency (*dunamis*) of the coalescent whole of reality enriching all finite differences within the scope of a horizon that surpasses them all. As such, Presence comprises but is not the universe; it is not the total system. Even as it extends throughout all things, Presence is not accounted for in monistic or pantheist frameworks. For these preclude possibility by swallowing up differences into the stasis of a totalizing system. Presence is a verb more than a noun, a living horizonal matrix of possibility more than a static substance. It is a transgressive limit-term toward which humans stand in being ushered into the between. Thus, Presence is the gratuitous space of possibility in which the other's presence gives itself, the opening *es gibt* of the between. It connotes the primal creative potency of relation and distance, filling all things but found in none.

In a word, *Presence is the infinite openness of the between, the possibility of all things interfused distinctly, the ambience of an irreducible and elusive promise sounded in being-with.* The infinity of Presence is the universal solidarity of differences. Thus, it is the omega point toward which trust directs itself in all finite acts of dwelling, the living universality toward which localized affirmations are directed, the telos of conversational solidarity, the uncircumscribable and open whole that is more than itself and mysterious. The sway of Presence inscribes itself in every finite presence as the Other of the other.

Let us draw out some summary observations. First, what I have been exploring here is not simply a speculative way of accounting for the presence of the other. The infinite sweep of the whole as Presence is neither a metaphysical ground nor an abstract postulate that renders being-with intelligible. It is an inescapable existential presupposition, a point of departure, a kind of eschatological affirmation built into the praxis of availability. Insofar as we are disposed beyond ourselves, opened to the other, we anticipate and so already extend into the transcendent horizon of Presence, coaffirming its infinity in the local happening of the other's presence. For in seeking ontological weight, held out into the excessive through a trust that wagers on the trustworthiness of things, we fallibly play out our openness toward the infinite power of being-with. Every experience of astonishment and wonderment attests to the plentitude of this encompassing yet difference-bearing context, a context that contextualizes us beyond totality.

Second, our inescapable need for orientation is an ontological exigency reaching for the empowering fullness of the living whole as Presence. Hence, contrary to Richard Rorty, our final vocabularies—while finite, as localized universals—do indeed insinuate and make an appeal to something genuine about the character of human being in the world: the other as the harbinger of an infinite being-with. The experience of the other is more than mundane happening; it invokes an affirmative thrust that outreaches itself, and in so doing, expresses an original confidence that meaning and vitality lie at the heart of things. When we encounter the presence of the other, we cannot help but say, "it is good," drawing near in letting it be, a relation that cannot help but also to will its good. And in this event we implicitly affirm the surpassing goodness of all things together. Esse qua esse bonum est—this is a statement marking the impact of Presence. Our lives grow into ontological weight by waiting upon and becoming answerable to Presence in the call of presence, summoned into deeper and richer moments of being-with. Thus, availability is a reflection of the potency of *interest* infused in all things, a courageous giving of oneself over to the between of relation and distance, a life lived with and for the other. Availability not only lets-be and draws-near the other, as a fidelity toward the other; it is an absolute affectedness that trusts the whole.

Finally, while the whole is broken and pluralized, we can see that this need not entail an ironic desacralization. The broken whole marks the disclosure and openness of Presence, releasing us into an infinite horizon of meaningful and vitalizing possibility. And this comes to pass as a dynamism rippling through each existent. Indeed, the world is enchanted, full of gods. It is infused with a transgressive pulse. The most minimal of perceptions is an opening toward the most maximal of horizons. The unavoidable narrowness of finite human experience, trained as it is on events limited in scope, is simultaneously a gesture toward the infinite openness of the whole.

Affirming Presence in Absence: The Fullness of Emptiness

Keeping the post-Nietzschean destruction of traditional metaphysics in mind, however, we must underscore that the openness of availability never guarantees Presence as a fixed point of reference. It is neither a determinate origin nor end, for its superabundance admits an effacing power, an absence. In this sense, affirmation is an erasure. The universality of Presence recedes infinitely even as it is extended in local presences, never becoming a specified content or delimited object, a concrete being among others. As the ambience of a room is elusive and cannot be grasped as an object, sounding only with the reverberation of particular voices and instruments, so too does Presence only leave its trace in the between invoked by the presence of the other.

Interrupting all closures and totalizing reductions, Presence remains qualitatively distant as an implicit limit-horizon anticipated in trust. Employing the terminology of Schleiermacher, we might say that Presence is the unspecifiable and undesignate "Whence"—the "from which"—of the promise of meaningful vitality affirmed in trust.[34] Only here it might be equally appropriate to see Presence as a "Whither" or "toward which," an eschatological "already not yet," anticipated in the gesture of availability. Hence, dialogical reason can never jump over the distance to apprehend and signify Presence. As infinite, the qualitative difference of Presence perpetually defers and iconoclastically relativizes all finite acts of being-with, eluding possessive grasp. It paradoxically summons us outward by an absence that bespeaks fundamental relation but never fully grants it. Presence withstands reduction and prevails as a relentless hiddenness. It outstrips and unsettles our efforts to comprehend; it breaks the hold of the Hegelian Begriff that would encompass everything in a totality. The dialectical movement is evident. We partake in the infinity of Presence by not having it. It "has" us.

Thus, Presence is both an absolute decentering and the ultimate potential of being-with. It is simultaneously absolute interruption and absolute promise. The infinite whole is itself a centrifugal centripetality. For infinity has no finite place, no local center that can be mapped out and determined; its fulcrum is everywhere and nowhere. It is a pure, and therefore impossible, possibility. In this case we might then say that Presence is an empty nothing, not as the homogenizing vacuity of a void, nor as the chaotic dissemination of sheer heterogeneity—each of which is the flip side of each other—but rather as the plentitude of infinite openness. This is precisely why the infinite is not subject to onto-theological closure. The sway of Presence cannot be reduced to the loaded universalism of a "metaphysics of presence." Yet we are not left with the residual empty universalism of hyper-reflexivity. For the infinity of Presence is both an undesignate nothing and a horizon of possibility opened up by local presences.

We are back to Giordano Bruno's polycentric centerlessness. Only now, we can view it as a positive state—as a difference-bearing openness that simultaneously grants and relativizes all concrete value as an anticipation of a promise that is both already and not yet a reality. In this way, too, we can agree with Emmanuel Levinas's statement that the infinite is "transcendent to the point of absence," to the degree of a "possible confusion with the agitation of the *there is* [*il y a*]"—that is, the nothingness of indeterminate being.[35] Only I would again stress that if the infinite were utterly indeterminate, a paralyzing undecidability would remain. Yes, the *between* "could be" an abyssal chasm instead of Presence. Derrida's reading of Levinas, which emphasizes an undecidability between the *there is* and the infinite, points this out with great insight.[36] But if this is the case, what then counts positively for the plentitude of promise that I have suggested lies in the experience of the other's difference? Trust and its opposite—horror and/or despair—become equally weighted responses to excess, and dialogue itself becomes reduced to hyper-reflexive rhetorical play. In my view, availability and its trust are existential criteria of discrimination for marking the finite trace of a context of surplus that is wholly transcendent yet also bears ontological weight. Undecidability trivializes the fact that humans are beings who cannot remain indifferent toward existence. And more, as per the discussion in chapter 2, such undecidability trivializes the unique worth of differences and the possible violation of that worth. It offers no productive counterweight to evil.

In sum, this is why I have argued (1) that the ingression of the other radiates outwardly and intimates a maximally inclusive, open, and transcendent horizon of possibility—Presence; (2) that trust is an absolute affectedness arising through the presence of the other and toward Presence; and (3) that only as a passion for the concrete other, in its singularity, is availability opened to the infinite universality of Presence. The ordinary is extraordinary, shot through with transgressive resonance. The broken whole is an open whole, mysterious, and gratuitous. It is this paradox that grants mere empirical plurality the status of a plentitude of differences-in-relation, an integral pluralism. It is this paradox that opens to the religious, but not as a panacea. For trust occurs only amidst the absence of Presence, amidst the unsettledness of not-having. We remain interrupted.

THE CONDITIONS OF THE RELIGIOUS: ELEMENTAL TRUST AND ANXIETY

Finite and temporal, human beings have no ready-made or immediate access to the open whole as an infinite possibility of meaningful vitality. Trust is an anticipatory dynamism that follows the trace of a promise but does not guarantee or possess it. It remains unhinged. There is then a tragic instability built into the structure of being-with and the availability that accompanies it. As contingent beings open to possibility, we stand vulnerable to negation and dissolution.[37] Hence, insofar as the ontological exigency implies a distance, a not-having, in its affirmative thrust, *anxiety* over the threat of non-being—of destruction in the shape of the meaninglessness of anomic dispersion (sheer heterogeneity) and the vitalitylessness of repetition and fate (sheer homogenization)—always remains poignantly intermingled with trust.

"Anxiety," as I am using the term, is neither merely neurotic phobia nor fear of a specific object, but rather a fundamental feature of contingency: the awareness of non-being built into the character of all finite human experience.[38] For each finite fulfillment is a nonfulfillment of sorts, a provisional and fallible stopping point along a way marked temporally by incompletion. Hence, as an exigency for ontological weight, trust is an anticipatory dynamism that is disproportionate to itself, a great disparity existing between its intention and its fulfillment. Trust aspires to more than it achieves; it cannot equal its own exigency. Caught in the tension of the in-between, of distance and relation, trust only has by not-having, at best awaiting in fidelity a future projected in hopeful expectation. Consequently, a limiting condition of ambiguity and vulnerability prevails over all human experience. We are constantly interrupted, confronted with limitations, moved by events not of our making and outside the province of our control, by circumstances that threaten us with non-being and that run counter to meaningful vitality.

Anxiety means that trust is fallible. This makes possible two negative modes of orientation toward the presence of the other: horror and despair. Whereas horror marks a fearful flight from the other perceived in dismay as an overwhelming menace to the self, despair indicates a listless disillusionment over the preciouslessness of the other perceived as an overdetermined, sterile, and banal repetition of the same. These two different responses, the terrified recoil of horror and the melancholic fatalism of despair, respectively, are the inverse images of what I have called "astonishment" and "wonderment." And both are nagging twin companions of anxiety, perpetually alienating trust from its intentionality. They are persistent because the sense of promise affirmed in the ontological exigency remains ever deferred by the reality of suffering, frustration, and eventual death, bringing with it a sense of loss, betrayal, and disappointment.

As an absolute affectedness, trust desires a clarity and assurance it simply cannot have. And this creates an abiding disease. Things indeed are not what they seem. The basic existential question then is: can we trust in the trustworthiness of things? Perhaps not. Perhaps we are flickers of light momentarily suspended over the darkness of a yawning nothingness, the desire for meaning and vitality an ironic absurdity playing out against a senseless cosmos that actually holds no promise, no ontological weight. Perhaps oppression, brokenness, and deception lie at the heart of human sociality, our lives a breeding ground for distrust. Trust cannot help but acknowledge such negation as an immanent possibility, for the anticipation that animates it evidences an absence, a lack. There is a nothingness at the heart of mortal human existence. We are unfinished, distanced from that which we desire. The fullness of meaningful vitality is incomplete.

But despite not-having, the prevailing winds of contingency and ambiguity blowing as they will, human beings cannot help but refuse the final victory of senselessness over sense and of fate over creative freedom—that is, of non-being over being-with. Despite never being completely assured, trust rises tenaciously like grass through asphalt. We do not remain content with discontent, complacent about our imperiled condition. The very character of anxiety itself bears testimony to the fact that we are unable to be indifferent toward existence, which itself connotes a passion that outruns negation. For in seeking orientation and ontological weight, human beings are always already drawn to meaningful vitality, and this is what makes the negative disposition of anxiety a positive intimation of a more fundamental exigency toward the infinite as a surplus of possibility, as Presence.[39] Pessimism and cynicism are derivative, their apparent resolve stemming from a frustration that bespeaks an affirmative passion surpassing its own annulment. The experience of the "not yet" suggests an anticipatory grasp of that plentitude toward which it aspires, a participative "already" in the space of its lack. This is why we resist non being. And the fact of such resistance signifies that trust is an eschatological intentionality, a passionate forward momentum toward the possibility of things being otherwise than tragic.

Thus, while tragedy is our condition, it is neither the primary nor final word of existence. Anxiety is infused with a pulse signifying an affirmative power already at work efficaciously in the experience of "lack." Ineluctably mixed into the fragile crucible of human experience, anxiety depends upon a deeper and irrepressible trust that precedes it. As H. Richard Niebuhr points out, "distrust is only possible where the conditions of trust have first been established."[40] The disease of anxiety is parasitic; horror and despair are erosions of a more basic fidelity and hope constituted by trust. Why do human beings seek ontological weight? Why do we resist horror and despair? Because, amidst the intractable ambiguity of not-having, the relational character of dwelling in the world affirms the capacity of life to sustain ontological weight. It follows after the promise of meaning over against the meaninglessness of utter chaos and heterogeneity (i.e., horror) and the promise of vitality over against the vitalitylessness of utter repetition and homogeneity (i.e., despair).

While it is never guaranteed fully, trust concretely surfaces as a courageous affirmation of meaningful vitality "in spite of" anxiety, or as Paul Ricoeur puts it, a radical affirmation of being made in the space of a lack of being, one that indicates that it has already been grasped by a fullness, the superabundance of sense over nonsense.[41] The prior affectedness of trust is why we struggle against struggle, hope against hope, and refuse refusal.[42] Trust is elemental, the condition of possibility for anxiety.

Toward the Recovery of Trust

But since humans are temporal beings enframed by contingency, such elemental trust neither fully grants itself nor subsists indeterminately; it must be self-consciously recovered and actualized concretely, won over anxiety. Out of elemental trust, yet in the throes of anxiety, we posture ourselves through fidelity and hope toward localized universals (i.e., values, ideals, and meanings) through which our lives may become meaningful and vitalized. Three factors display this kind of recovery process.

First, perhaps the most ubiquitous example of trust asserting itself is found in the asking of *limit-questions*.[43] In an existential condition of not-having, we are driven to ask questions that push against the boundaries of what is manageable and taken for granted and propel us into the mystery of things, questions about the ultimate nature and worth of the whole of reality and human life in it, questions of origin and destiny that assume the dispositional primacy of trust insofar as they seek to resist negation and thematize the trustworthiness of things. But this is not simply cognitive play or speculative musing. It is the desire for a practical wisdom or *phronesis*, a hunger for an existential resolution to the problem of living. Limit-questions embody an elemental trust that seeks to understand itself, which seeks to establish its own priority over anxiety. Questions like, "Is life precious?" "Why is truth worth seeking?" or "Why is the good worth pursuing?" work toward thematizing the mystery of the whole. They indicate that we have to some degree already trespassed the limits of negation and extend into the infinite limit-horizon of the whole as Presence.

Thus it is, second, that we stretch for an evocative language of surplus value housing those elements in our lives that call forth affirmation over negation, being over non-being. *Limit-expressions* are the result, the intensification of fields of semantic power and their conversational matrixes in directions that exceed their ordinary or mundane context and, through poetic suspension and figuration, seek to disclose the infinite economy of the whole as trustworthy.[44] In so doing they become the interpretive fulcrum of local languages, thrusting them toward a universal import. Such expressions involve diverse linguistic forms—stories, parables, metaphors, images, symbols, and concepts—all of which function in this case to map a territory of transgressive value and invoke the praxis of a correlative fidelity and hope. In this, limit-expressions serve imaginatively to generate and preserve frameworks of meaningful vitality—that is, worlds. They are loci around which concrete acts of trust congeal. As the correlative "answer" to limit-questions, limit-expressions hold the power of ontological weight.

With this we are led to a third point, namely, that limit-expressions have the character of a *theodicy*. Broadly conceived, theodicy addresses the disease over not-having by giving voice to the possibility of something more, reaffirming and concretizing trust.[45] Representing the intuition that somehow all is not right and could be other than what it is, all human formulations that resist what negates the possibility of worth and value in human dwelling together (i.e., frustration, oppressive violence, and death) have the character of theodicy, legitimating fidelity and hope in the midst of struggle and brokenness, empowering the courage of resistance in the face of suffering or injustice.[46] The tragic instability of the ontological exigency makes such posturing inescapable. For the need for orientation in dwelling together radiates from an irrepressible affirmation within the space of an ongoing lack.[47] In this space, human beings seek reassurance against the possibility of final dissolution and negation, moved by an originary confidence that life is indeed worthwhile and full of the promise of meaningful vitality.

In sum, limit-questions are the presentation of trust seeking understanding, and the limit-expressions of theodicy are the tangible consequence, founding dwelling places of focused value and so filling-in trust with specific content that inspires ongoing fidelity and hope in the midst of the ambiguity of not-having.

THE RELIGIOUS SENSIBILITY AND FAITH AS A CONCRETE APPEAL TO TRANSCENDENCE

It is here that explicitly religious themes emerge. As an absolute affectedness, trust seeks to recover the sense of its hyberbolic excess. This gives it the distinct capacity for taking on religious form. That is, trust is a religious capacity or sensibility: a capacity that is manifest concretely in localized appeals to transcendence. In the vein of Schleiermacher, then, by "religious sensibility" I mean to indicate not a specific experience or content but a kind of aptitude or "sensibility and taste for the infinite"—*a generic anthropological potency that becomes actualized only as it is modified by an appeal to transcendence that is historically specific and situated in a community of discourse.*[48] Faith is such a modification. And it becomes an issue precisely with the penchant for theodicy, where limit-questions create semantic room for the reception of what is designated the limit-of existence and so is of universal import—that is, as transcendent. Let us discuss these ideas in further detail.

First, given the foregoing analysis, it can be said that human beings seek relation to that which refuses negation, quells the crippling power of anxiety, and confirms or "founds" trust.[49] We do not believe that existence is good in the abstract; its goodness is conferred by something upon which we rely and place our confidence.[50] Some kind of categorical leverage is needed. As concrete orientation in a particular framework of value is inescapable, the absolute affectedness of trust calls for a concrete content. Faith, then, is trust modified locally by certain material contents—that is, images, symbols, and narratives—that are projected to invoke an order of existence of universal, indeed unconditional, import. Such contents, in orienting humans to the infinite whole, stretch local linguistic conventions and idioms poetically into *limit-expressions* that designate transcendence. These limit-expressions operate as loci around which beliefs, practices, and relations are constructed. They are the means by which we fill-in trust's infinitizing sweep and affirm that life is worthwhile despite its perils. And when we affirm that life is worthwhile, by the same act we make universal reference to the whole as itself worthwhile.[51] We are thereby empowered to project a future of infinite potential—that is, we hope.

In this way, religious faith functions as a medium of Presence, not directly but indirectly, as a peculiar modification of the absolute affectedness of trust. What I am suggesting, therefore, is that Presence is the horizon of possibility in which the concern for a concrete form of transcendence arises, beckoning forth faith as a particular way of living toward an infinite possibility. Insofar as our lives have been opened up to finite presences in astonishment and wonderment, the possibility of faith as an appeal to transcendence is inescapable, for human beings are opened to the infinite whole in a way that summons response. Human religiosity is therefore not only a viable but an inevitable option in the course of human dwelling together.[52]

Limit-expressions, however, only have the power they do because trust, as an extension of availability, is an anticipatory dynamism insufficient to itself. It is compelled to go outside and beyond itself for its own completion. But here is the rub: in the final analysis, only a specific relation to the power of the mystery of the whole, to Presence, can authentically offer such a possibility. Only that which is elevated to an unconditioned relevance can confirm the unconditional character of the concern that animates elemental trust, disclosing the trustworthiness of things. Precisely this is what enables trust to resist non-being.

However, this presents a problem. Opened up toward infinity, no finite object or set of objects can adequately fulfill the exigency of trust, rendering it equal to its own momentum. And yet this is the inmost aspiration of all concrete human activity—to have a value-center that fills in trust's gaping hole, as it were. All contingent objects and relations that would potentially recover and sustain our inexpungeable trust in the possible meaningful vitality of life display contextual limitations that can be falsified by the existential conditions imposed by the finitude of life. As an absolute affectedness, trust gestures past all penultimate sources of confirmation, a dynamism driven outward beyond the frontiers of finitude. *Because of this, an explicit appeal to transcendence is required, a motion toward the infinite that effectively relativizes all finite goods as guarantors of trust and opens up to the whole.*[53] Such an appeal, riding the arc of a transgressive pulse, lies immanent in the performance of any and all acts of human dwelling. For human beings are suspended between the finite and the infinite, the local and the genuinely universal.[54]

Accordingly, we ask limit-questions because we in some sense already exist beyond the limitations of not-having; we are exposed to a dimension that exceeds non-being, and to which trust bears a remote but correlative affinity. And it is in this "exposure" and in the space of the failure of things ordinary to satisfy the fundamental impetus of trust that limit-expressions come to be, able to exert their semantic power. Here, following after the trace of infinity in localized forms, language is perpetually pushed—metaphorically and poetically—to trespass its conventional modes of signification toward opening up the whole of reality itself as trustworthy, signaling a surplus dimension of possibility that presents trust with its ownmost possibilities. As it reflects the anticipatory momentum of trust, such language seeks connective potency, aspiring to invoke that through which trust participates in the meaningful vitality of things. On the basis of such generative vigor, limit-expressions invariably become saturated with illuminative power. They are the self-consciousness of trust's stretch toward the infinite.

The ultimate trustworthiness of things, then, is envisioned via a designate content that confirms trust's original confidence, and so becomes a founding value-center of transcendent import, calling forth faith. Yet, as historical beings, we can do this only on the basis of some focused center of value that is thematized and affirmed locally within a particular field of semantic power. A categorical, dare I say onto-theological, discourse is required. Indeed it is unavoidable. The religious sensibility, as an anthropological potency, becomes actualized in the appeal to an ascribed dimension of transcendence that confirms, represents, and concretizes the transgressive pulse of elemental trust in explicit form. A specific limit-expression—an image or term of ultimacy qualitatively distinct in its possibilizing power—names the power of the economy of the whole, refracting that which in reality calls forth and justifies our original, unavoidable confidence in the abiding and final worth of things.[55] In religious faith, trust is recovered and founded—preserved by fidelity and nourished by hope—by way of an historically circumscribed anticipatory relation to the infinite whole as trustworthy.

Such a relation is what I mean by "faith," and it is mediated *through* what is imagined and received by a community as the final limit-of existence. Because we always already exist *past* the limitations of a local point of view or perspective, we are compelled to designate and establish relation to the resource of this capacity. *Originating by way of reference to a framework's field of semantic power in a particular cultural horizon or form of life, limit-expressions, insofar as they evoke the perception of some transcendent and ultimate order of meaningful vitality, represent and fill-in the absolute affectedness of elemental trust with semantic density, thus orienting human beings to the whole by offering a theodicy that upholds the promise of ontological weight. Religious language is ordinary language transformed past its mundane circumscription as an anticipation of that possibility that bestows ultimate value.*[56]

With this in mind, rather than saying that religious faith constitutes or causes trust, it is perhaps more appropriate to say that it is its confirmation, the effect of trust seeking understanding, indeed the modification and amplification of trust in the direction of an affirmation of transcendence.[57] Faith presupposes the absolute affectedness of trust as its condition of possibility, a trust that surfaces in the midst of a situation of disease and that resists determination by that disease. Schubert Ogden puts it in the following way: "Logically prior to every particular religious assertion is an original confidence in the meaning and worth of life, through which not simply all our religious answers, but even our religious questions first become possible or have a sense."[58] The recognition and reception of some particular transcendent reality presupposes an anthropological potency—elemental trust—that opens up the possibility of such recognition and reception. And this designate transcendent then confirms and makes real the unconditionality of trust, calling forth faith.

Faith, then, is a response that assumes that the subjective condition of trust's resistance to anxiety is based in an assigned referentiality, an objective reality. That is, faith is conscious of itself as related to a transcendence taken to be actual, not merely fictional or illusory. The religious sensibility, therefore, is bipolar: (1) faith is the existential, subjective (noetic) pole of which (2) a designated transcendent is the correlative objective (noematic) pole. Faith without concrete orientation toward a transcendent referent does not exist; but without being received by faith as a lived option promising an ultimate fulfillment, such a referent is an empty and meaningless nihil. The two poles are existentially interwoven.[59] And the localized yet universaling thrust of limit-expressions are the mediating glue (1) invoking an ultimate value-center and (2) evoking a corresponding trust.

We can therefore say that religious faith is an intentional act of being grasped by a specified content that founds and precipitates unconditional trust by offering the assurance of an unconditioned meaningful vitality. This content is experienced as "transcendent" insofar as it indicates and participates in a transgressive, inexhaustible dimension of reality that showers the whole of life with ontological weight, opening human beings up to the final trustworthiness of things. And if by "reality" we mean that which is relevant and of which we are compelled to take account, then a designated transcendent functions as an "ultimate reality." It is in this way that faith augments trust in the direction of an explicit affirmation that siphons Presence. And through the power of limit-expressions to imagine and concretize transcendence, faith projects an ultimate context for dwelling together in reference to the mystery of the whole, unifying all concerns and organizing all experiences. This acts as a powerful force shaping human dispositions, motivations, and activities. Faith experiences its transcendent referent *as* the possibilizing power of the whole, ordering all events and showering existence with value.[60]

Faith interprets all things through the eyes of limit-expressions and thus is a kind of "seeing as."[61] Limit-expressions and faith are dialectically related. This is why limit-expressions are not experienced merely as fictional devices; their "fictions" are disclosive interpretations that make a genuine claim upon human beings. And such claims are found emanating from certain objects, forces, events, subjective states, and/or persons that have the charismatic power and disclosive capacity to radiate transcendent value to everything around them. They have the potency of the "gods," evoking what Clifford Geertz calls an "aura of factuality" that establishes a religious world.[62]

And these gods reveal themselves. This makes sense of the fact that religious traditions often appeal to an authoritative revelation of some sort. At base, revelation is a modality of worldly life that manifests unconditioned meaning and vitality. It is the experience of the "givenness" of a designate transcendence, a site of divine disclosure that presents a way of "seeing-as." Revelation thus is a manifestation that summons its recipients into a "more real" level of existence. And the evocative poetic power of limit-expressions both creates the interpretive context for such "manifestations" and governs their reception in testimonial "proclamations."[63] Thus, faith emerges as the total response to a summoning disclosure-event that announces a reality content, drawing attention to a certain state of affairs infused with the promise of an unconditioned fulfillment. So while elemental trust may be the condition of possibility for faith, it is faith that actualizes trust concretely by representing it in terms of an appeal to transcendence.

Consequently, faith is not strictly cognitive assent to a state of affairs, a belief (*fides*) in some form of transcendence, for it also involves a confident clinging of the heart (*fiducia*), an assurance that involves hope and also a correlative praxis of allegiance and fidelity (*fidelitas*). Belief, hope, confidence, and fidelity are not isolated activities, but one interrelated movement occurring in focused relation to an object that promises to confer value to one's particular life with others through conferring value to the whole of reality in general.[64] Knowing, being, and doing "religiously" are inseparably linked.[65]

Religious Faith as a "Saving" Performance Anticipating Presence

Human religiosity provides an answer to the problem of anxiety. It is an explicit actualization and concretization of elemental trust as a relation to the whole, to Presence. Religious faith "places" us—as a conversational community—in a trustworthy and gratuitous ultimate environment, one that resists falsification by the conditions of finitude by offering strength in the midst of struggle, comfort in the midst of sorrow, enduring purpose and ontological weight. Insofar as this placement happens, the limit-expressions of a religious faith have soteriological power. Religion, therefore, must be measured according to its own distinct criteria of relevance and appropriateness, in terms not just of what it says but of what it does.

When trust is mediated and founded, a deliverance or "salvation" comes to pass. This entails a liberative assurance of possibility against the final triumph of dissolution and negation. But this is neither the evasion nor the erasure of anxiety, for nothing can render us invulnerable to the conditions of finitude. Rather, it is a move *through* anxiety to a recovery of trust, a courageous "in spite of" that sets us free from the negation of non-being by anchoring trust in a value-center that transcends and encompasses existence, accordingly showering all experience with a significance that empowers fidelity and hope in the midst of ambiguity. Trust is now reconciled with its own infinitizing impulse, freed to risk asserting itself in the space of not-having, of not being guaranteed, by being assured of its ontological weight.

Faith thus evidences the relational freedom of an openness to existence as trustworthy in its plentitude and difference. The anticipatory promise of ontological weight is thereby proclaimed as a real possibility, an "already not-yet," held out in a vision of the whole as infused with surpassing fulfillment and joy. But at the fundamental level, this is not a deliverance *from* existence, though it might be secondarily characterized as such in some theodicies; rather, it is a deliverance *into* existence, into the depth of being-with, into the gratuitous meaningful vitality of the ever-extensive between of distance and relation.[66] And herein lies the ethical praxis of openness that is characteristic of availability, which affirms and wills the goodness of the whole as a creative and difference-bearing fulcrum of being-with. A founded trust is not a passive self-enclosure against the world, but an active being-with, a performance that anticipates Presence.[67] All this has radical implications that will be more fully discussed in chapter 6. For now it is enough to note the soteriological heft of faith as a founding confirmation of elemental trust.

But in assigning trust a referentiality clothed with an "aura of factuality," and despite its soteriological efficaciousness, the religious sensibility provides no access to Presence. We do not ever simply experience "the" infinite whole; it is only intimated indirectly in trust. Recall that Presence is not deliverable as a specifiable faith-content or limit-expression. As all limit-expressions are formulated in finite fields of semantic power, they accordingly fail to present or designate infinity as such. What a limit-expression of transcendent value does do, however, as a "seeing as," is *present us to* infinity, naming and evoking a human performance. That which is thematized in religious faith, then, is not Presence but elemental trust as a passion for the infinite, which only anticipates Presence.[68]

Given this, the ascription of transcendence to something is the product of trust seeking understanding, the imagined corollary of a human anticipation projected onto reality, not a revelation of *the* transcendent. It is the way we fill-in the infinitizing dynamism of trust, rendering it equal to itself, commensurate with it own exigency. But despite its Feuerbachian ring, this is only a partial capitulation to reducing transcendence to anthropology, for recall that the heft of elemental trust signifies that reality always already presents itself as capable of bearing such projections. So while Presence is never given as the transcendent, paradoxically, neither is it unrelated to religious faith. As the surplus ambience of the whole, Presence is the impinging qualitative space in which the concrete appeal to transcendence becomes a concern. The anticipatory outstretch of trust bears the imprint of Presence's ingression via presences. And it is because of this structural imprint—as an absolute affectedness—that we are opened up to the possibility of historically mediated shapes of transcendence.

We might say that the impression of Presence creates an anthropological cast with such a peculiar design and shape that only what is taken to be of transcendent power and value is capable of mediating and filling it. A limit-expression that is received as ultimate indirectly signals and evidences the reality of Presence insofar as it imaginatively projects, represents, and configures the passion for the infinite characteristic of elemental trust. So faith does involve a reality claim, but only as a saving performance and not directly or wholly in overt referential claims and significations. Religious truth lies in the efficacy of faith in a transcendent value, and this can happen within widely variant interpretive orientations.

Two basic conclusions follow. First, the appeal to transcendence is not a thematization of Presence but rather of the human trust that bears its imprint. Second, faith is a modification of trust, a performance expressing the passion for the infinite. Here, Presence is implicitly anticipated, but only locally and provisionally in the shape of a mediation of elemental trust and its universal outstretch. In short, *the religious sensibility is a gesture toward Presence in that it aspires to found trust, a drama or performance actualized via localized universals, which, as limit-expressions of transcendent import, call forth faith by naming the whole as trustworthy.* While the material content of such a sensibility varies, its generic contour as an anthropological potency is cross-cultural.

Thus, Presence is not *the* divine as defined by one religious tradition or another, but its infinite possibility is the condition for the impetus to imagine the divine in all religious traditions. It is ultimate Reality—the "God" beyond ascriptive discourse, which exceeds the configured and anthropomorphic God of historic theism.[69] There is no common essence that reduces all religions to a univocal, core content. Yet there is a common human potential for the infinite: the anticipatory gesture of trust toward Presence, which ushers into motion a human activity flowering in many ways. The appeal to transcendence takes on a plurality of forms and induces a variety of experiences. But the many religions are not devolutions of an original revelation of *the* transcendent—that is, God or Brahman or Nirvana. Rather, they constitute unique modifications of trust, each resonating to, and in its own way anticipating the living fecundity of, the whole as Presence. The Christian "God" is one such modification, an appeal to transcendence in theistic form. Thus, we can sympathize with words penned by Wilfred Cantwell Smith, themselves echoing the influence of Schleiermacher: "faith differs in form, but not kind."[70] Faith is a representative reassurance of the elemental trust that precedes it.

The Shape of Transcendence: Wisdom and Creativity

It is the enduring disposition of trust that predisposes human beings toward the religious. Through faith's appeal to transcendence, trust is modified, filled-in, and given determinate semantic content in a variety of ways, like different paths in the same forest, each of which functions similarly to orient humans by placing everyday experiences in an encompassing and ultimate interpretive context. Religious faith is trust experienced with peculiar semantic density, a density given by way of a transcendent reference. It is a manner of dwelling in which the entirety of life is seen as having to do with the "really real," the depth dimension to reality.

Thus it is that images of transcendence are not mere arbitrary constructions, but rather have a certain comparative intelligibility. Insofar as they represent and confirm trust's anticipation of Presence, its way of following after the infinite possibility of meaningful vitality, such images will quite naturally display not merely an empty transcendence, but a transcendence reflecting (1) complementarity and harmony, on the one hand; and (2) empowering vitality, on the other. I propose the terms "wisdom" and "creativity" to indicate such an interpretive shape. They are, respectively, correlates of meaning and vitality.

Wisdom is the possibilizing power of the whole as meaningful. In *Religion in the Making*, Alfred North Whitehead suggests that religion begins and ends with the vision of wisdom deep down in things.[71] Elsewhere, he eloquently expands the point:

> Religion is the vision of something which stands beyond, behind, and within, the passing flux of immediate things; something which is real, and yet waiting to be realized; something which is a remote possibility, and yet the greatest of present facts; something that gives meaning to all that passes, and yet eludes apprehension; something whose possession is the final good, and yet the hopeless quest. . . . The fact of the religious vision, and its history of persistent expansion, is our one ground for optimism. Apart from it, human life is a flash of occasional enjoyments lighting up a mass of pain and misery, a bagatelle of transient experience.[72]

This description corroborates the way in which we have described trust as an absolutely affected disposition that anticipates the ultimate "why" and "how" of the trustworthiness of things. Indeed, such trustworthiness can be seen as an unconditioned "wisdom"—the ultimate intelligibility and significance of the whole as a display of ordered and determinate potentiality.

But wisdom without vitality is sterile conformity and necessity. Also implied by the appeal to transcendence, therefore, is a supplement to wisdom—an empowering and directional *creativity*.[73] Gordan Kaufman illustrates the point boldly:

> [C]reativity is the only proper object of worship, devotion, and faith today, the only proper ultimate point of reference for our valuing. Everything other than the ultimate mystery of creativity is a finite created reality that may indeed by valued and appreciated (within certain limits) but is itself always subject to distortion, corruption, and disintergration and thus must be relativized by the creativity manifest in the coming into being (and the ultimate dissolution) of all finite realities—that alone may be characterized as "ultimate."[74]

The trustworthiness of things implies an ultimate coordination of contrasts. This is neither sheer homogeneity nor heterogeneity, but relational differentiation. Such creativity is *empowering* in that its novelty yields vitality, not as a chaotic free play but as an interrelational intensity. It is also *directional* in that its ordering potency yields meaning, not as a determinism but as a configuring harmony, a wisdom. Any designate image of transcendence will bear witness to wisdom and creativity.

Such wisdom and creativity can be found in three forms: theistic, cosmic, and acosmic.[75] These are conceptual types, different ways of imaginatively representing trust's anticipatory gesture *as* confirmed by reality itself. The theistic option (and this includes polytheism) projects transcendence in anthropomorphic guise as a being or beings, god or gods with distinct personalistic qualities somehow distinct from, yet related to, the world as causal powers. The cosmic view, on the other hand, projects transcendence as a world-ordering force or experience (e.g., the Tao). Different still, the acosmic position holds that this world is mere name and form—in more extreme views, an illusion—behind which a more real unity subsists as a force or experience (e.g., Brahman or Nirvana). While we cannot unpack these options here in the nuanced comparative detail they deserve, the point is that an empowering creativity and directional wisdom is assumed in all. But these shapes of transcendence also contain a strong relativizing feature that resists idolatry. Chapter 6 shall take up precisely this point.

Conclusion

Based upon what has been said thus far in a more abstract way, it might be assumed that the religious sensibility is an entirely subjective, individualistic affair. In actuality, nothing could be further from the truth. As trust occurs only in being-with, intersubjectively constituted in a linguistically saturated field of semantic power, so too does the appeal to transcendence. The religious sensibility comes to the fore only in the particular and varied performances of coalescent faith-traditions. Thus, we must supplement this discussion to underscore how religious faith becomes what it is only in cultural systems, taking historical shape in pluriform renderings. In doing so, we shall be able to see in chapter 6 how trust—and so the religious sensibility—can become subject to distortion, becoming self-enclosed, idolatrous, and exclusivist. But more fundamentally, we will be in a better position to understand how faith, as an appeal to transcendence, implies an ethical imperative summoning an availability opened out toward the whole in hospitality. And this openness is made concrete in welcoming the other, who is our neighbor, the stranger in our midst.

The soteriological impulse of religious faith, in founding trust, effects a localized universal affirmation that cannot help but will the good of the whole and so binds us to the dialogical praxis of a potentially universal human community of benevolent solidarity. Local horizons are thus opened from within to a translocal potentiality. The "truth" of religious faith is found not in a self-enclosed and passive trust, but in a trust-inspired praxis of love and justice.

CHAPTER 6

MAKING THE DIFFERENCE: RETHINKING RELIGIOUS PLURALISM IN LOCAL AND UNIVERSAL HORIZONS

All things are full of gods.[1]

The appeal to transcendence as a source of meaningful vitality—that is, God, Krishna, Nirvana, the Tao, Wakan Tanka, and so forth—is an inherently finite and social act. As we explored in chapter 5, elemental trust is never fully guaranteed and exists amidst the fundamental ambiguity of not-having. Thus, it must be self-consciously recovered against the pull of anxiety. It is in the work of such recovery that limit-expressions emerge and take thematic shape in theodicies of one sort or another. But limit-expressions are not derivatives of some inviolable core experience that is everywhere the same. There is no predetermined or deductive passage from fundamental trust to thematic expression. Yet neither are limit-expression wafted into existence ex nihilo. They are imaginative interpretations and as such are wedded to the localized world-building enterprise of specific communities of discourse.

It should be no surprise then that theodicies bear the stamp of particular fields of semantic power, providing orientation to a trustworthy cosmos in light of the exigencies and concerns that draw into focus a particular community's stability and well-being. Recall that Presence is never given immediately in some "pure" revelation. Its trace is inscribed in trust as an absolute affectedness, which invokes the anticipatory affirmation of a universal and unconditional horizon of trustworthiness. But this affirmation is only actualized as an appeal to transcendence from within a particular framework and its historical heft. The local and the universal exist in tension, side by side in a mutually fructifying relation.

The discussion in this chapter seeks to harness the generative power in this tension as a potentially global form of being faithful to one's own tradition while remaining opened up to the genuine value of others. There is a kind of double vision at work here. David Tracy captures the idea eloquently: "[S]tay faithful to your own tradition; go deeper and deeper into its particularities; defend and clarify its identity. At the same time, wander, Ulysses-like, willingly, even eagerly, among other great traditions and ways; try to learn something of their beauty and truth; concentrate on their otherness and difference as the new route to communality."[2] In a similar spirit, I advocate an ongoing and dialogical search for what is similar in our differences and different in our similarities. Indeed, the universal is realized only in the particular and local; yet the local itself is universalizing, opened out to an inclusive matrix of a sharing solidarity. Such solidarity, however, is no easy alliance. While it is inevitable that convergent truths will emerge from dialogue, it is also the case that differences will become accented, disorienting and sharpening each other, calling each other into accountability by exposing false closures or idolatries.[3] What remains is a discordant concordance, a dialectical pluralism.

Broadly conceived, this chapter is composed of three sections. The basic argument of section one is that there is no solitary actualization of trust, for we find ourselves already along the way with others, inescapably located in the public space of a given cultural-historical horizon that shapes the way in which we configure human life and its capacity for meaningful vitality. Trust emerges concretely as already overdetermined. And this means that, in its religious formation, trust necessarily displays diverse configurations, pluralized through and through. But I do not wish to conclude with the mere fact of plurality. For, in the second section, I suggest that trust can become distorted and indeed idolatrous. Based upon this, the discussion takes a turn toward outlining the contours of a nonidolatrous religious faith, in its condition of plurality, as an imaginative and double-visioned opening toward translocal difference. How so? Through an *availability* facilitated by what I call the "iconic" power of the appeal to transcendence, a power that "makes a difference" in being "difference making." In the final section, then, I contend against polemical, monistic, and historicist understandings of religious pluralism that a *dialectical* pluralism of solidarity best suits the very character of the religious sensibility.

LOCAL HORIZONS: RELIGIOUS FAITH AS A COMMUNAL EVENT

We acquire the tools for concretely realizing trust by inheriting a designate language from which we "discover" our place in a given world. But *discovery* in this sense is too strong a word. Explicit trust comes to the fore more in the act of "being interpreted"—of being socialized into a certain outlook wherein we internalize assurances that have already been placed before us—than in "finding."

We always already talk and reason together *from* these assurances and the linguistic conventions that mediate them. It is the interpretive jurisdiction of these conventions—with their authoritative codifications and "canonical" stories and symbols—that provides distinguishable semantic structure to limit-expressions, marking focus and identifiable perimeters that circumnavigate a collective value-center. This is true of a nation, a business corporation, a sports team, and so forth.

The Traditional Nature of Trust

Accordingly, a self-conscious trust is a trust that inherits an ongoing past and is tradition-bound, taken hold of, and formed contemporaneously by, the narrative-oriented conversation of a community of discourse.[4] Without this, trust is an empty and indeterminate capacity, a mere *potentia*. Anthony Giddens sums up the point succinctly: "Tradition . . . contributes in basic fashion to ontological security insofar as it sustains trust in the continuity of past, present, and future, and connects such trust to routinized social practices."[5] Tradition is not merely a representation of trust; it is a constitutive condition for trust. Trust, as a being-with, is always already communally instantiated.

Given this, we can see how a tradition's identity, and so the constitution of trust, can become imperiled by forgetfulness and disintegration.[6] Without being managed, maintained, and carried by stable signposts reminding us of who we are, the semantic boundaries of a shared world fall into oblivion, creating the anxiety of discord and senselessness, indeed the horror of self-diffusion. Like a cell without a membrane, the collective resonance of a community collapses into shapeless noise without the definiteness of systematic channels of flow and constraint organized around an established value-center.[7] Though this often rings with negative, imperialistic connotations, limits are in fact indispensable in their *productive* ability to give life together a distinctive shape and character. Trust requires the restrictive self-definition of narrative traditions to assure the reliable transmission of values through the passage of time.

It is no wonder, then, that communities of trust tend to show a centripetal, "conservative," and self-protective side that resists the vagueness of diffusion or the disruption of fragmentation. Clear boundaries of normative import are necessary to negotiate a trustworthy world, boundaries that make a community definite and set it apart from others. Thus it is that social institutions (i.e., organizing and governing authorities) and performative technologies (i.e., rituals and routinized practices) are created as vehicles enabling a community to remember and carry forward its corporate gestalt. For, in the end, an unbounded and unstructured world is an unintelligible world, compromising the very need for orientation that animates a tradition's relevance and plausibility.

Sociality and the Religious Sensibility

It is in the struggle for communal synthesis that the appeal to transcendence becomes especially pertinent. As trust is a covenantal and co-inhabiting event, so too is the religious faith that represents and founds it, giving enduring plausibility to a community's public reality by appealing to transcendence. Thus, religious faith is not some prethematic, inner, and spiritual experience that is subsequently expressed. Rather, it names a certain way of being-toward the whole that is a way of being-with others. As such, faith is already linguistically saturated. How so?

Due to their imaginative and world-generating power, limit-expressions have a tendency to sacralize or project into transcendent status the identity forming values of a tradition. This projection reflects the infinitizing dynamism of trust, which, stopping at nothing short of an unconditional affirmation and mediated by a tradition's field of semantic power, intensifies, pushes, and so transforms this mediation into a transgressive signification event naming a dimension of surplus beyond itself. In this connection, a peculiar social world—marked by its unique interpretation of the various powers that bear down upon it and demand account—becomes housed within an ultimate and cosmic frame of reference, invoking an orientation toward the whole as trustworthy. A local community's value-center becomes extended into transcendence and given concentrated paradigmatic vigor.[8]

And this means that value-center takes shape as a designated image of the transcendent. Such an image—a limit-expression—gains sway as a configuration of the power of a shared whole, a localized universal with unconditioned import. The promise of meaningful vitality in dwelling together is thereby transferred to a universal and ultimate horizon that circumscribes and so transfigures all things within its interpretive sway according to its image. Here, the anxiety inherent in the condition of finitude and in all the circumstances of human life is assuaged by the security of dwelling in a field of semantic power that manifests transcendent power. Such power, which can take many semantic forms, is of unconditioned relevance insofar as it resonates with what a particular community finds as significant to the founding of trust. Hence, particular objects, natural forces, persons, subjective states, and/or historical events come to take on special import as having a disclosive power conferring value and meaning to everything around them.

We must stress, however, that such disclosive power never happens "in itself." It is wedded to a communal identity. For example, religious "symbols" do not have an inherent meaning that is everywhere and always the same; they are given meaning in a social context. Hence, not only do the limit-expressions of faith's appeal to transcendence (1) display the distinguishing marks of a communal identity, they also (2) operate heuristically to draw out and bring into focus that identity, construing disclosures or manifestations of transcendence in a manner that establishes and regulates a ritualized semantic space or territory mediating and so recovering the unconditioned character of trust. And this plays out, furthermore, as (3) the temporal extension of such a space is interpreted as an emplotted episode in a sacred time, its basic narrative sociality imitating by being so rooted in the universal nature of things. We can therefore see how cultic performances of remembering and reaffirming, fidelity, and hope, become invested with a transgressive and sacramental power, referred to a transcendent center of orientation that is embodied and carried forward in a living community of faithful persons.

Through this kind of activity, *religious traditions* become historically embedded and local traditions of trust. *Religious traditions are those communities in which limit-expressions have become sacralized—that is, cosmicized and universalized—to the degree that faith in some specific shape of transcendence has been generated.* In this way, religious communities experience themselves as an *ecclesial* existence "called" into being. Bound by a transcendent imperative, a distinct corporate intentionality is created wherein human beings become tied to, and accountable for, each other.[9] And this corporate intentionality is charged with a ritual and liturgical focus marked conspicuously by mythical and narrative contours. One only has to think of the liturgical calendar of the Christian community, the Islamic holy month of Ramadan, the Jewish Passover, or various rites of passage to find examples of the tie between myth and ritual. Persons of faith not only tell their formative stories, they dramatize them so as to participate in the power they represent. All this designates a common dwelling space organized around a shared appeal to transcendence. That religion is social means it is an ethical praxis and ritual performance shaped by a narrative field of semantic power.

Accordingly, one becomes religious not in the abstract, but by participating in an ongoing line of narrative power and so becoming rooted in its particular appeal to transcendence. There is neither "religion in general" nor a way of being "religious without religion." Only through the material mediation of historical life can the formal potency of the religious sensibility be opened up and actualized concretely. Speaking metaphorically, we might say that if limit-expressions are the music of the religious sensibility, then history is the instrument being played. The religious sensibility is an open-ended capacity that is filled in and modified in a variety of ways, coming to pass in specific historical horizons shaped by peculiar fields of semantic power.

A religious person is then one who acquires certain interpretive skills that relate her or him to a designate image of transcendence through a social-linguistic practice.[10] Indeed, one discovers what salvation is by being socialized into its specified meaning for a particular social situation. This is why Buddhist enlightenment and Christian atonement should be understood as two distinctly different kinds of saving experiences. For in the end, as a modification and founding of trust, religious faith is a thoroughly intratextual and traditioned affair. It begins in the middle, so to speak, within the finite narrowness of narrative self-description.

This helps us understand how religious traditions are not only plural, historically embedded in local sociocultural traditions, but also can jealously guard their *ecclesia* against interruption by differences. Negotiating a trustworthy world requires semantic limits that protect traditions from imperilment—whether by forgetfulness, vagueness, obsolescence, or fragmentation. The appeal to transcendence only confirms and sharpens this fact, granting communal boundary markers an unconditioned, sacralized status. Confessions of faith display precisely this point. For empirically speaking, there is "no salvation outside the church" because only *within* a religious tradition and its self-described and "given" world can trust be mediated and founded.[11] Adherents of different religions do not simply express the same experience in diverse forms; they have widely variant experiences intrinsic to their own unique contexts.[12]

The question for us now is how to properly understand this universalizing momentum of trust as a concrete appeal to transcendence. Are we left with a defensive and polemical religious pluralism that either (1) imperialistically aims to swallow all differences into one normative and universal mold, one saving way of being religious, or (2) tribalistically disperses all differences into local, self-enclosed narrative monads appropriate universally only insofar as they provide consensual conformity for their own traditioned context? I suggest not, for both indicate something disingenuous at work, something that indeed distorts trust. Therefore these postures must be resisted. To understanding why, however, we now push beyond the previous discussion, still underscoring the need for communal boundedness and narrative identity.

TOWARD A UNIVERSAL HORIZON OF RELIGIOUS PLURALITY

Is human religiosity an inherently conservative and totalizing force? Does faith's need for conviction necessitate a plurality of traditions resistant to acknowledging genuine pluralism, instead breeding intolerance or at best indifference? Given the universalizing penchant of the appeal to transcendence, it would seem frighteningly so. Yet I propose to argue the contrary. Of all kinds of communal witnesses, religious traditions *can* and *should* be the most open to innovation, the most hospitable toward difference. On what basis, then, do I make such an audacious claim, running counter to the mass of historical evidence that implicates religion as a source of hostility and divisiveness?

In order to answer this question, we must first sweep together some key themes drawn out earlier in this book. Recall that, empirically speaking, human beings do not inhabit a single, internally consistent and intratextual social world. *While it is true that we stand within the social-linguistic context of a tradition, it is equally true that we stand so at the marginal meeting-place of multiple horizons.* We dwell together in many places at once, our identities the product of a series of hyphenations.

The same, of course, is true of religious identities. There is no way around this fact. For religious traditions are hybrid amalgamations of various practices adapting to, and borrowing from, extraneous elements, informed continually by the precarious crisscrossing of cultural boundaries. One only has to give a cursory glance at the history of religions to find examples—from Santaria and Rastifarianism to the religions of Japan and India, even to Christianity itself. Traditionally, scholars have used the word *syncretism* to indicate such blending and incorporative processes.[13] Now, however, many also talk of "inculturation" as a way of describing how a religious tradition can develop new ways of self-identification as it encounters other cultures and religions, even as it retains an integral focus. Inculteration marks how a tradition draws from resources initially foreign in order to address new needs and issues in different geographic and/or cultural contexts.[14] However we might understand the phenomenon—as syncretism or as inculturation—some form of cross-fertilization is inevitable, especially in a globalizing context in which cultures and peoples become "mixed," sharing multiple heritages and allegiances. An intensification of this is what some Hispanic American writers call *mestizaje*, the experience of having a double identity, of being at home nowhere, caught in the indeterminate zone of being not quite the "same" and yet not quite the "other."[15]

The point is: *religious traditions are not single dimensioned and monophonic wholes, but richly complex, polyphonic, and tension-filled entanglements of multiple conversational threads, each feeding contrapuntally off the other in a wide array of what might be called "intertextualities."* Even though the phenomenon of global connectedness may be new, it serves instructively in a more general sense to bring out and radicalize features (and possibilities) of communal dwelling that have always been there, lying within the character of intersubjectivity itself. Insofar as any community involves discrete agents engaged with one another, the in-between zone of distance and relation is primary, rendering difference not just peripheral but integral. As postcolonial studies underscores, differences do not merely occur outside a purified and self-enclosed communal circle of the same, but unavoidably exist within its self-referential space, contaminating it, so to speak.[16] Postmodern pluralistic consciousness dramatizes the point with dizzying poignancy.

This fact alone mitigates any solid and fixed sense of identity, any sense of stable concordance or enduring coherence. It renders all configurations of a religious "we" fluid, provisional, and unstable. To speak of narrative singularity or self-descriptive enclosure, then, is to promulgate a misconception going against the very conversational texture of the way in which humans dwell together. Like the corner of a busy urban intersection, traditions are not selfsame but rather are comprised of many converging narratives. Plurality is not only something "out there," it is also "in here." Nonidentity is built into the fabric of identity. Integration is always qualified by disintegration. And only because of this does pluralism become possible in its broader and more ethical sense.[17] But how do we reconcile such pluralism with the existential need to dwell together in an interpretive framework that is tradition-bound, especially in the case of religious faith?

Roughly speaking, there are two ways of negotiating the question, both of which entail specific modifications of trust's universalizing affirmation, its need to dwell in a trustworthy world. The first way seeks the immediacy of an identity-over/against-difference by universalizing the local; the second seeks a mediated identity-in-difference by localizing the universal. One way sees difference as a force of diffusion and chaos; the other sees difference as the richness of a plentitude. The first involves a *polemical* posture conditioned by a monological vision, the second, a posture of open *availability* conditioned by a dialogical vision. Both imply an exposure to difference from within the narrative sway of some communal envisagement, some form of intersubjective placement. And more, both receive their universalizing stimulus from local horizons, the openness of trust always concretely embedded. But whereas the former aspires to the closure of satiation, endeavoring to establish itself as complete and thus invulnerable by prioritizing having over not-having, the latter consents to its own finitude in not-having and thereby opens itself to a universality of nonclosure, accordingly granting space for difference.

The polemical stance begins locally and ends locally, universalizing from closed and reified borders, deeming itself absolute. In this, it falsifies and betrays its own internal plurality, deforming trust by conceding to anxiety as its principle motivating force. Availability, to the contrary, gestures universally from borders opened outward toward a horizon that is maximally inclusive in scope, thus inviting the praxis of a dialogical solidarity among the widest variants. Such a gesture is dialectic or double-visioned in that it both affirms and denies its own traditioned position. It stands centered within a centripetal framework that is simultaneously self-surpassing, thrust centrifugally into the exterior, into the liminal in-between of distance and relation. It gains ontological weight in a way that relativizes its own perspective, leaving space for doubt and insecurity. Availability marks the recovery of trust's absolute affectedness, its infinite openness as anticipation of Presence.

The religious sensibility, therefore, is most genuinely displayed in the posture of availability. Indeed, a nonpolemical form of religious universalism *can* be defended. Let us now unpack some of these nuanced distinctions in more detail, highlighting how faith's appeal to transcendence functions in both polemical and available gestures toward difference.

Distorted Trust: Succumbing and Idolatry

I begin with a thesis: the desire for communal closure signifies a trust that has become distorted by turning inward. While it is true that dwelling together requires the limiting character of boundaries that mark a shared value-center and define a collective space of inhabitance, it is also (frighteningly) true that these boundaries can become artificially overextended and ossified to insure corporate integration and preservation. After all, disintegration and forgetfulness remain the nemeses of tradition. The point seems obvious. When called into question or jeopardized, communities of trust can become nostalgic for a return to origins, jealously protecting their narrative identity in a defensive display of "fight or flight."

Especially because of its boundary-erasing and deterritorializing momentum, our global context presents ample opportunity for such a reaction. Most contemporary fundamentalisms and resurgent movements display a hunger for stable orientation, seeking with stubborn and perhaps militant zeal to rid themselves of "foreign" intrusions and to foster a "purified" and hyperdifferentiated identity. This kind of defensive maneuvering is itself a symptom of imperilment by disruption and instability, conflict and change.[18] Ironically, however, it mirrors the very mechanisms of homogenization that it resists: namely, those fostered by the neocolonialism of global capitalism and its bureaucratic institutions. For built into the fabric of reactionary resistance movements is the desire for homogenizing selfsameness. True, the macrologic of globalization is identitarian, trained on "one world" (a "Westernized" hyperculture of consumption epitomized by powerful entertainment, clothing, and food conglomerates), but so are the micrologics of reactionary movements. The former is assimilative and the latter is exclusivist. In both, however, differences become instrumentalized and rendered subservient to a system of transaction caught under the spell of totality. Like a cementing cast, such a totalizing dynamic places a stranglehold on the play of differences.

Communities trained upon the reification of their identity employ the appeal to transcendence in a way that cannot help but become oppressive, a hegemonic violence deforming the mutual recognition of differences that mediates the fabric of being-with. In order to guarantee preservation against disintegration, a redundancy and repetition is introduced that drowns out the indeterminacy and novelty created by relational counterpoint. And the result is an "overextending" religious monotony that falsely constricts polyphony. Indeed, an image of transcendence can devour differences, digesting all to preserve itself. This violence is often seen in both globalizing religious movements and in their reactionary counterparts. But how does this display a distortion of trust?

To the extent that it affirms *meaning* in refusing the anomie of chaos, the reification of identity sacrifices the qualitative power of *vitality* that is the primary correlate of trust's initial anticipatory orientation toward the promise of meaningful vitality. Recall that the creative vitality produced by the play of genuine individual differences is an essential ingredient in trust's elemental affirmation of the trustworthiness of things. Negatively, this arises as an existential refusal: trust's openness resists the suffocating banality of sheer repetition, of a totalizing fate, of external manipulation and domination. Hence, insofar as embedded communities of trust seek to totalize their localized anticipation of the whole, they distort trust by nullifying its dual thrust toward both the harmony of differences drawn-together in complementarity (meaning) and the fertility of differences let-be (vitality). Reacting to the fear of diffusion, traditions that become self-duplicating economies of meaning also become incapable of the freedom of novelty. And thus, they become instruments of violence that subjugate the "distance" of real difference for the sake of assuring the ordered "relation" of identity. The difference of the other becomes a source of contempt or disregard.

Let us now be a bit more specific about what brings about this distortion of trust and what its implications are for religious faith. As has already been indicated, because of its condition of not-having, trust is a disproportionate exigency that aspires to more than it can achieve. This makes it intrinsically unstable and asymmetrical—top-heavy, as it were. Building upon this, I introduce a modifying thesis: *when trust feigns a clarity incompatible with its intrinsic state of not-having, it demonstrates a willful capitulation to anxiety (to the fear of non-being in horror and despair), and as such, fundamentally obscures its original affirmation.* I propose to call this process "succumbing." The word here connotes a brokenness and fault, having both a passive and active component. It is passive in that it submits or gives in to a pressure, a temptation: the closure of immediacy and self-sameness. But it is only such as an activity, a will-to-control that yields to the pressure for closure, bringing about a corresponding renunciation of difference and invoking a kind of death.[19]

Broadly speaking, the act of succumbing is essentially a defensive maneuver that seeks a false assurance, one that diminishes trust by denying the instability of not-having and refusing the fragility of finite being-with. How does this occur? Ironically, it is empowered by the fact that trust is always already propelled beyond finitude. Because of its universalizing outstretch, its opening to infinity, trust surpasses all finite mediations as guarantors of trustworthiness, of the promise of meaningful vitality. And yet, insofar as it is suspended between the finite and infinite, trust cannot escape its embodied condition of finitude and the non-being that besets it. There is a tension or double-bind here, the asymmetry of which effects a pervasive sense of disease and restlessness and creates the conditions for anxiety.[20] Nothing can fill the gaping hole deep in the heart of trust's self-surpassing capacity: nothing, that is, except the unconditioned itself, the truly unlimited and universal. Accordingly, trust of its own accord is driven to make an appeal to transcendence. This appeal itself, however, does not signify a deformed or faulted situation; recall that it is the condition of possibility for the recovery and founding of trust.

Yet it is precisely in the affirmative stretch toward transcendence that the impulse toward succumbing begins. The unconditioned, as the anticipated Whence of the promise of meaningful vitality, cannot be mediated, assured, and possessed as a content among others. As the correlate of trust's absolute affectedness, its infinitude is a relentless and content-surpassing absence. Insofar as it tastes this abysmal absence within its own outstretch, trust recognizes itself as vulnerable and open to dissolution, suffering, and frustration. Disproportionately "top-heavy," the perennial temptation, then, is for trust to resist the pull of non-being by denying its own finitude, rendering itself complete and therefore invulnerable by presenting its own immediate resolution. And it does so by placing a finite object or set of objects in the position of the infinite, "filling-in" its own infinitizing sweep, as it were. Insofar as this temptation is unavoidable, it is what makes human beings fallible.[21] For trust's affirmative exigency, as an embodied passion incomplete of itself, carries the germ of its own deformation, a deformation brought about through the act of succumbing.

Inevitably—though not necessarily—the anxiety of not-having becomes too much to bear, and in a desperate gesture of control, trust seeks to equal its own exigency by forcing the hand of infinity, founding itself.[22] When it capitulates to anxiety in this way, trust indicates a will-to-control or impulse to master that falsifies its openness by closing it in on itself. Trust negates its absolute affectedness. Accordingly, trust is diminished into a posture of insistence, a desire for the immediacy of absolute foundations.[23] Instead of remaining anticipatory, trust now resorts to possessing. It not only wants to have, it demands the closure of having. Through insistence, trust prematurely stakes claim to its eschatological telos, presuming the promise of meaningful vitality as a reality possessed here and now.

Thus, trust refuses its ownmost possibility as an anticipatory openness Presence. This refusal is a paradoxical double negation in that it (1) negates finitude, seeking to deny by overcoming contingency; and (2) negates the infinite, suppressing the absolute affectedness that houses trust's original affirmation. Succumbing is accordingly a perversion of trust, a striving curved in on itself to assure its own self-security in the face of vulnerability. It is a self-aggrandizing attempt (born out of insecurity) to gain identity by pulling all into its gravitational force field and admitting to nothing outside. It aspires to the existential solipsism of homeostasis, a *concupiscentia* seeking to possess the whole as a manageable content, a totality. It thereby halts the tensional play of distance and relation. And in this, the fundamental postures of astonishment and wonderment are suppressed, ironically cutting trust off from its own animating power. Succumbing belies the originary and relational event of being-with.

In order to guarantee the identity of selfsameness, succumbing refuses relatedness by universalizing the local, insisting the finite play the role of the infinite, a role it simply cannot play without become a totality. A penultimate and mundane good is projected as ultimate good and fixated upon—*fetishized*—as if it offered final relief from the instability of not-having, bringing satiation and closure. Conversely, the openness of the infinite is reduced to the finite—to a belief, class status, ethnicity, gender, material acquisitions, social cause, mythical story, nation, history, event, and so forth. This is the dynamic that the Hebrew prophets named *idolatry*.[24]

Succumbing and idolatry are internal moments of one another. In succumbing, trust fashions a god unto itself, raising the contingent to an absolute dimension in and for itself, thereby masking its contingency. The idolatry of succumbing happens as trust seeks the immediacy of self-sufficiency, wishing not only to see but to fully possess its own localized image reflected back as ultimate. By infinitizing the finite, a local value-center or limit-expression is authorized as universally privileged and adequate unto itself, the exhaustive and controlling center of gravity for all meaningful affairs. "Our" framework of orientation is "the" one, universal, fixed, and true way. In the idol, the finite is not merely referred to an ultimate point of reference; it *is* that ultimate point of reference. An *immediate correspondence* is created between the infinite and the finite, the latter alleged to grant the former. But in taking the finite for the infinite, idolatry is in effect not only (1) a refusal of the truly infinite, Presence, but (2) a refusal to let the finite be finite, relative, and relational. The two refusals are interrelated, corresponding to the double negation of succumbing. And they have a pathological effect: the denial of embodied relationality, of being-with.

The logic of immediate correspondence, with its double refusal, has a debilitative narrowing effect on relationality in three ways, all of which, I suggest, are reflected in the polemical attitude. First, in refusing to let the finite be finite, the idol obscures difference, mobilizing a constrictive and totalizing sense of identity that falsifies that identity's own liminality and pluralized relativity by putting boundaries around all in its purview as a means of asserting and safeguarding its own integrity. And by feigning such comprehensive sway, the idol creates an ideological blindness by which genuine difference becomes systematically put out of play (i.e., excluded and denied any value) or put in its place (i.e., instrumentalized and assimilated). The idol is thus opaque; it stops the flow of differences in relation, admitting nothing beyond itself. It evacuates and in effect erases the between of distance and relation, claiming self-related sufficiency. The result is heteronomy, a slavish subduing of difference.

Second, the idol has a narrowing effect in that it is deceptive, hiding the truth about contingency in general and about its own insufficient, limited status in particular. It claims a certitude and finality it does not possess, wielding a false power over differences. Even more subtle, the idol prevails unconscious of its own deceit. It holds sway over a trust that remains unaware that it has been seduced into identitarian closure. Self-deceptively opaque, the idol is incapable of self-criticism and therefore unable to face dissent and the possibility of supplementation, enrichment, or reform. The psychology of this is circular. To have the power to deceive others, one must have already deceived oneself. Accordingly, deceiving others becomes an ongoing effort to convince oneself of the lie. And in this process, one is invariably (and tragically) led to distrust others as equally deceptive. Hence, because of deceit, a rampant sense of distrust and alienation accompanies the idolatrous act, breeding fear of, isolation from, and contempt for all others.

Related to this, a third point emerges. The idol is narrowing in that it functions ironically to exacerbate the very anxiety it purports to quell. Like an iron cage, it traps its adherents inside by facilitating further and greater acts of closure. Why? Because finite goods cannot ultimately deliver the assurance anticipated by trust. The idol is dubious, fragile, and weak, and thus in need of constant maintenance and protection from exposure. It requires purification and adornment, its trustworthy power *made* efficacious through fatiguing narrative and ritualized consecrations, which sacrifice the difference of the other and eschew genuine being-with. Indeed, the idol has a stabilizing sway as a closure only insofar as it is fetishized, made rigid, and cemented in place, injected with authoritative power by the posture of insistence.[25] Even here, however, it can never finally convince. An awareness of the idol's natural vulnerability—the fact that even amidst deceit it plays a role it cannot play without failure—accompanies succumbing. And this breeds further and further insecurity. Hence, like a vicious circle, idolatry creates more anxiety, and in so doing fuels a *polemical* attitude toward all that would threaten its sacrosanct status and undermine the false security it yields. The idol cannot help but bread accommodation and conformity over and against creativity and innovation.

Hence, in these three narrowing effects, succumbing to idolatry has dramatic moral consequences, breaking apart the capacity for availability. It is the font of moral evil. It induces heteronomous relations and a correlative xenophobia that justifies wrongdoing against the other and so against the infinite, Presence. By erasing the liminality of the between, it nullifies the dialectic of distance and relation, inducing the performance of a polemical logic. For the difference of the other becomes an object either for violation, trespass, subjugation, and takeover (in an absorbing relation without distance) or for expulsion, rejection, abandonment, and indifference (in an isolating distance without relation). Perhaps, then, we might call idolatrous actions "sinful" because they betray being-with, signifying and further exacerbating a broken relatedness with others and, accordingly, with the whole. "Sin" violates another by causing suffering.[26] It is not strictly agential, however, for systemic structures of oppression are objectifications of this violation. They too cause suffering and broken relatedness, but on a larger, societal scale. Indeed, given the social character of faith, systemic objectifications of succumbing are more insidious, and often more subtle.

The point here is: when trust succumbs to an idol, it becomes corrupted and morally culpable, bringing about a pernicious feedback loop that perpetuates the very disease it aims to overcome. Given this, we can see the real value of the deconstructive critique of metaphysics, for it calls into radical questioning the artificiality of preemptive closure, undermining the subterfuge of polemical logics, the sway of totalizing identities, and thus setting free (letting-be) differences. Deconstruction is anti-idolatrous and antipolemical. In the best sense of the word, it is nonconformist. It aids in exposing the idolatry not only of nationalist neo-imperialism and globalizing forms of capitalism and consumer culture, but also of their reactive counterpulses in the forms of fundamentalism or neotribalism.

But unless a new idol is merely to supplant an old one, something with positive and determinate weight must replace the idol. Freedom is not merely a freedom-from; it is also a freedom-for. What is the true object of freedom, of trust's original affirmation? It is no object at all. It is the infinite ambience of the between as a limit-dimension of the open whole itself—the pure possibility of Presence.

Religious Faith: Idolatrous and/or Available?

What then of the religious sensibility and of faith's appeal to transcendence? It would appear that it is inherently idolatrous, the consequence of succumbing. I wish, however, to declare that the religious sensibility contains a relativizing iconoclasm that resists the closure of the idol, having a deconstructive thrust. While it would be absurdly naive to claim that religious faith *never* displays idolatrous tendencies, it would be irresponsible—and indeed cause for defeatist pessimism—to claim therefore that it *always* does, that nothing holds the power to break the hold of idols and act as a founding of trust, that we are inevitably bound to idolatry and determined toward its violence. The key is to know when a specific appeal to transcendence is not merely idolatrous.

Of course, we have argued that all religious value is a human projection, and so, taking this into consideration, the idol must not be understood simply as a "human construct" compared to some "truly divine" reality that somehow descends from the sky and gives itself to us. I cannot be more emphatic here: there is no self-authenticating and authoritative revelatory moment in history that destroys the idol, no absolute revelation that outlines itself in such a way that it supplies us with its own nonidolatrous interpretive apparatus. All appeals to transcendence are unavoidably conditioned and finite. So if we take the meaning of idolatry in a strictly positive sense, all faith is idolatrous. But asserting this does not get us very far. For in the pejorative sense I have employed here, an idol is a "false god" because it implies a distortion of the relational openness of trust, falsely naming the power of the whole as something that can be possessed, mastered, and manipulated. *Eschewing idolatry is not then merely a matter of substituting an idolatrous image with one that is "really" the transcendent. It is, rather, a matter of pacifying the will-to-control and opening up trust to the fullness of its original intentionality.*

But are there any grounds to negotiate the difference between an idol and something that authentically represents the transgressive impulse of trust and anticipates Presence? If so, it cannot lie in the circularity of a positivistic appeal to some specific revelation. For this simply obfuscates the problem by reintroducing the closure of a sacrosanct authority.[27] Neither, however, can it lie in a monistic appeal to Presence as some universal content or metaphysical ground, an abstract criteriological foundation by which all faith should be measured. Avoiding these options requires that we take an anthropological turn and look to a soteriological and ethical criterion: *availability*.[28] A trust that is truly concretized, recovered, and founded is one that will display the liberative character of nonclosure. It will be a faith that demonstrates itself in its works, *in the praxis of a performance.* I put forth a thesis: *religious faith, as an appeal to transcendence, is nonidolatrous, authentic, and true when it both (1) serves to found trust and (2) generates the corresponding disposition of availability.*[29]

In negative terms, then, we can recognize idolatry in a religious tradition insofar as it specifically expresses and nurtures acts of succumbing, the appeal to transcendence trained upon closure. The existence of such closure is evidenced in claims to finality and displayed in polemical acts that denigrate alternate faith positions. But if we grant the contingency and plurality of human life, there can be no transparent access to the unconditioned. And if we grant that trust is an *anticipatory* dynamism that neither possesses nor equals its telos, there can be no conclusive rendering of transcendence without succumbing. It is, therefore, idolatrous to equate one's own religious identity with the infinite, regarding it as the absolute or divine, asserting the finality of its unique claim to revelation.[30] Such is to universalize the local and assert a particular image, along with its traditioned narrative and/or confession, as definitive. It is to make sacred one's community to the degree that being "saved" means being "like us," absorbed into the idol's sway. It is to mistake one's finite appeal to transcendence for the unconditioned itself, denying by artificially filling in the qualitative distance between the finite and infinite. Thus, in the name of religion, the idol ironically promulgates the irreligious. How then does trust resist the idol and become authentically founded?

The answer lies in the character of the transcendence to which trust appeals. Recall, a trust that is authentically recovered is not constituted as selfsame. For this would be to falsify its self-surpassing relationality, its absolute affectedness, rendering it solipsistic and sufficient unto itself. Because elemental trust is a participative openness toward the whole as meaningful and vital, the concrete actualization of its universal stretch can only be anticipatory, not total, arising in the relational potency of being-with, not the stasis of closure. This then leads to a key point.

Any image or limit-expression that is received as transcendent, insofar as it projects and names the trustworthiness of the whole and founds trust, must itself be a self-surpassing nonclosure. It must hold open a space between the finite and infinite if it is not to negate the self-surpassing exigency of trust, which is driven beyond the frontiers of finitude. This is required by the fact that the basic tilt of trust's affirmation functions to relativize all contingent values as guarantors of trustworthiness. Built into trust is a leveling iconoclasm, for no finite content can render trust equal to its own momentum. No determinate image or limit-expression can be *the* transcendent. No place, object, person, status, order, or anything else, can stabilize and constitute the trace of the original promise that inaugurates trust as a passion seeking its own recovery. Trust remains an absolute affectedness.

The promise of meaningful vitality calls forth an appeal to transcendence, not because it acts as a foundational ground or substance guaranteeing trust, but because it exceeds and escapes all such guarantees, all totalities, all acts of closure, as an absence perpetually deferring the immediacy of referential signification. Indeed, as I have argued, its call, perceived in the throes of presence, bursts open interiority toward the possibility of an infinite being-with. Accordingly, any image that adequately represents the promise of meaningful vitality must galvanize a double vision, a fundamentally dialectical structure. It must (1) confer value and significance as it simultaneously (2) defers away from itself. It must recover trust while relativizing itself in the process. Only in this kind of dual intentionality can trust resist succumbing and break away from the opacity of the idol, becoming founded in faith. A limit-expression or image suggests genuine transcendence, then, not only because it affirms existence as worthwhile by naming the possibility of the whole as trustworthy, but because it does so in a way that is dialectical and self-surpassing. Like trust, it has by not-having.

In this way, asserting that the concrete appeal to transcendence is self-relativizing is not the same as asserting an empty iconoclasm. It is not tantamount to a desacralizing "death of God" that wipes the horizon of the whole clean of its ability to evoke the projection of transcendence. This kind of Nietzschean move would essentially nullify the universalizing modality of trust, rendering its original affirmation banal and ironic (recall Richard Rorty's ironist). It would not uphold the dialectic between having and not-having, the anticipatory moment of the appeal to transcendence sublated "infinitely" by a second moment of deferral (recall Jacques Derrida's *différance*), indeed dissemination (recall Michel Foucault).[31] But deferral itself is only possible because of an anticipatory gesture that affirms some kind of promise that exceeds closure and that functions as the "toward-which" of deferral. Otherwise deferral has no initiative, and in effect, no erasive power. While Derrida's later writings seek to address this issue by stressing the always "to come" of the *messianic*, such eschatological promise is left in the desertified landscape (*khora*) of waiting for an anonymous "any" other, we know not whom.[32]

Consequently, I have suggested that exposure to the promise of ontological weight tilts us in a certain direction, suggesting interpretive possibilities. Why? Because it comes to pass as a superabundance of meaning over chaos and vitality over repetition, as an excess having the character not of an indefinite abyss but of the openness of infinity. Thus it is that the explicit appeal to a nonidolatrous shape of transcendence designates a shape that is self-surpassing, reflective of the nonclosure of the infinite.

And this event of "designation" is an implicit referral, an indirect and oblique allusion, to the Whence of trust's absolute affectedness—namely, Presence. That is to say, it is a way into the surplus possibility of being-with that empowers a courageous consent to finitude in the space of not-having. Only as it defers and negates itself (as a closure) can a designated image of transcendence open desire to the possibilizing power and mystery of the whole. The unconditioned character of the infinite limits the claims of all local affirmations as it bursts them open toward universality. Such universality is never fully instantiated. For we are talking about an absolute future that can never become confused or identified with any item of localized peculiarity, whether as a content or experience. It remains unsaid, unthought as such. It is anticipated as an eschatological possibility always "to come," a *potentia* never fully actualized or granted.[33] Hence, the universality of an image of transcendence stems from an appeal that is transgressive in its forward stretch. It is not the inwardly turned closure of an immediate correspondence. Universality is, paradoxically, an always-already not-yet, a correlate of trust's participative openness.

Iconoclasm in this way corresponds to a sacramentalism, an exposure to a surplus that opens up all local value toward the infinite horizon of the whole, an absolute possibility that is a deferred reference, present as an absence, disclosed as an impenetrable mystery. Universality, as a sacramental fullness, and iconoclasm are internally related as coaffirmations.[34] Together they suggest a center without a center, a decentering center, a difference-bearing plentitude that knows no circumnavigating boundary and thus places all in the liminal between of relation and distance. *Hence, insofar as it is double-visioned, a nonidolatrous appeal to transcendence projects the meaningful vitality of the whole itself as an infinite being-with.* In this lies its religious value, its capacity to found trust. For trust's basic affirmation of meaningful vitality is only recovered and actualized by being held open, only conferred by being deferred in a dialectical performance that anticipates and so intimates—that is, obliquely signifies—Presence. Religious faith is dialectical, a *sacramental iconoclasm.*

The Projective Imagination: Limit-Expressions, Metaphor, and the Icon

An example of this dialectical structure is found in the very nature of limit-expressions. Carried along by the anticipatory momentum of trust, seeking to recognize the whole as worthy of its promise, the language of limit is an excessive language transgressing its local boundedness. For as trust has by not-having, limit language refers by nonreference. It is an indirect presentation, an action that is more an invocative performance than a static description, functioning in a poetic and metaphoric way to break open a surplus dimension of reality and invite faithful adherence. And, in this, the role of the creative imagination is prominent. A designate shape of transcendence, as a limit-expression, gains its dialectical power as the product of the *projective imagination*. As Paul Avis suggests, "Through imagination we are enabled to indwell the world of religious belief and to obtain a glimpse of what it might be like to live as though it were true."[35] And, I would add, it is the "as though" that marks the imagination projective and metaphoric at base. Words are not idols, directly rising out of and immediately corresponding to things, but rather are living emblems of participative openness, mediating worlds that galvanize perceptions and actualize our orientation toward the whole. As such, they have a potentially unlimited suggestiveness. Contra Ludwig Wittgenstein's statement in the *Tractatus*, the limits of a language do not define the limits of a world. As George Steiner suggests, even a single sentence is elastic and always means more, expanding outward.[36]

There is an indeterminate element of surplus value always at work in fields of semantic power. Why? Because the dialogical nature of language itself displays differential potency, exposing the betwixt and between of being-with, of distance and relation. It shows that we are not linguistic determinates of an enclosed communal world. We are creative bearers of an openness that exceeds "us" and makes relative all closures. And the imagination itself is the carrier of that openness, a poetic capacity of infinite projective power.[37] The imagination is a structuring and destructuring potency. It structures in that it envisions and draws together things into momentary configurations or closures; but it destructures in that it reopens these closures to the vitality of difference.[38] The projective imagination is the house of meaningful vitality.

This is demonstrated in the character of metaphor. As Paul Ricoeur suggests, the metaphor—the "is" and "is not" coupling of an affirmative designation—is the root of all linguistic meaning.[39] As a community's identity only happens in the productive togetherness of differences in relation, as a dia-logos, the metaphor incarnates this linguistically; it is an event in which two semantic mediums are reciprocally juxtaposed, placed together in a simultaneity of neither conflation nor separation. Neither reducing what is different to the similar and already known, nor simply allowing the different to slip into an impenetrable alterity, metaphors indicate the poetic capacity to stretch out and "stand in-between" the familiar and the foreign. In the metaphor, a tensional interaction takes place between similarity and strangeness, like and unlike, from which occurs not merely a repetition of taken-for-granted meanings but a novel configuration of meaning. Two semantic horizons are fused, to use Hans-Georg Gadamer's terminology, and through their free exchange, ordinary ways of looking at things are suspended, and we are disposed toward seeing something new.[40] Through this transference of meanings a fresh gestalt appears. Something is "seen as" something else.[41] The familiar is seen through the unfamiliar and the unfamiliar is seen through the familiar. Here, there is neither the dispersal nor the self-sameness of meaning, but rather the liminal between of proximity in remoteness, congruity in incongruity, identity in difference.

Thus it is that metaphoric meaning itself displays the dialectical qualities of living conversation. It emerges as the afterimage of an event of being-with. And within the metaphor, ordinary reality is redescribed and enriched, supplemented and enlarged. But this is no mere flowery embellishment of an already established and stable fact. Rather, the metaphor is an iconic or image-producing act of creative synthesis that excites and releases meaning in and through letting-be the vitalizing dialectic of differences in relation.[42] It is a rapprochement that reveals a "kinship," an interconnection and complementarity, between heterogeneous elements.[43] The metaphor, then, is an imaginative projection of meaningful vitality, revealing the character of a trust in the relational differentiation of things. Indeed, it is a poetic vehicle through which we generate and indwell a world together, sharing understanding. "Poetic" because it exhibits feeling elevated and transformed into "fiction" as an attributive figuration of sense, a projection of new possibilities.[44] Stated differently, the metaphor is poetic in that it opens up what Ricoeur calls "the field of a nondescriptive reference" to existence, a reference to the way we belong to the universe as an embodied desire: what Gabriel Marcel calls "fundamental feeling."[45] *Elemental trust, then, as an enduring affective disposition, is a metaphoric instinct with innovative semantic potency.*

This is further borne out in that trust's "not-having" is analogous to the metaphoric "is not." Because of the "is not," the metaphor itself contains a destructuring moment, becoming intrinsically unstable and open to supplementation. The juxtaposition of two terms creates what Ricoeur calls a "tensive" truth, an iconic "is" that at once signifies both similarity and difference.[46] Here the distance of difference is not annulled by the nearness of relation, but is dialectically affirmed. Remoteness is preserved in proximity, for to see a relation of likeness is to see similarity in and through difference.[47] And metaphor attends to that difference, letting it be. This is what makes its meaning an innovative vitality opened outward as a nonclosure, more a suggestiveness than a definitiveness. A relativizing *via negativa* or apophatism accompanies the iconic status of metaphoric attribution, creating the liminality of an in-between, a having that is a not-having.

Without such a not-having, the metaphor dies—that is, loses its vitality—becoming subsumed into taken-for-granted meanings. The conservative pull of a narrative tradition can threaten the metaphoric imagination in precisely this way. It can close itself off to innovation by too rigidly holding to an identity. We must remember, then, that narratives too, in that they are metaphoric, are open to the distance of difference. Ricoeur argues the point in stating that narratives display a "flexible dialectic between innovation and sedimentation," an emplotment that hovers between servile repetition and sheer deviance.[48] Any event of storytelling involves a dimension of indeterminacy, for its reception and retelling mediates a reference that is constantly deferred and open to a variety of interpretive deployments. Revisionment is thus an inescapable part of narrative, ruling out stable closure.[49] And this is so because the metaphor itself stands on the boundary between the closed and the open. Never selfsame, it suspends identity as it gives identity.

Thus, the character of metaphor displays the very dialectic or double vision we have ascribed to trust's representation in a nonidolatrous appeal to transcendence. As limit-expressions are themselves metaphoric, a self-limiting apophatism will necessarily accompany all projective figurations of transcendence. Trust's anticipatory impulse emerges concretely as a metaphoric event, perhaps *the* metaphoric event, in that it aspires through the means of ordinary language to disclose the infinite relational power of the whole. Language is thereby brought to excess, saying more than it can say as it names the limit-horizon of existence, not as a static description of immediate referential status, but as a nonconclusive dialectical performance between the local and the universal.

For this reason, I suggest that limit-expressions serve as *icons*.[50] The authentic logic of the appeal to transcendence is iconic, not idolatrous. For a designate limit-expression or image that is received as transcendent can only be so as a self-surpassing content attesting to the qualitative difference of the finite and infinite. Whereas the idol is opaque and definitive, the icon is diffuse and suggestive, deferring away from itself as it simultaneously configures meaning and vitality. Containing a self-relativizing and "iconoclastic" moment of nonclosure, an icon is disclosive, an image that is received as transparent. It is an open closure. It orients by disorienting and reorienting beyond itself, its reference not intrinsic to or immediately given in itself. Because the icon discloses an economy of asymmetrical value and superabundance, it demands a concomitant negative qualification. Indeed, the fact of such negative qualification is proof of its disclosive power. *Icons usher us metaphorically into the remoteness/discontinuity of an infinite promise via the proximity/continuity of concrete images and categories drawn from finite experience. But they do so only by effecting a reversal, ushering us anew into the proximate as relativized by its capacity to evoke the remote.*

Icons evoke interest, inspire vision, and radiate value as harbingers of a power not inherent or reducible to themselves. That is what makes them disclosive in a heuristic more than descriptive sense. They anticipate—that is, they point to and participate in—a power beyond themselves, an asymmetrical power of qualitative difference that cannot be determined and measured by, or reduced to, local construals. This is why images of the sacred often carry within them a disruptive element that neutralizes any attempt at referential closure, negating the positive pull of attributive language.[51] For the unconditioned power of the whole is affirmed in all things only as a possibility distinct from them. This is also why images of the sacred invoke multiple strands of interpretation, even multiple traditions. The icon is infinitely open to interpretation.

Therefore, we can say that icons are localized universals: they mediate the universal (i.e., the infinite) from a local (i.e., finite) condition yet do so as a universalizing that returns full circle to open up, contextualize, and relativize the local. In this way, limit-expressions explode language from the inside toward the limit-horizon of existence, displaying the impulse of trust's passion for connection in differentiation. The givenness of an image of transcendence, as a disclosive event, provides orientation and ontological weight while at the same time invoking a disorientation that precludes self-enclosure. Hence, *the icon marks a nonconclusive dialectic that is difference-making. It makes difference paradoxically in that it (1) founds trust precisely as (2) an opening of trust to its original affirmation. And this opening takes the shape of an availability to and for difference.*

RELIGIOUS FAITH AS AVAILABILITY AND THE DIALOGICAL PRAXIS OF SOLIDARITY

The concrete appeal to a designate transcendence need not universalize the local from closed borders, invoking slavish submission, subdual, or exclusion. To the contrary, precisely as iconic and metaphoric, such localized universalizing invokes the liminal border-dwelling of a potentially unlimited relationality, empowering resistance against succumbing and idolatry. Certainly, we universalize from embedded local conditions. Yet insofar as this act represents the pulse of trust, it transgresses local boundaries, breaking open any and all closures. We stand within a tradition and yet from such a place are thrust outward toward a universal horizon of maximal solidarity. It is this double vision that both reflects and grants a space for difference *within* local dwelling places, which allows for identity in difference.

Moreover, its nonclosure necessitates dialogical supplementation from *outside* its space, meaning that we are open to all potential "others," to other traditions and to their unique claims, readjusting our perspective as we attend to and take account of theirs. While each may reflect its impact, none fully grasps the possibilizing power of the whole as Presence. Rosemary Radford Ruether makes the point eloquently:

> True universality lies not in trying to make one cultural synthesis that can embrace all possibilities. Such a synthesis will always be limited, and thus become a new cultural imperialism that ignores or

> denies truth outside its limited construct. True universality lies in *accepting* one's own finiteness, one's own particularity and, in so doing, not making that particularity the only true faith, but *allowing* other particularities to stand side by side with yours as having equal integrity. Each is limited and particular, and yet each is, in its own way, an adequate way of experiencing the whole for a particular people at a particular time.[52]

True universality is thus a difference-making performance, an "accepting" of finitude that at the same time "allows" its particularities to remain distinct in being integrally related. Indeed, it is because of this acceptance that differences are let-be. But even more fundamentally, it is because of the "always already thereness" of difference that this acceptance emerges. For trust emerges as an original affirmation of differences-in-relation as a meaningful vitality.

Thus, I contend that the religious actualization and recovery—that is, the founding—of trust in faith will necessarily display the characteristics of availability to and for difference. As we have stated in chapters 3 and 4, availability—in Gabriel Marcel's sense of the French word, *disponibilité*—means the ability to respond sympathetically to, to actively take-in and appreciatively dispose oneself to, the presence of an "other."[53] It is the full actualization of being-with. Because of this, the ethical moment of availability is the crucial test through which the dialectic of a sacramental iconoclasm must pass. Availability does not stop with the acknowledgment of finitude. It flowers into an ethical relation with the other, a way of being toward the other as precious and beautiful in its own right. Just as the bodhisattva in Mahayana Buddhism pours out love in a boundless compassion (*karuna*) that seeks the well-being of all life, attending to and saving others, availability is a self-transcending giving to the other.[54] It is the stuff of the moral character—that is, the goodness, mercy, compassion, loving kindness, and so forth—that characterizes the "saint."

In drawing-near and letting-be the difference of the other, availability cannot help but participate in and will the other's good. And this act of *willing another's good* is the loving hospitality and freedom-making justice, the reconciling reciprocity, which fuels a dialogical praxis of solidarity. A "we" is created that is an open circle, a community of identity in difference. There is neither reductive absorption nor exclusion from relation. For the other is received as bearing its own initiative and intrinsic preciousness. This is the ideal praxis of being-with. It is the telos of elemental trust. Indeed, it is the harbinger of the infinite, the anticipation of Presence as the unconditioned possibility of presences being-with one another.

Accordingly, availability is the fruit of the dialectical power of the icon. It exhibits human openness to the difference-bearing fecundity of the whole in and through the local. How so? Because all that is finite and limited is both equally near and equally remote from the undesignate Whence of the promise of meaningful vitality. Stated negatively, no particular reality within the finite sphere of localized relations can be said to be "closer" to the infinite and universal than any other.[55] *Yet far from negating the icon, consent to not-having affirms the icon, opening up the qualitative difference of the infinite, thereby letting the finite be what it in fact is: finite, and as such, diverse.* The infinite is a context without a context, a context that contextualizes the finite as such. And in letting the finite be finite, a space for the distance and relation of genuine difference is allotted. For it is only in refusing the finite condition of not-having that the problem of succumbing and idolatry emerges.

Stated positively, then, as the corollary of the fact that *no* finite content establishes immediate or exhaustive connection with the infinite, *all* finite being is equally related to, and participates in, the infinite. All things, in their difference and richness, are full of gods. All finite limits are held infinitely open; they are comprehended by something larger than themselves. Far from denying limit, then, trust's appeal to transcendence attests to limit and sanctions it, making its closure a relative nonclosure. It is this iconic affirmation of the infinite that affirms the finite in a way that resists succumbing and its refusal. For nothing is constituted completely selfsame; everything is interrelated. Accordingly, each iconic representation is incomplete and open to supplementation.

Religious faith, therefore, at its best, exercises not only a resistance to the dispersive anomie of chaos, but also, in the words of David Tracy, "extraordinary powers of resistance . . . to more of the same," to the overdetermination of homogeneity.[56] The infinite can never become monopolized as a self-enclosed totality. Its qualitative difference resists and explodes all onto-theological contents from the inside. The icon holds open the gap between the finite and infinite, and does so by affirming both dialectically—in their difference and unity. For the infinite is disclosed only via the anticipation of an unconditional promise; and this happens in and through conditional events of being-with. Religious faith is such an anticipation, and availability is its correlate mode of being-with.

Availability is trust transposed beyond anxiety toward participating in the goodness of the difference-bearing whole. But it is so only in faith's openness to the possibility of value in all concrete differences. This renders all religious acts of being-with an unfinished and outward momentum rather than a closed circle of relation. Availability, then, is a performance hearkening to the call of the infinite in the finite, reflecting and coaffirming Presence, in that it exists liminally on the boundary between closedness and openness, between the local and the universal. It arises always and everywhere as tradition-bound, but is at the same time thrust beyond itself by resisting both dispersive anarchy (meaninglessness) and homogeneous repetition (vitalitylessness). And in this twin resistance, it affirms the whole as an interdependent complementarity of relations (as meaningful) energized by the varied particularity of difference (as vitality). Each difference is integral yet related, none having its own-being yet none absorbed into the same. There is neither the chaos of dispersion nor the static unity of totality. Rather, there is a *pluralism* of differences-in-relation.

In sum, availability plays out essentially as a self-surpassing readiness for the other—an acceptance of finitude and a willingness to live without self-security in the creative between of distance and relation. *In the mode of availability, particular acts of being-with are a localized enactment of the potentially universal communion to which trust's anticipation of Presence is the call.* What is such communion but the sharing of differences in solidarity. This is no amoral drama. To the contrary, it evokes an interest that wills the good of the other, a desire that goes out to (1) embrace and (2) release its dignity as different. "Embrace" and "release" are two interwoven and communion-producing actions reflecting the reconciling reciprocity of the infinite whole. Let us examine these terms in further detail.

Embrace: Loving Regard

The dynamic of *embrace* is one of drawing near, of attending to, of accepting, and offering hospitality.[57] It has a reconciliatory momentum that resists dispersion and isolation and seeks relation with the other. The opposite of exclusion, it is love, a passion for connection, and its affective impulse is that of wonderment. For the other allures and hearkens interest as a preciousness to be savored and preserved, a gift radiating the promise of a meaningful vitality. Such a promise functions as an affirmation of complementarity—of likeness or similitude—that draws together and informs a relation of sharing. Arms stretched open, embrace responds to the other with hospitality, creating room for its difference within a now shared space of co-inhabitance. It indicates an identity/self not "full" of, or sufficient to, itself. For embrace receives the other's difference as contributive, valuable, and good. And in so doing, it wills the good of the other as part of its own, sympathetically aligned with its difference. It suffers with the other, seeking the fulfillment of the other as part of its own fulfillment. Thus, we might say that embrace takes the shape of an inclusive *care*, not simply as a heteronomous "ought," but as an existential kinship with the other that evokes acts of waiting upon and tending to its good as part of something shared.

But this does not happen in a vacuum. Indeed, care's sympathetic alignment with another is related to the universalizing impulse of trust's anticipatory gesture, itself a passion for the limit-horizon of the whole as Presence. The care of embrace implies an infinite relation of sharing complementarity, of similarity between differences. It coaffirms Presence. Put axiomatically, embrace is an "arms stretched open" that gestures toward a particular being in a given situation because it is at the same time an "arms stretched open" to potentially *all* particular beings—in their specificity—as kindred participants in an unconditioned matrix of sheer gratuity and unlimited preciousness. Embrace is not merely a generalized obligation or disinterested act, abstractly willing another's good from a distance. It plays out locally as a loving care, an attentiveness to, and admiration of, *this* concrete other recognized as such in the relational context of the goodness and trustworthiness of all potential others. In this way, the uniqueness of the other is received as infinitely valuable. The other participates in a universal good that we all share, or better, in which we all share. The local other is a glimpse into the universal Other: Presence.

Availability as embrace is an invitation to dwell together in the most expansive solidarity possible, not as a closure but as a transregional and fluid zone of encounter. It resists alienation and isolation. It is a self-surpassing or nonegocentric desire to create a space in oneself for the other precisely as a way of entering the space of the other. The care of embrace, then, is the sharing of multiple spaces as one's own. And the liminality of this condition is *communion*, neither a coercive domination nor assimilative inclusion, but rather a gesture of hospitality whereby one's world is enlarged and reconfigured toward a universal being-with. When I will the good of a concrete other, I make an affirmation willing the universal good of the whole itself. But I don't will the good of the other "in order to" will the good of the whole, nor vice versa. I do both simultaneously. We are all interrelated, joined in kinship from the macro- to the microlevel. The implicit telos of embrace is relational flourishing in the widest sense imaginable.

Release: Deferential Regard

But the drama of embrace does not suffocate difference in its hold. Its care does not cling to the other in symbiotic attachment. Nor does it seek merely to enhance or enlarge self-enclosure by absorbing the other's distinctness within itself. Embrace does not possess. Rather, it *releases* the other to let it be genuinely other, exterior, and at a distance. It prepares a space for the other, but not as a cage. For the drama of embrace requires a not-having, an unbinding and liberative moment that lets the other be free. Without oscillating into release, embrace is not embrace but obsessive clutching, an anxiety-driven and egocentric will-to-control that gives impetus to the totalizing pseudo-fulfillment of idolatry. Such clutching evacuates distance, denies the independent integrity of the other, and so snuffs out vitality.

In contrast, the reconciling embrace of love lets be distinctness in a freedom-making relation of reciprocity. "Letting be" does not negate embrace, dispersing connective relations into the sheer distance of isolation. Rather, it supplements by suspending embrace. It is a waiting upon the other that is a *waiting for* the other: not a will-to-control grasping for closure—which can only spawn violence—but a nonviolent relinquishing of the will-to-control, an openness that lets the other make its own presence felt.[58] On the other hand, waiting for the other is not the equivalent of self-denial or abnegation, the disappearance of the "I" into the "we." As embrace does not mean to transform the other into oneself, neither does it mean to diffuse oneself and so to transform oneself into the other. The logic of absorption is resisted by embrace's release. For it is an active receptivity that goes out of itself to welcome the other as one with aims and needs not coincident with my own, preserving individuality and distinctness.

Release is a gesture of hospitality that preserves the mystery of another's strangeness even in its familiarity. It wills the good of another in yielding to its own concrete capacity to reciprocate in ever-new ways. As the dialectical correlate of embrace, release highlights the awe-inspired distance through which relational kinship is made possible and vitalized, a distance that signifies the freedom and unique character of the other as independent from my gaze. Indeed, my own gaze is relativized by the unique "in-itself-ness" of the presence of the other. The other stands before me empowered to be its own, with the capacity to embrace (or equally resist embrace) on its own. Hence, the care of embrace entails the acknowledgment and preservation of *distance* in relation. It exists in the between, a between that is infinitizing. In release, availability reflects the infinite vitality of reciprocity in the whole itself, which upholds distance in relation, distinction in complementarity, separateness in kinship. Release is the gratuitous letting-be of difference that characterizes Presence as the power of being-with.

A truly universal solidarity, then, rather than being grouped around a univocal center, can only be polycentric, a community of communities. This is what makes it communion rather than uniformity. Similarity cannot be imposed in advance; it is discovered in the process of finding what we share in our differences. And such sharing is polyphonic. Care for humanity means caring for the richness of all variations in an ad hoc and ever-increasing reciprocity, beginning from the particular and local but implicitly extending outward toward a potentially universal horizon of sharing. But such reciprocity does not automatically come whenever humans dwell together. It must be won and actualized as the toward-which of all acts of dwelling together. It is a possibility inherent in being-with.

Ethically speaking, reciprocity begins in the praxis of recognizing and paying careful attention to the other. In brief, it means to give *respect* to the other. Respect is to care as release is to embrace, a dialectical associate. Care without respect is either sentimental overattachment or pity-like condescension. It invokes no reciprocity and indeed can victimize and become oppressive. Simultaneously, respect is not merely tolerance, a disinterested posture of noninterference that puts the other at a distance without engaging it. Tolerance, while feigning nobility, can often exercise a subtle totalizing impulse, "putting up with" differences from a position of dominance or self-security.

By respect, then, I mean to indicate *deferential regard*, a regard that defers itself, pays heed to, and esteems the distinctness of the other, granting it the right to be. Respect considers the other as having its own dignity. More than merely leaving the other as other, however, respect is a "response-ableness" to the other's value, for the preciousness of the other has the character of an address, in principle calling out to and making a claim upon all others. What is the nature of this claim? Fundamentally, it is call for recognition as something of worth.[59] But this worth does not rise in terms of an economy of interchangability, the other's value being reduced to a utilitarian functionalism. Rather, recognition acknowledges the other as a being also—that is, like me—desiring meaningful vitality, capable of its own unique perspective.

The claim of the other, then, has force in that it sets before me, apart from me and yet related to me, a noninterchangeable difference vulnerable to misrecognition and disrespect. Taking on and owning up to this claim, respect exhibits genuine commerce with the other in the form of an accountability, a moral culpability, a responsibility. It responds "here I am" to an other who exclaims, "love *me*," and in so doing, attends to the superabundant dignity of something precious and good before me.[60] Put succinctly, respect is a responsibility that wills the meaningful vitality of the other. It eschews and indeed resists instrumentalizing techniques that serve to exclude the other. When I care for others, I do not reduce them to a doppelgänger, a mere reflection of my own image; I respect them and become (and remain) responsible for their own distinct flourishing, willing their own good as separate or distinguishable from mine, even as I am sympathetically aligned with it. The other, precisely as a gift of preciousness, is also a source of obligation.

With such relational accountability in mind, I suggest that localized respect is an anticipation of a potentially universal symmetrical reciprocity of relation, for an inclusive *justice*. The ethical praxis of respect implies an expectation of justice. And justice is a call for respect on the widest of relational scales—a universal sociality. Justice reflects respect and mutuality in willing the good of all potential others.[61] It is the golden rule writ large, indicating responsibility as a commitment to reciprocity in general. Implied in the "golden rule" is both kinship and separateness. It is not simply a demand for disinterested obligation; it suggests that I am on a relational par with others and so am accountable. As a logic of equivalence, it grants each difference recognition and equal treatment, forging a space for sharing reciprocity universally.[62] Indeed, without the justice of symmetrical reciprocity, there can be no genuinely reconciling embrace. Without justice, the distance of difference is denied, the relational par of kinship distorted. But it is this distance of differences that holds at bay the temptation to heteronomous closure.

Justice, then, is a relativizing prophetic call that emerges from the acknowledgment of the other released through respect. It comes forth as a universalization of the call of the concrete other. Indeed, responsibility is a harkening to justice, to preserve the distinctness of differences in the kinship of participative interconnectedness. Justice is a critique of all closures that would confuse the finite with the infinite and so distort relational liminality. Accordingly, it resists and calls into question idolatrous systems of domination and subjugation—whose modality is that of disrespectful assimilation—by seeking to subvert any and all totalizing logics of identity. Such resistance is also an affirmation summoning caring regard for those who are not embraced, who are displaced, despised, discarded, marginalized, and in a word, excluded. It seeks to restore reciprocity and mutual recognition, bringing about the liberative release of those violated and victimized.

But the very universalizing character of the call for justice indicates that the historical negotiation of genuine differences can never produce the definitiveness of a final resolution. Justice is never societally or institutionally actualized. If so, it would be a totalizing collective egoism, for as Reinhold Niebuhr notes, "no scheme of justice can do full justice to all the variable factors which the freedom of man introduces into human history."[63] No calculation of proportionality can exhaust the difference-making novelty of the other's self-initiating potency and its constant shifting about. Justice then remains always already in-front, a hope yet to be achieved.[64] It functions as destructuring and open-ended telos, the goal or ideal of dwelling together. A truly reconciling reciprocity can only be ongoing and fluid, held open in the equalizing force of justice. It is justice that ensures relational novelty and vitality, for it is through the dissonance of difference that we become alive to the new. And it is through the social task-making of justice that solidarity, as a mutual recognition between differences, can blossom.

Dialectical Pluralism: A Communion of Justice-Making Love

We can now make a summary statement, raising the discussion to a final swell. Embrace and release together, as twin modes of an availability nurtured by faith's iconic appeal to transcendence, serve to inculcate a *justice-making love* between differences. And justice-making love is the foundation of pluralism, as an ethical configuration. Contra the polemical attitude, which holds difference at bay, embrace and release promote communion as a tensional praxis of reconciling reciprocity—drawing together while letting-be differences. Hence, it is the stuff of a dialectical pluralism of solidarity versus that of dispersion (merely letting differences be) or identity (merely drawing differences together).

As embrace and release, love's reconciliatory gesture and justice's call to reciprocity are bipolar moments internal to each other. Without justice, love can become facile and sentimental and/or identitarian and instrumentalist. Justice calls love into accountability and preserves it from asserting identity over difference, from becoming a logic of absorption, heteronomously denying the freedom of the other to be different. Without love, however, justice can become a banal and utilitarian relativizing of differences under calculated equivalency, an abstract "this for that," means-end relation that homogenizes differences.[65] Love keeps justice from emptying the other of singular value. Taken together, love and justice resist each other's propensity to perversion. Only in love is justice truly just and not difference-blind, is the other tended to and embraced in ways appropriate to its novelty and difference.[66] And only in justice is love attentive to the other as such, a distance-affirming stretch toward the embrace of true difference. As love draws near in hearkening to the other as precious and full of value, justice qualifies that drawing near by holding open the between zone of distance in a symmetrical relation of mutuality. A justice-making love forges relation and preserves distance in the shape of a similarity in difference, a kinship in distinctness—at base, an intersubjectively constituted meaningful vitality—through the praxis of an ever-deepening and widening belonging together. Put briefly, it is a fidelity to, and hope for, a potentially universal communion of communities.

Thus, in the mode of availability, religious communities are not closed circles of faith, but rather are embedded and provincial openings outward toward a transprovincial horizon of ongoing *mutual transformation* between communities. By "mutual transformation" I mean something similar to Gadamer's "fusion of horizons," wherein different interpretive horizons become conversationally interwoven and reciprocally enriched; only now it is important to add the element of justice-making love. Through a dialectic of differences in relation, interpretive horizons intersect or become "fused" in the dance of embrace and release, resisting both totalized universality and fragmented isolation. This event, however, does not signify the negation of faith. To the contrary, it facilitates faith's enlargement. Faith is local and traditioned, having a communal form, but as such it is a world-openness of its own accord invited into an ever-larger space of mutual belonging. Recall that the icon is self-deferring and open to supplementation. It points toward and participates in that which is more than itself. This fact propels faith outward to an extrinsic value. Faith is exposed to the open, to the liminality of the between.

In being so exposed, faith is simultaneously centering and self-surpassing, a centrifugal centripetality disposed toward being-with in the most inclusive and universal sense. Such a disposition is availability. But availability does not leave its bounded tradition behind as some skin to be shed. It rather reaches from and through the local toward the universal, not as a disembedded perspective to be achieved but as an anticipatory mode of self-transcendence propelled by the projective imagination. And this anticipatory reach is the condition for a dialogical openness to other faith traditions in the mode of justice-making love.

Hence, in the loving regard of embrace, dialogical openness involves a sixfold aptitude: a willingness (1) to *listen* attentively to what another has to say; (2) to *discover value* in another's way of naming and relating to the mystery of the whole; (3) to *appreciate* and so uphold its value, not remaining indifferent, but imaginatively (metaphorically) entering into its uniqueness as it might be seen by the other; (4) to be *challenged* by the encounter, facing up to the limitations of one's perspective in light of the other; and finally (5) to be *changed* by it, to let one's own perspective be supplemented and enriched as a consequence of stepping into the border zone of engagement. Yet in all these forms of "willingness," embrace, precisely as an offering of oneself, means (6) not to efface or deny but to *give witness* to one's own particular standpoint. Indeed, embrace only is possible *from* a position. There is no universal perspective; there is only the open-ended dialectic of differences in relation.

In dialogue we explore together from our different origination points, and in the process these origination points not only become enriched individually, they also form a larger and more inclusive nexus of relationship by which we begin to rethink our individuality as a belonging together, a solidarity in which differences are complementary and not merely contradictory. A logic of partnership and collaboration thus emerges over competition and distrust, one that is democratic, open, and public. Universality is found only in and among the many. For religious truth is thoroughly kaleidoscopic and plural, the fullest picture only emerging piecemeal in a constantly shifting, changing, and realigning landscape of solidarity.[67] And dialogue is the locus of convergence that bears the weight of such solidarity, building networks of interdependence shaped and reshaped by the creative tension of contrasts.

Dialogue is then an "adventure," to borrow a term from Alfred North Whitehead, which has no end other than itself. It is a process restlessly moving beyond the narrow and homogeneous toward wider, more intense forms of harmony or ordered novelty. Perhaps we could even go further with Whitehead's language to suggest that communion itself is a collective work of *beauty*, an enlivening "harmony of contrasts."[68] Dialogue is human creativity at work.

But structural or systemic communicative distortions do in practice dampen such beauty, inhibiting the full harmony of equal reciprocity between contrasting voices. Tragically, not all differences make a positive difference. There are discursive practices that are overtly antagonistic to the prospect of mutuality, maintaining a polemical logic of assimilation or exclusion by which others suffer. Accordingly, relational symmetry and mutual understanding must never be simply assumed as a given. They must instead be seen as "ideals" animating and preserving the conversation, functioning as prophetic tools for critique and resistance when idolatry is put into motion and reciprocity thwarted. It is no accident, then, that religious traditions not only speak of love and kinship, but also of justice and deferential regard, calling into question dehumanizing corruptions. This makes critical judgment a requirement of any dialogue.

Resources for such judgment can be found in the justice-making mode of release. Indeed, dialogical openness involves an interrelated set of five criteria that supplement the six criteria just mentioned. These are: a determination (1) to let no particular center of value become *the* favored or privileged center for all others, all of "us" equally decentered as an other to each other; (2) to celebrate and work through conflict, dissensus, and disagreement when they occur (as they invariably do) as a healthy and vitalizing moment in the throe of conversation itself, an outcome of genuine mutuality in setting forth claims, not a perversion of it; (3) to preserve through dialogical reason a co-inhabited public space for such conflict to take a robust yet nonviolent and peaceful course toward reconciliatory resolution; thus (4) to eschew and resist coercive or instrumental techniques of consensual power, dominance, or pacification that preempt conflict by ruling differences out of play; and finally, (5) to work side by side together, even in disagreement over the formulation of justice, to facilitate the liberative social conditions for the maximally inclusive reciprocity that the very openness of conversation itself anticipates, forging greater and greater horizons of mutuality and recognition for every possible participant. While cultures and religions may differ on their conceptions of justice, each in their own way trades on a notion of mutuality and reciprocity.

There are key overlapping characteristics in all five of these elements. Most importantly, the integral distance of difference is let be and preserved, neither dispersed nor erased. This implies, I suggest, an option for, or a hermeneutical privileging of, the victimized, the poor, the suffering, the nonperson—those whose difference has been heretofore marginalized. Truly, if the religious sensibility seeks a salvation, a founding of trust, then the emancipatory impulse of justice to "let be" must be a fundamental ingredient in this process.[69] Dialogue is not merely a luxury, a disattached curiosity, but rather an enlivening responsibility. In light of this, moreover, when any of the five elements are compromised, the call for justice must emerge in the dialogue as a critical voice exposing, judging, and resisting those forces that would do violence to and subjugate differences, differences that make the continuation of an inclusive dialogue possible. Still further, the call for justice in dialogue also entails the critical standard of measurement proffered by a "dangerous memory," a remembrance of failures in the past and a retrieval of positive and empowering histories that enliven the power to resist, keep hope alive, and engender solidarity in the process.[70] Last, presumed in all of this is a confidence in the emancipatory power of dialogical reason to overcome both loaded universalisms (polemics), which repress difference, and empty universalisms (historicisms), which simply revel in sheer difference.[71]

Thus, an interreligious dialogue without a justice-making praxis is either a naive dialogue presuming that love has preemptive status or a disinterested one in which the other makes no real claim. In the former, injustice is blithely passed over or ignored in favor of superficial similarities. In the latter, differences simply go their own way without evoking respect or responsibility. Solidarity among differences is a justice-making enterprise. The undeniable fact of an increasingly interconnected global economic and political situation makes this point especially apropos, for pressures toward homogeneity or fragmentation threaten the fabric of what has become a necessity—a planetary way of belonging together.

It is this planetary way of belonging together, in the shape of a dialogical praxis of solidarity among religious traditions, which is the inner telos of faith's availability: as a justice making love. Recovered in faith, trust is an availability that anticipates the fecund universality of Presence itself as the promise of meaningful vitality, the reconciling reciprocity of the open whole beckoning us into the between of relation (love) and distance (justice) in every concrete gesture of being-with. A trust fully actualized is one that affirms differences in relation in the mode of availability.

Being faithful to one's own religious tradition, then, should not simply promote hostility and xenophobia. It can be a paradigm case of being-with. For through the metaphoric and dialectical power of an iconic source of transcendent value, religious faith can yield fidelity to, and hope for, a truly universal community of love and justice. It can open up the power of dialogical reason, resist succumbing, and by recovering trust, inculcate a self-transcending solidarity with difference. *Religious faith evokes meaningful vitality, granting ontological weight by founding trust, but it does so as it exposes and resists idolatry and invokes the performance of availability as an ethical relation of being-with in being-for the other.*

The fruition of this, however, remains possible only in the concrete task of ongoing dialogue itself. This is where mere plurality becomes configured as a pluralism, or better, to use Anselm Kyongsuk Min's term, a "dialectical pluralism"—that is, a "concrete *historical* process that creates the *solidarity* of others."[72] Such solidarity is not an "us" in the provincial sense of "us versus them," but a transprovincial "us" of the "both/and," an "us" drawn together in our differences as a concordant discordance, a resonating vitality of meaningful interrelation, "the distinct participating in each other," to employ Theodor W. Adorno's apt phrase.[73] This is a wider and more vibrant universalism—an ongoing harmony of contrasts restlessly configuring and reconfiguring itself into novel shapes.

Pluralism, then, is much more than a descriptive fact; it is an imaginative, productive, and public task to be achieved. And the religious sensibility goes a long way toward establishing the conditions for making this task a real possibility, intimating a decentering center that in the final analysis is the communion of the whole itself, the omega point toward which all acts of being-with point. *The truth of human religiosity is not the property of one tradition, but rather the capacity in each to surpass itself in creating a universal mode of belonging together.*

Conclusion: Into the Breach

Truly, our life together is charged with a creative pulse that displays the life force of the gods, awakening in us a trust in the fundamental trustworthiness of things. As the trace of Presence passes in presences, we are bathed in an original call to be-with, and our lives become a response to the call. From the very first encounter with the presence of another, we are exposed to a surplus horizon much larger than ourselves, and our human task is to participate fully in it. In this, various appeals to transcendence—as modifications of the religious sensibility—can be seen as humanizing and difference-making, constructively shaping the landscape of a planet in need of love and justice. Indeed, a global and polycentric solidarity is our highest human hope, a hope with no closure or resting place but with an infinite horizon awaiting ahead of itself.

The broken whole is an open whole, a possibilizing surplus flowering creatively in multiple places and in myriad ways. The "many" ways that human faith reflects this should not be seen as devolutions or perversions of a more original unity, nor as a competition between otherwise isolated tribes, each marching to its own drummer and obstinately defending its own territory and possessions. Rather, religious traditions are bearers of gifts, prizes to be exchanged and shared in a now planetary Umwelt. The local horizons of particular communities open out to a universal possibility; herein lies their viability, their hope, and in the end, their redemption. Indeed the cross-cultural migrations of an expansive global situation could spawn a great cultural and religious renaissance, forging a shared destiny among the most diverse historical horizons, a decentering but fertile matrix of creativity and mutual flourishing. But this destiny is fragile, indeed tension-filled, and must be won by a gentle and resolute working toward peace. Pluralism is not the absence of tension, the opposite of order; it is the harmonic resonance of contrasts sounding together. It is the nature of reality itself.

Let us forge ahead together, then, making a difference amidst and through our differences. For in this, we reflect the infinite and open whole, which is unconditionally difference-making. Indeed, there is a wisdom and a creativity shimmering from the depths of all, summoning us into a horizon of unremitting excess. All things are full of gods.

Notes

INTRODUCTION

1. Recently there has been a proliferation of books dealing specifically with the increasingly important issue of religion and violence. For instance, see Mark Juergensmeyer's *Terror in the Mind of God: The Global Rise of Religious Violence* (Berkeley: University of California Press, 2000); Leo D. Lefebure's *Revelation, The Religions, and Violence* (Maryknoll, NY: Orbis Books, 2000); and Marc H. Ellis's *Unholy Alliance: Religion and Atrocity in Our Time* (Minneapolis: Fortress Press, 1997).

2. See Paul Ricoeur, *Figuring the Sacred: Religion, Narrative and Imagination*, trans. David Pellauer, ed. Mark I. Wallace (Minneapolis: Fortress Press, 1995), 61.

3. Peter Berger, *The Heretical Imperative* (New York: Anchor Press, 1979), xi. Berger makes the same point in a recent book, *Questions of Faith: A Skeptical Affirmation of Christianity* (Oxford: Blackwell Publishing, 2004), 4–5.

4. Hans Küng argues such a point in *Global Responsibility: In Search of a New World Ethic* (New York: Crossroad, 1991). See also Jonathan Sacks, *The Dignity of Difference: How to Avoid the Clash of Civilizations* (New York: Continuum, 2002).

5. See Ricoeur, "Philosophy and Religious Language," in *Figuring the Sacred*, 35–47.

6. Jacque Dupuis, *Toward a Christian Theology of Religious Pluralism* (Maryknoll, NY: Orbis Books, 1997), see 1–19.

7. For examples, see the essays in *Christian Uniqueness Reconsidered: The Myth of a Pluralistic Theology of Religions*, ed. Gavin D'Costa (Maryknoll, NY: Orbis Books, 1990).

8. This is the basic point made by most of the authors contributing to *The Myth of Christian Uniqueness: Toward a Pluralistic Theology of Religions*, eds. John Hick and Paul F. Knitter (Maryknoll, NY: Orbis Books, 1989).

9. For a superb treatment of these problems, see James M. Gustafson's recent book, *An Examined Faith: The Grace of Self-Doubt* (Minneapolis: Fortress Press, 2004).

10. On this idea, see the essays by Gordon D. Kaufman and Langdon Gilkey in *The Myth of Christian Uniqueness*.

11. In Paul Tillich, *Christianity and the Encounter of World Religions* (Minneapolis: Fortress Press, 1994), 63–79.

12. Ibid., 67.

13. See Gustafson, *An Examined Faith*, 67–77.

14. On this "revisionist" method of mutually critical correlation, see David Tracy, *Blessed Rage for Order: The New Pluralism in Theology* (New York: Seabury, 1975), 45ff. Tracy here draws from and modifies Tillich's famous method of correlation in *Systematic Theology*, Vol. 1 (Chicago: University of Chicago Press, 1951), 8, 30–31, 34, 59–66.

15. On the nonfoundationalist theological use of a "wide reflective equilibrium," see Francis Schüssler Fiorenza, *Foundational Theology: Jesus and the Church* (New York: Crossroad, 1992), 301ff.

16. See Charles Taylor, "Comparison, History, Truth," in *Philosophical Arguments* (Cambridge: Harvard University Press, 1995), 152–53; and "Understanding and Ethnocentricity," in *Philosophy and the Human Sciences, Philosophical Papers*, Vol. 2 (Cambridge: Cambridge University Press, 1985), 125f.

17. I have loosely compiled these five criteria from David Tracy's discussion in *Plurality and Ambiguity* (San Francisco: Harper, 1987), see 22f. and ch. 2.

18. Taylor, "Social Theory as Practice," in *Philosophical Papers*, Vol. 2, 111.

CHAPTER ONE. PLURALITY AND HISTORICAL CONSCIOUSNESS: FROM HETERONOMOUS BELONGING TO A TRADITIONED BELONGING TO HISTORY

1. William James, *A Pluralistic Universe* (Cambridge: Harvard University Press, 1977), 27.

2. Giordano Bruno, "On the Infinite Universe and Worlds," (1584) trans. Dorothea Waley Singer, in Dorothea Waley Singer, *Giordano Bruno: His Life and Thought* (New York: Greenwood, 1968), 280.

3. For an example of this, see David Tracy, *Plurality and Ambiguity* (San Francisco: Harper, 1987), 35f. See also Van A. Harvey's classic study, *The Historian and the Believer* (New York: Macmillan, 1966).

4. Hans-Georg Gadamer, "The Problem of Historical Consciousness," in *Interpretive Social Science: A Reader*, eds. Paul Rabinow and William A. Sullivan (Berkeley: University of California Press, 1979), 109. Gadamer associates this with philosophical developments in Germany up through Wilhelm Dilthey (104).

5. On this transition see Bernard Lonergan, *Method in Theology* (New York: Herder and Herder, 1972), 301, 326–27; and Kathryn Tanner, *Theories of Culture: A New Agenda for Theology* (Minneapolis: Fortress Press, 1997), esp. 18–24.

6. For examples, see Gordon D. Kaufman, *God, Mystery, Diversity* (Minneapolis: Fortress Press, 1996), 33f., 54–67; Paul Knitter, *Jesus and Other Names* (Maryknoll, NY: Orbis Books, 1996), 29; Peter Hodgson, *Winds of the Spirit: A Constructive Christian Theology* (Louisville: Westminster John Knox Press, 1994), 104; and Leonard Swindler's essay in *Death or Dialogue*, eds. Leonard Swindler et al. (Philadelphia: Trinity Press International, 1990), 58. Ernst Troeltsch expressed similar ideas some eighty years ago in his essay, "Christianity among World Religions," in *Christian Thought: Its History and Application* (1923), ed. Baron von Hugel (New York: Meridian Books, 1957), 35–63.

7. On this point, see Louis Dupré, *Passage to Modernity: An Essay in the Hermeneutics of Nature and Culture* (New Haven: Yale University Press, 1993), part 1; Steven Toulmin, *Cosmopolis: The Hidden Agenda of Modernity* (New York: Free Press, 1990), ch. 1;

and Charles Taylor, *Sources of the Self: The Making of Modern Identity* (Cambridge: Harvard University Press, 1989), esp. 199–202. For an excellent survey of the decentering influence of the Renaissance sciences, see Alexandre Koyré, *From the Closed World to the Infinite Universe* (New York: Harper, 1958).

8. Though the Bible was "liberated" in an certain sense from dogma, later Protestant thinkers fell back into a dogmatism and orthodoxy of their own. The difference, however, was that biblical interpretation had now been problematized, giving rise to the need for rules of interpretation in order to insure the proper reading of sacred texts on their own terms rather than in service of ecclesiastical and dogmatic authority.

9. Immanuel Kant, "An Answer to the Question: What Is Enlightenment?" (1784), trans. Lewis White Black, in *Foundations of the Metaphysics of Morals and What Is Enlightenment?* (Indianapolis: Bobbs, 1959), 85–92. It is worth quoting the celebrated passage at length to make the point:

> Enlightenment is man's release from his self-incurred tutelage. Tutelage is man's inability to make use of his understanding without direction from another. It is self-incurred when its cause lies not in lack of understanding but in lack of resolution and courage to use it without direction from another. *Sapere aude*! 'Have the courage to exercise your own understanding!'—that is the motto of enlightenment. . . . For this enlightenment, however, nothing is required but freedom . . . freedom to make public use of one's reason at every point. (90, 92)

10. Of course Kant in his essay is referring to freedom of thought and religious belief, extolling the virtues of Fredrick the Great as an enlightened despot, but not questioning the veracity of monarchical rule itself. Carried further than Kant, however, this "first moment" lies behind the ethic of individual rights that fueled the French and American revolutions. Adorno and Horkheimer suggest, "In the most general sense of progressive thought, the Enlightenment has always aimed at liberating men from fear and establishing their sovereignty" (*The Dialectic of the Enlightenment* [1944], trans. John Cumming [New York: Herder and Herder, 1972], 3). Of course the very next sentence in this text introduces a paradoxical qualification, one that we must in chapter 2 explore in some detail: "the fully enlightened earth radiates disaster triumphant."

11. See Giddens, *The Consequences of Modernity* (Stanford: Stanford University Press, 1990), 36ff.

12. On this point, see Jurgen Habermas, *The Philosophical Discourse of Modernity*, trans. Frederick Lawrence (Cambridge: Massachusetts Institute of Technology Press, 1995), 6–7, 15; and Michel Foucault, "What Is Enlightenment?" trans. Catherine Porter, in *The Foucault Reader*, ed. Paul Rabinow (New York: Pantheon, 1984), 33–34.

13. Foucault, "What Is Enlightenment?" 40–41, 50.

14. Habermas, *The Philosophical Discourse of Modernity*, 7.

15. Foucault, "What Is Enlightenment?" 42.

16. See Paragraph 1 of the First Meditation in *Meditation on First Philosophy*, ed. and trans. George Heffernan (Notre Dame, IN: University of Notre Dame Press, 1990), 87. Another example is found in his "Discourse on the Method," in *The Philosophical Writings of Descartes*, Vol. 1, trans. John Cottingham et al. (Cambridge: Cambridge University Press, 1985), 155–16.

17. Immanuel Kant, *Critique of Judgment* (1790), trans. Pluhar (Indianapolis: Hackett, 1987), 161 (par. 40).

18. See Cassirer, *The Philosophy of the Enlightenment*, trans. Fritz C. A. Koelln and James P. Pettegrove (Boston: Beacon, 1960), 160ff.

19. Toulmin, *Cosmopolis*, 33.

20. See Habermas, *The Philosophical Discourse of Modernity*, 16f. and ch. 2.

21. Cited in Peter Gay, *The Enlightenment, an Interpretation: The Science of Freedom*, Vol. 2 (New York: Norton, 1977), 13.

22. Giddens, *The Consequences of Modernity*, 17ff.

23. Giddens (ibid., 22–28) notes how the rational organization of time and space in disembedded systems necessitates the creation of (1) symbolic tokens of interchange between local contexts and (2) expert systems that reorganize and negotiate many such contexts. An example of the former is capital or money, an abstraction that enables the exchange of goods and services by substituting them with an impersonal standard unit of measurement. Expert systems are those systems of technical proficiency or professional specialization that organize large sectors of the material and social environments in which persons live, providing assurances of expectations across time and space (e.g., doctors, lawyers, architects, and bankers). See also Peter Berger, Brigitte Berger, and Hansfried Kellner, *The Homeless Mind: Modernization and Consciousness* (New York: Vintage Books, 1974), chs. 1–2.

24. Ibid., 21.

25. Ibid., 36–45. The following discussion widens the scope of Giddens's viewpoint to serve the purposes of my own argument.

26. Ibid., 38.

27. Kant, *Critique of Pure Reason*, trans. Norman Kemp Smith (New York: St. Martin's, 1965), 58ff.

28. A more social or institutional example of this reflexivity is the self-regulating systems of political or corporate bureaucratic networks. The bureaucracy is caught up in an endless cycle of self-monitoring and adaptation, rolling social life away from the sway of tradition. Preoccupied as bureaucracies are with their own perpetuation, they become in a way modern surrogates for tradition, only they trade on anonymity and standardized relations, which force a tenuous breach between (1) public/professional and (2) private life. See Berger and Berger, *The Homeless Mind*, ch. 2.

29. Giddens, *The Consequences of Modernity*, 39f.

30. Habermas, *The Philosophical Discourse of Modernity*, ch. 1, esp. 7–8.

31. Dupré, *Passage to Modernity*, 152.

32. Ibid., 156.

33. Cassirer, *An Essay on Man* (New Haven: Yale University Press, 1944), 176.

34. For a similar treatment of the problem, see Walter Lowe, *Theology and Difference: The Wound of Reason* (Bloomington: Indiana University Press, 1993), 25.

35. Cassirer, *The Philosophy of the Enlightenment*, 182–83,197–99. See also Karl Barth, *Protestant Thought: From Rousseau to Ritschl*, trans. Brian Cozens (New York: Harper, 1959), 35ff. Lowe's treatment of the Enlightenment (its "idealist diamond") tends to overlook this crucial point (see *Theology and Difference*, 25ff.).

36. I follow Ernst Troeltsch's view here. See "Historical and Dogmatic Method in Theology," in *Religion and History*, trans. James Luther Adams and Walter F. Bense (Minneapolis: Fortress Press, 1991), 24–25.

37. Edward Farley, *Ecclesial Reflection* (Philadelphia: Fortress Press, 1982), 165–68.

38. See Cassirer, *The Philosophy of the Enlightenment*, 199–209. Bayle's subsequent impact on the French Encyclopedists was significant.

39. See Van A. Harvey, *The Historian and the Believer*, 39–42, 69ff.

40. Cassirer, *The Philosophy of the Enlightenment*, 183.

41. For a discussion of Reimarus's method, see Roy A. Harrisville and Walter Sundberg, *The Bible in Modern Culture: Theology and Historical-Critical Method from Spinoza to Käsemann* (Grand Rapids, MI: William B. Eerdmans Publishing Company, 1995), ch. 3.

42. Cassirer, *Philosophy of the Enlightenment*, 209–23.

43. Gotthold Lessing, "On the Proof of the Spirit and of Power," in *Lessing's Theological Writings*, ed. and trans. Henry Chadwick (Stanford: Stanford University Press, 1956), 53.

44. Ibid., 55.

45. Ibid., 83.

46. Ibid., 89, 94.

47. Ibid., 95.

48, On this point see the excellent study by Henry E. Allison, *Lessing and the Enlightenment* (Ann Arbor: University of Michigan Press, 1966), 133ff.

49. In "The Education of the Human Race" (see *Lessing's Theological Writings*, 82ff). Lessing displays this idea by marking three contextual stages in the development of the religious ideal: its Jewish, Christian, and future exemplification beyond both in the rational "eternal gospel," wherein virtue would be loved for its own sake. Whether this third stage would itself express a positive historical revelation through which reason would actualize its own truth most completely remains ambiguous in Lessing's text, though a reference is made to the Spiritual Franciscans as pointing the way (97). Lessing is also unclear as to whether the religion of pure reason is ever attainable, or whether it remains an ideal always out in front of history. Given the historical character of his thought, consistency would seem to weigh on the side of an elusive yet present ideal propelling history forward. It is clear, however, that Lessing thought the Enlightenment witness was as close as history has yet come to realizing the eternal gospel.

50. Cassirer thinks Lessing in this way builds a bridge across the "ugly, broad ditch" (*Philosophy of the Enlightenment*, 194). Allison agrees but thinks that Cassirer exaggerates Lessing's resolution of the problem, for too many ambiguities remain (see *Lessing and the Enlightenment*, 205, note 2). Chadwick concurs (see "Introduction," in *Lessing's Theological Writings*, 37–38), placing Lessing more in line with the Enlightenment tradition of rationalism.

51. Johann Gottfried Herder, "Ideas toward a Philosophy of History," in Marcia Bunge, *Against Pure Reason*, trans. and ed. Marcia Bunge (Minneapolis: Fortress Press, 1993), 49. "As ready as human beings are to imagine that they are self-made, they are nevertheless dependent on others for the development of their capacities" (48).

52. Ibid., see 49–52.

53. Ibid., 51.

54. See "Yet Another Philosophy of History," in *Against Pure Reason*, 38.

55. Ibid., 43.

56. Ibid., 39.

57. Herder states: "The universal, philosophical, philanthropic tone of our century readily applies 'our own ideal' of virtue and happiness to each distant nation, to each

remote period in history. But can one such single ideal be the sole standard for judging, condemning, or praising the customs of other nations or periods?" (ibid., 44).

58. Hans-Georg Gadamer, *Truth and Method*, 2nd revised ed., trans. Joel Weinsheimer and Donald G. Marshall (New York: Crossroad, 1992), 200–01. Herder's pioneering notion of history anticipated many of Gadamer's key formulations, a fact that Gadamer acknowledges.

59. Herder states, "In this way they (the rationalists) invented the fiction of the 'universal, progressive improvement of the world' which no one believed, at least not the true student of history and the human heart" ("Yet Another Philosophy of History," 44).

60. See Cassirer, *Philosophy of the Enlightenment*, 231.

61. Georg G. Iggers, *The German Conception of History* (Middletown, CT: Wesleyan University Press, 1968), 37.

62. Friedrich Meinecke, *Historicism: The Rise of a New Historical Outlook*, trans. J. E. Anderson (New York: Herder and Herder, 1972), lv–lvi.

63. See Iggers, *The German Conception of History*, 4–5; see also Meinecke, *Historicism*, lv–lvii. Iggers has a helpful footnote denoting some of the many uses of the word *historicism* (see 287–90).

64. See Wilhelm Dilthey, *Dilthey: Selected Writings*, ed. and trans. H. P. Rickman (Cambridge: Cambridge University Press, 1976); and H. A. Hodges, *The Philosophy of Wilhelm Dilthey* (1952; reprint, Westport, CN: Greenwood, 1974).

65. Gadamer, "The Problem of Historical Consciousness," in *Interpretive Social Science: A Reader*, eds. Paul Rabinow and William A. Sullivan (Berkeley: University of California Press, 1979), 109.

66. I am indebted to Gadamer's interpretation here. See ibid., 110–11.

67. Ibid., 110.

68. This is my own interpretation of Gadamer's suggestion that "Enlightenment philosophy is carried out in historical consciousness" ("The Problem of Historical Consciousness," in *Interpretive Social Science: A Reader*, 126).

CHAPTER TWO. PLURALISTIC CONSCIOUSNESS: FROM HISTORICAL BELONGING TO THE CHALLENGE OF RADICAL CONTINGENCY AND DIFFERENCE

1. John D. Caputo, *Radical Hermeneutics: Repetition, Deconstruction, and the Hermeneutic Project* (Bloomington: Indiana University Press, 1987), 235.

2. Hans-Georg Gadamer, "The Problem of Historical Consciousness," in *Interpretive Social Science: A Reader*, eds. Paul Rabinow and William A. Sullivan (Berkeley: University of California Press, 1979), 109.

3, On this point, see Craig Calhoun, *Critical Social Theory* (Cambridge: Blackwell Publishers, 1995), 218–19.

4. Charles Taylor, "The Politics of Recognition," in *Multiculturalism*, ed. Amy Gutmann (Princeton: Princeton University Press, 1994), 71. See also his, *The Ethics of Authenticity* (Cambridge: Harvard University Press, 1991), 51f.

5. See Robert D'Amico, *Historicism and Knowledge* (New York: Routledge, 1989), xi–xiv, 147f. For a detailed account of the German response, see Georg G. Iggers,

The German Conception of History (Middletown, CT: Wesleyan University Press, 1968), chs. 6 and 7.

6. Of course relativism has been around since Protagoras and has taken many different forms with many subtle variations. Here I refer to it as a consequence of historicist contextualism.

7. Paul Ricoeur, "Civilization and National Cultures," in *History and Truth*, trans. Chas A. Kelbley (Evanston, IL: Northwestern University Press, 1965), 278.

8. Ibid., 283.

9. Calhoun, *Critical Social Theory*, 74–75.

10. Ibid., 193; and Charles Taylor, *The Ethics of Authenticity* (Cambridge: Harvard University Press, 1991), 52.

11. For a discussion of reflexivity, see Hilary Lawson's *Reflexivity: The Post-modern Predicament* (LaSalle, IL: Open Court, 1985); see esp. ch. 1. Though dependent on Lawson, I am underscoring the self-referential character of "reflexivity" with a slightly more "historicist" set of concerns in mind.

12. Karl Marx, "Theses on Feuerbach," in *The Marx-Engels Reader*, 2nd ed., ed. Robert C. Tucker (New York: Norton, 1978), 144.

13. Gadamer, *Truth and Method*, 2nd revised ed., trans. Joel Weinsheimer and Donald G. Marshall (New York: Crossroad, 1992), 279. This point underlies his criticism of Dilthey's latent Cartesianism.

14. Susan Sontag, " 'Thinking against Oneself': Reflections on Cioran," in *Styles of Radical Will* (New York: Anchor Books, 1969), 74.

15. See "Yet another Philosophy of History," in *Against Pure Reason*, trans. and ed. Marcia Bunge (Minneapolis: Fortress Press, 1993), 43ff.; and also Bunge's "Introduction," 14.

16. Kathryn Tanner, *Theories of Culture: A New Agenda for Theology* (Minneapolis: Fortress Press, 1997), 36–37.

17. Michel Foucault, "What Is Enlightenment?" trans. Catherine Porter, in *The Foucault Reader*, ed. Paul Rabinow (New York: Pantheon, 1984), 42.

18. Ibid., 50.

19. Foucault, "The Art of Telling the Truth," in *Critique and Power: Recasting the Foucault-Habermas Debate*, ed. Michael Kelly (Cambridge: Massachusetts Institute of Technology Press, 1994), 148.

20. Examples of this line of critique are Max Weber's *Protestant Ethic and the Spirit of Capitalism*; Martin Heidegger's "Question Concerning Technology," in *Martin Heidegger: Basic Writings*, ed. and trans. David F. Krell (New York: Harper, 1977), 283–318; Horkheimer and Adorno's, *Dialectic of the Enlightenment*, trans. John Cumming (New York: Herder and Herder, 1972); and Max Horkheimer's *Eclipse of Reason* [1947] (New York: Continuum, 1992).

21. Borrowing the term from Hegel, but with a more pessimistic outcome, this is what Horkheimer and Adorno call the "dialectic of the Enlightenment," which on the one hand brings the positive progress of self-critical and freedom-making thought ("We are wholly convinced—and therein lies our *petitio principii*—that social freedom is inseparable from Enlightened thought" [*Dialectic of the Enlightenment*, xiii]), yet on the other unleashes a regressive dehumanizing and instrumental form of rationality that is totalitarian, reducing everything in its path to value-neutral and interchangeable cogs in a vast

administrative network ("Enlightenment is totalitarian. . . . [I]ts ideal is the system from which all and everything follows. . . . To the Enlightenment, that which does not reduce to numbers, and ultimately to the one, becomes an illusion" [6–7]). In its latter mode, the Enlightenment becomes self-destructive.

22. Postmodernity then represents not the wholesale negation of modernity (i.e., antimodernity) but a furtherance of certain dynamics set in play by critical consciousness. Though I do not think, as Habermas seems to, that modernity's ideal project is one of unifying the varieties of human discourses, I do think it appropriate—on the grounds I have just indicated—to say that modernity is an "incomplete project." On Jürgen Habermas's position, see "Modernity—An Incomplete Project," trans. S. Ben-Habib, in *Postmodernism: A Reader*, ed. Patrician Waugh (New York: Edward Arnold, 1992), 160–70, originally published in *Postmodern Culture*, ed. Hal Foster (London and Sydney: Pluto Press, 1985).

23. Here, borrowing from Terry Eagleton, I am referring to "postmodernity" as a cognitive style and mood more than a cultural sensibility or epochal historical shift, reserving the term "postmodernism" for depicting the latter—though this distinction is somewhat arbitrary (see *The Illusions of Postmodernism* [Cambridge: Blackwell Publishers, 1996], vii–viii). On postmodernity as a "mood," see Richard J. Bernstein, *The New Constellation: The Ethical-Political Horizons of Modernity/Postmodernity* (Cambridge: Massachusetts Institute of Technology Press, 1991), 11. In the most general way postmodernity indicates, as its prefix signifies, a relation to modernity by way of a completion, exhaustion, eclipse, or outright rejection of the latter. But the term has been used, perhaps overused and abused, in so many different ways it is difficult to find a stable entryway into its salient features. As a caveat, some authors suggest that this is precisely the point, citing its playful eclecticism as an intentional breaking-up of modern unitary ways of thinking (see *Zeitgeist in Babel: The Post-Modernist Controversy*, ed. Ingeborg Hoesterey [Bloomington: Indiana University Press, 1991]). For a helpful survey of the many uses of "postmodern," see *The Post-Modern Reader*, ed. Charles Jencks (New York: St. Martin's, 1992). See also Paul Lakeland, *Postmodernity: Christian Identity in a Fragmented Age* (Minneapolis: Fortress Press, 1997), esp. 12–18.

24. See Ihab Hassan, *The Postmodern Turn: Essays in Postmodern Theory and Culture* (Columbus: Ohio State University Press, 1987), 168–73. See also, David Harvey, *The Condition of Postmodernity* (Cambridge: Blackwell Publishers, 1989), 44f.

25. See the essays in *The New Historicism*, ed. H. Aram Veeser (New York: Routledge, 1989), and also William Dean's essay, "The Challenge of the New Historicism," *Journal of Religion* 66 (July 1986): 261–81.

26. John D. Caputo, *Radical Hermeneutics*, 209. See also his recent rejoiner, *More Radical Hermeneutics* (Bloomington: Indiana University Press, 2000).

27. See Todd May, *Reconsidering Difference* (University Park: Pennsylvania State University Press, 1997), 4ff. On the theme of resistance, see Hal Foster's "postmodernism of resistance," which is deconstructive of modernity and a counterpractice to the status quo, avoiding what he calls the "postmodernism of reaction" that characterizes a neoconservative return to tradition and the status quo (*The Anti-Aesthetic: Essays on Postmodern Culture*, ed. Hal Foster [Port Townsend, WA: Bay Press, 1983], vii).

28. Jean-Francois Lyotard, *The Postmodern Condition: A Report on Knowledge*, trans. Geoff Bennington and Brian Massumi (Minneapolis: University of Minnesota Press, 1984), xxiii–xxiv.

29. Richard J. Bernstein, *The New Constellation*, 32–33.

30. Caputo, *Radical Hermeneutics*, 260–61.

31. Lyotard, *The Postmodern Condition*, 82.

32. Michel Foucault, *The Order of Things: An Archeology of the Human Sciences* (New York: Pantheon, 1970), xviii.

33. Lyotard, *The Postmodern Condition*, xxv.

34. Jencks, "The Post-Modern Agenda," in *The Postmodern Reader*, 11. See also Eagleton, *The Illusions of Postmodernity*, vii.

35. Lyotard, *The Postmodern Condition*, 43.

36. Ibid., 79. This position is corroborated by David Harvey, *The Condition of Postmodernity*, 116f., and Calhoun, *Critical Social Theory*, 104ff.

37. Anthony Giddens, *The Consequences of Modernity* (Stanford: Stanford University Press, 1990), 49.

38. Habermas, *Postmetaphysical Thinking*, trans. William Mark Hohengarten (Cambridge: Massachusetts Institute of Technology Press, 1992), 139.

39. Richard Rorty, *Philosophy and the Mirror of Nature* (Princeton: Princeton University Press, 1979), 373–79.

40. Ibid., 315–16.

41. Friedrich Nietzsche, *The Will to Power*, trans. Walter Kaufmann and R. J. Hollingdale, ed. Walter Kaufmann (New York: Vintage Books, 1967), 330, #616.

42. Rorty, *The Consequences of Pragmatism* (Minneapolis: University of Minnesota Press, 1982), xlii. Indeed, "man finds in things nothing but what he himself has imported into them" (Nietzsche, *The Will to Power*, 327, #606).

43. Ibid., 172.

44. See Rorty, "Solidarity or Objectivity," in *Relativism: Interpretation and Confrontation*, ed. Michael Krausz (Notre Dame, IN: University of Notre Dame Press, 1989), 35–50.

45. Ibid., 37.

46. Ibid., 43ff. See also *Contingency, Irony, and Solidarity* (Cambridge: Cambridge University Press, 1989), 189–98.

47. Rorty, *Contingency, Irony, and Solidarity*, 73.

48. Ibid.

49. Ibid., 73–74.

50. Ibid., 1–69. Rorty's argument trades on the later Wittgenstein.

51. Ibid., 97. The obvious dependence on Nietzsche's idea of truth as a "will to power" is important, for Nietzsche is one of Rorty's exemplary ironists (see Nietzsche, *The Will to Power*, 298, #552; 290, #534).

52. Ibid., 78–80.

53. Ibid., 77.

54. Ibid. 52.

55. Ibid., 20, 53ff.

56. Isaiah Berlin, *Four Essays on Liberty* (Oxford: Oxford University Press, 1969), 172; quoted in Rorty, *Contingency, Irony, and Solidarity*, 46.

57. Rorty, *The Consequences of Pragmatism*, 166.

58. Ibid., 172.

59. Rorty, *Contingency, Irony, and Solidarity*, 52, 60, 84.

60. Ibid., 60–61. Elsewhere, referring to J. S. Mill, Rorty admits his "favorite utopia is the liberal one described in *On Liberty*: a world in which nothing remains sacred save the freedom to lead your life by your own lights, and nothing is forbidden which does not interfere with the freedom of others" ("Afterward: Pragmatism, Pluralism and Postmodernism," in *Philosophy and Social Hope* [New York: Penguin Books, 1999] 271).

61. Ibid., 68, 196–97.

62. Rorty, "Truth without Correspondence to Reality," in *Philosophy and Social Hope*, 23–46. See also *Contingency, Irony, and Solidarity*, ch. 1.

63. Rorty, "Solidarity or Objectivity," 43, 44.

64. See Rorty, *Contingency, Irony, and Solidarity*, 48ff.

65. Rorty, "Solidarity or Objectivity," 37; "Truth without Correspondence to Reality," 33; and "Relativism—Finding and Making," in *Debating the State of Philosophy*, eds. Jozef Niznik and John T. Sanders (Westport, CN: Praeger, 1996), 37ff.

66. Rorty, *Contingency, Irony, and Solidarity*, 60.

67. Rorty, "Solidarity or Objectivity," 42. See also *Contingency, Irony, and Solidarity*, 67f.

68. Rorty, *Contingency, Irony, and Solidarity*, 198.

69. Rorty, "Globalization, the Politics of Identity and Social Hope," *Philosophy and Social Hope*, 237.

70. Early in *Contingency, Irony, and Solidarity*, Rorty conforms to his own precepts, conflating the useful and the true, stating: "I am not going to offer arguments against the vocabulary I want to replace. Instead, I am going to try to make the vocabulary I favor look attractive by showing how it may be used to describe a variety of topics" (9). In this way, Rorty claims to outflank his opponents by not "arguing" on their terms (see esp. 44–45).

71. See Donald Davidson, "On the Very Idea of a Conceptual Scheme," *Proceedings of the American Philosophical Association* 47 (1973–74): 5–20, esp. 20. Rorty makes use of Davidson's argument in "Solidarity or Objectivity" and in *Contingency, Irony, and Solidarity*, ch. 1. For an excellent general discussion of this issue, see Richard J. Bernstein, *Beyond Objectivism and Relativism* (Philadelphia: University of Pennsylvania Press, 1983), 51–108.

72. Rorty, *Contingency, Irony, and Solidarity*, 177.

73. Ibid., 91.

74. Ibid., 192.

75. Ibid., 85ff.

76. Ibid., 177.

77. In fact, in one of his more affirmative moods, Rorty states: "What matters for pragmatists is devising ways of diminishing human suffering and increasing human equality, increasing the ability of all human children to start life with an equal chance of happiness" ("Relativism—Finding and Making," 44).

78. Rorty, "Solidarity or Objectivity," 44. Rorty even suggests that those who helped the Jews in World War II probably did so less out of a perception of them as fellow human beings than as part of the same local group or defining community—a city, profession, and so on (*Contingency, Irony, and Solidarity*, 190–91). But this kind of ethnocentric logic works just as well for Nazi sympathizers whose "us" did not include Jews. As Terry Eagleton comments, for Rorty, morality "is really just a species of patriotism" motivated by a sense of "one of us" (*The Illusions of Postmodernism*, 114–15).

79. Anindita Nigoyi Baslev, *Cultural Otherness: Correspondence with Richard Rorty*, 2nd. ed (Atlanta: Scholars Press, 1999), 63.

80. See Rorty, "Solidarity and Objectivity," 45: "We Western liberal intellectuals should accept the fact that we have to start where we are, and that this means that there are lots of views which we simply cannot take seriously."

81. Ibid., 37, 39, 44. "[The] ethnocentrism of 'we' ('we liberals') . . . is dedicated to enlargening itself, to creating an ever larger and more variegated *ethnos*" (*Contingency, Irony, and Solidarity*, 198).

82. Rorty, *Contingency, Irony, and Solidarity*, 48.

83. Rorty's answer is "improved self-description" (ibid., 52f.). But again what constitutes "improved" or better remains a product of intracultural or intralinguistic circularity. There is no way to "get to" the "other" except by co-opting or dismissing it. Rorty comes close to admitting this in *Consequences of Pragmatism*: " 'undistorted' means employing *our* criterion of relevance, where *we* are the people who" are educated in a certain Western tradition and can recognize the contingency of all starting-points (173).

84. Foucault himself is critical of Rorty's facile use of the term "we," which must be carefully and critically probed before it can be instructive. See "Polemics, Politics, and Problemizations: An Interview," in *The Foucault Reader*, ed. Paul Rabinow (New York: Pantheon, 1984), 385.

85. In his dialogue with Baslev in *Cultural Otherness*, Rorty makes a telling confession on page 70: "I agree that one person's mild ethnocentrism is another's secondary narcissism or cultural imperialism. . . . I cannot offer what you call for: a 'direct response' to charge of cultural imperialism." He goes on to state that "the vocabulary of the 'twentieth century Western social democratic intellectuals' may well be the best anybody has yet come up with. I assuredly have no argument for this claim, and have no idea in what vocabulary such an argument could be phrased. . . . But, until another batch of people more experienced and skilled at tolerance comes to my attention, I probably shall not change my mind."

One could press Rorty here. Why is tolerance such a noble ideal? Why avoid parochialism if that is where we start from and must inevitably end up? Rorty's response is:

> I agree that ethnocentrism is a ladder which we eventually hope to throw away. But, unless one is a full-fledged Platonist essentialist, there is no other ladder available to use. So, as a good pragmatist, I think that we should use it—should play off *our* preferred ethnic against others, rather than comparing them all with something that is not a set of actual, or at least concretely imagined, human practices. (73–74, italics added)

Baslev reacts to the apparent duplicity in Rorty's notion of "ethnocentrism" by asking: "If we can hope to do away with it, is ethnocentrism then a description of a provisional state of human inter-relationship or is it an idiom one clings to for want of a more adequate one?" (87)

86. This is Habermas's critique of Rorty in *Postmetaphysical Thinking*, 137–38.

87. For examples, see *Cultural Otherness*, 41f, and *Contingency, Irony, and Solidarity*, 80f. Though, in his defense, Rorty claims that an ironist develops a "skill in imaginative identification" with others, this does not rescue him from the charges of an operative assimilative logic in his ethnocentrism (see *Contingency, Irony, and Solidarity*, 93).

88. Rorty, *Achieving Our Country* (Cambridge: Harvard University Press, 1998), 17–18.

89. See Caputo's criticisms in *More Radical Hermeneutics*, 116ff.

90. Rorty, *Achieving Our Country*, 18–19, 24.

91. Rorty, "Pragmatism and Romantic Polytheism," in *The Revival of Pragmatism: New Essays in Social Thought, Law, and Culture*, ed. Morris Dickstein (Durham, NC: Duke University Press, 1998), 21–36. See also his, "Religious Faith, Intellectual Responsibility and Romance," *American Journal of Theology and Philosophy* 17/2 (1996): 121–40.

92. Rorty, *Achieving Our Country*, 132ff.

93. Ibid., 29.

94. Jason Boffetti, "How Richard Rorty Found Religion," *First Things* 143 (May 2004): 30.

95. See Bernstein's charge of fideism in *The New Constellation*, 278ff. The discussion here is indebted to Berstein's extensive and nuanced critique of Rorty (see 230–92).

96. Rorty, *Contingency, Irony, and Solidarity*, 67.

97. In *Cultural Otherness*, Rorty admits (ironically) that the pragmatist is not suited to producing normative judgments about the character of a global community (95, 100–01).

98. Quoted by Baslev, ibid., 27.

99. See Bernstein, *The New Constellation*, 287.

100. Lyotard, *The Postmodern Condition*, 82.

101. See Immanuel Levinas, *Totality and Infinity*, trans. Alphonso Lingus (Pittsburgh: Duquesne University Press, 1969), 21–22; and *Ethics and Infinity*, trans. Richard A. Cohen (Pittsburgh: Duquesne University Press, 1985), 75–76, 91. It is no accident that Levinas, in the preface to *Totality and Infinity*, likens "totality" to "war," for there is an inherent violence to individuals when they are usurped by the whole (21). Hence, Lyotard's subversive reversal of this dynamic in claiming a "war" on totality.

102. Of course the literature on Marx is extensive, and I can only lightly touch here on several prominent themes. For useful introductions, see David McLellan, *The Thought of Karl Marx: An Introduction* (New York: Harper, 1971); and John Plamenatz, *Karl Marx's Philosophy of Man* (Oxford: Oxford University Press, 1975).

103. For instance, Marx states: "The mode of production in material life determines the general character of the social, political and spiritual processes of life. It is not the consciousness of men that determines their being, but, on the contrary, their social being that determines their consciousness" ("A Contribution to the Critique of Political Economy," in *The Marx-Engels Reader*, 4). See also "The German Ideology," Ibid., 154–55.

104. Marx, "Manifesto of the Communist Party," ibid., 489.

105. Marx, "Theses on Feuerbach," ibid., 145.

106. See in particular the "Introduction" and "Asceticism and the Spirit of Capitalism" in Weber's *Protestant Ethic and the Spirit of Capitalism*, trans. Talcott Parsons (New York: Routledge, 1992), 13–31, 155–83. See also Bernstein's brief but very helpful discussion of Weber, in *The New Constellation*, 35–41; and Andrew Arato and Eike Gebhardt's introductory essay to "Esthetic Theory and Cultural Criticism" (*The Essential Frankfurt School Reader*, eds. Andrew Arato and Eike Gebhardt [New York: Continuum, 1995] esp. 91–93).

107. This is a central thesis in Horkheimer and Adorno's *Dialectic of Enlightenment*, and also appears in Horkheimer's *Eclipse of Reason* [1947] (New York: Continuum, 1992), and in Adorno's *Negative Dialectics* [1966], trans. E. B. Aston (New York: Seabury Press, 1973). For an excellent secondary source on Adorno, see Martin Jay, *Adorno* (Cambridge: Harvard University Press, 1984). See also Craig Calhoun's chapter on the history and import of the Frankfurt School: "Rethinking Critical Theory," in *Critical Social Theory*, 1–42.

108. The passage goes on to state: "A technological rationale is the rationale of domination itself" (ibid., 121). See also 145–46.

109. Ibid., 25. See Jay, *Adorno*, 68. In a similar vein, Martin Heidegger launches a critique of technology as Gestell (enframing), representing an "ontologizing" of the problem of technical reason (see "The Question Concerning Technology"). More recently, Jurgen Habermas has spoken of the "colonization of the lifeworld" as the product of societal rationalization. For example, see *The Theory of Communicative Action*, Vol. 2, *Lifeworld and System: A Critique of Functionalist Reason* (Boston: Beacon, 1988), ch. 8.

110. See Horkheimer, *Eclipse of Reason*, 3–57. He states, "if reason itself is instrumentalized, it takes on a kind of materiality and blindness, becomes a fetish, a magic entity that is accepted rather than intellectually experienced" (23–24).

111. Ibid., 30, 44, 56. It is no accident, then, that Horkheimer is intensely critical of pragmatism and its conception of truth as utility (see 42–55).

112. *Minima Moralia: Reflections from Damaged Life*, trans. E. F. N. Jephcott (New York: Verso, 1974), 33, as quoted in Jay, *Adorno*, 43.

113. Paul Rabinow puts Foucault in the trajectory of Weber, Heidegger, Horkheimer, and Adorno, all of whom thematize the dangers of rationalization (see his "Introduction," in *The Foucault Reader*, 13). Foucault at one point admits the affinity of his critique of rationality with that of the critical theorists: "If I had known about the Frankfurt School in time, I would have been saved a great deal of work. I would not have said a certain amount of nonsense and would not have taken so many false trails trying not to get lost, when the Frankfurt School had already cleared the way" (quoted in Calhoun, *Critical Social Theory*, 35).

114. See "Nietzsche, Genealogy, History," in *The Foucault Reader*, 76–100. On the constructed and discursive character of knowledge, see *The Order of Things: An Archeology of the Human Sciences*, trans Alan Scheridan-Smith (New York: Random, 1970), and *The Archeology of Knowledge and the Discourse on Language*, trans. Alan Scheridan-Smith (New York: Pantheon, 1972). Regarding the term "ideology," Foucault uses the word with circumspection because it implies a relationship, albeit a distorted one, with something considered to count as "truth," with something on the order of a "subject," and purports to relate to some specific material determinate, all of which are suspect from the Nietzscean point of view (see "Truth and Power," in *The Foucault Reader*, 60). On the concept of power and power relations, see the interview, "Truth and Power," and the monographs *Discipline and Punish: The Birth of the Prison*, trans. Alan Sheridan (New York: Vintage Books, 1977) and *The History of Sexuality*, Vol. 1, *An Introduction*, trans. Robert Hurley (New York: Vintage Books, 1980). For good secondary sources on Foucault and power, see the related chapter in Hubert L. Dreyfus and Paul Rabinow, *Michel Foucault: Beyond Structuralism and Hermeneutics*, 2nd ed. (Chicago: University of Chicago Press, 1983), ch. 9; and Joseph Rouse, "Power/Knowledge," in *The Cambridge Companion to Foucault* (Cambridge: Cambridge University Press, 1994), 92–114.

115. Foucault, *Discipline and Punish*, 28.

116. Foucault's understanding of power then is not merely juridical and negative, a constraining force. For it is productive and seductive as well: "it traverses and produces things, it induces pleasure, forms of knowledge, produces discourse. It needs to be considered as a productive network which runs through the whole social body, much more than as a negative instance whose function is repression" ("Truth and Power," 61). Power thus comes from the ground up as well as from the top down. We might say, however, that while productive, power inevitably and simultaneously invokes the negative effect of repression, as an action upon other actions. See "The Subject and Power," in *Michel Foucault*, 220.

117. Foucault, *The Archeology of Knowledge and the Discourse on Language*, 40–49. For example, the schizophrenic exist *for* the psychiatrist as objects of therapy. Even the "self," as a subject of universal human reason, is one such discursive invention, a product of Enlightenment humanism.

118. And, as Nietzsche said, "Knowledge works as a tool of power. . . . [I]t increases with every increase of power" (*The Will to Power*, 266, #480)

119. Foucault, "Truth and Power," 74. "Truth" then functions as a kind of ideological "regime" or "political economy." Again Foucault states, "Truth is a thing of this world: it is produced only by virtue of multiple forms of constraint" (ibid., 73).

120. This is Habermas's reading, see *The Philosophical Discourse of Modernity*, trans. Frederick G. Lawrence (Cambridge: Massachusetts Institute of Technology Press, 1987), 254ff.

121. Foucault, "Nietzsche, Genealogy, History," 85, 96.

122. See Foucault, *Discipline and Punish*, 30–31.

123. Foucault, "What Is Enlightenment?" 46. This is the self-critical ethos of the Enlightenment that Foucault in fact wants to preserve against its repressive "humanism."

124. Foucault, "Truth and Power," 56. In this way Foucault's genealogical design marks a departure from hermeneutics, which aims at the interpretive appropriation of meaning and in so doing keeps disparity and dissemination at a distance, imposing directions and thus, accordingly, participating in historical violence (see "Nietzsche, Genealogy, History," 86). Instead of illuminating contexts of meaning, for Foucault, there is an analysis of complexes of power, whose meaning lies in productive force.

125. Foucault, "Nietzsche, Genealogy, History," 85.

126. Ibid., 89–90, 93–97. For an excellent essay on Foucault's sense of history, see "Foucault's Mapping of History," in *The Cambridge Companion to Foucault*, 28–46.

127. Foucault, "What Is Enlightenment?" 46.

128. Foucault, "Nietzsche, Genealogy, History," esp. 76–77, 89. "What is found at the historical beginning of things is not the inviolable identity of their origin; it is the dissension of other things. It is disparity" (79).

129. Foucault, *The Archaeology of Knowledge and The Discourse on Language*, 131; see also 138–40.

130. Foucault, "Nietzsche, Genealogy, History," 88–89.

131. Ibid., 87.

132. Ibid., 90–93; See also "The History of Sexuality," in *Power/Knowledge: Selected Interviews and Other Writings, 1977–1984*, ed. Lawrence D. Kritzman, trans. Alan Sheridan et al. (New York: Routledge, 1988), 193; and "Interview with Lucette Finas," in *Michel Foucault: Power, Truth, Strategy*, eds. M. Morris and P. Patton (Sydney: Feral Publications, 1979), 75.

133. Foucault, "What Is Enlightenment?" 50.

134. Ibid., 47; Dreyfus and Rabinow, *Michel Foucault*, 203.

135. Ibid., 46.

136. See Rabinow, "Introduction," in *The Foucault Reader*, 6. Foucault states elsewhere: "It's not a matter of emancipating truth from every system of power (which would be a chimera, for truth is already power), but of detaching the power of truth from the forms of hegemony, social, economic, and cultural, within which it operates at the present time" ("Truth and Power," 74–75).

137. See Foucault's essay, "The Subject and Power," in *Michel Foucault*, 221.

138. Foucault, "What Is Enlightenment?" 47.

139. Ibid., 48.

140. Foucault, *The Order of Things*, xviii.

141. Habermas, *The Philosophical Discourse of Modernity*, 241.

142. Bernstein, *The New Constellation*, 162–63.

143. Foucault, "Polemics, Politics, and Problemizations," in *The Foucault Reader*, 381–82.

144. Foucault, "Politics and Ethics: An Interview," in ibid., 379.

145. Habermas, *The Philosophical Discourse of Modernity*, 276–86.

146. Ibid., 102, 125–26.

147. Calhoun, *Critical Social Theory*, 121.

148. Habermas, *The Philosophical Discourse of Modernity*, 126–27.

149. Ibid., 129–30. This is exemplified in Adorno's *Negative Dialectics* (see Jay, *Adorno*, ch. 2; and Calhoun, *Critical Social Theory*, 25–26).

150. Jacques Derrida, *Writing and Difference*, trans. Alan Bass (Chicago: University of Chicago Press, 1978), 280. I have chosen Foucault rather than Derrida as an exemplar of postmodernity in the form of resistance to totality mainly for his emancipatory slant. Derrida, however, would be an equally illuminating case study, especially in light of his later ethical considerations. For examples, see "Force of Law: The Mystical Foundations of Authority," trans. Mary Quaintance, in *Acts of Religion*, ed. Gil Anidjar (New York: Routlege, 2002), 230–98; and *Of Hospitality*, trans. Rachel Bowlby (Stanford: Stanford University Press, 2000).

151. Caputo, *More Radical Hermeneutics*, 172–73. See also his book, *Against Ethics* (Bloomington: Indiana University Press, 1993).

152. Calhoun, *Critical Social Theory*, 116.

153. Eagleton, *The Illusions of Postmodernism*, 67. See also 103ff. Eagleton proposes a more traditional form of Marxism to bolster his vision of plurality (65–66).

154. Adorno, "Introduction," in Adorno et al., *The Positivist Dispute in German Sociology*, trans. Glyn Adey and David Frisby (New York: Harper, 1976), 12, quoted by Jay, in *Adorno*, 66.

155. Eagleton, *The Illusions of Postmodernity*, 43, 114.

156. This is Calhoun's criticism, see *Critical Social Theory*, 98f., 115–16.

157. Ibid., 218–19. Taylor concurs; see "The Politics of Recognition," in *Multiculturalism*, 71.

158. Habermas, *Postmetaphysical Thinking*, 50.

159. Horkheimer warned of this possibility latent in relativism (*Eclipse of Reason*, 19).

160. Lyotard, *The Postmodern Condition*, xxv.

161. Langdon Gilkey, "Events, Meanings and the Current Tasks of Theology," *Journal of the American Academy of Religion* 53/3 (December, 1985): 727.

162. See Bruce O. Boston, "Doing Theology in a Planetary Age," in *Revolution of Spirit: Ecumenical Theology in a Global Context*, ed. Nantawan Boonprasat Lewis (Grand Rapids: William B. Eerdmans Publishing Company, 1998), 231–45.

163. Ricouer, *History and Truth*, 283.

164. Adorno, "Subject and Object," in *The Essential Frankfurt School Reader*, 500.

165. Ricouer, *History and Truth*, 283.

CHAPTER THREE. DWELLING TOGETHER: IDENTITY, DIFFERENCE, AND RELATION

1. Hans-Georg Gadamer, "Hermeneutics and Logocentrism," trans. Richard E. Palmer and Diane P. Michelfelder, in *Dialogue and Deconstruction: The Gadamer-Derrida Encounter*, eds. Diane P. Michelfelder and Richard E. Palmer (Albany: State University of New York Press, 1989), 125.

2. Thedor W. Adorno, "Subject and Object," in *The Essential Frankfurt School Reader*, eds. Andrew Arato and Eike Gebhardt (New York: Continuum, 1995), 500.

3. I use Alfred Schutz's term "lifeworld" to portray the everyday events that comprise a life together. See his posthumously published work, *The Structure of the Life-world*, trans. George Walsh et al. (Evanston, IL: Northwestern University Press, 1967).

4. Ludwig Wittgenstein, *Philosophical Investigations*, trans. G. E. M. Anscombe (New York: Macmillan, 1958), 123, 249, 630. Unless otherwise indicated, citations from the *Philosophical Investigations* will be noted by paragraph number. For an excellent study of the *Investigations*, see G. P. Baker and Peter M. S. Hacker, *An Analytical Commentary on the "Philosophical Investigations"* (Oxford: Basil Blackwell, 1980), esp. 97–98, which deal with "language games." Another good study of Wittgenstein's general work is A. C. Grayling, *Wittgenstein* (Oxford: Oxford University Press, 1988).

5. Ibid., 202, 262.

6. Ibid., 19, 23, 241, and pp.174, 226. Peter Winch, in his important and controversial monograph, *The Idea of a Social Science and Its Relation to Philosophy* (London: Routledge & Kegan Paul, 1958), develops Wittgenstein's understanding as related to social life.

7. See ibid., 241.

8. Charles Taylor, *Sources of the Self: The Making of Modern Identity* (Cambridge: Harvard University Press, 1989), chs. 1–2.

9. On this point, see the excellent study of Gaston Bachelard, *The Poetics of Space*, trans. Maria Jolas (Boston: Beacon, 1964), esp. xxxii, 46–47, 51.

10. On "world," see Martin Heidegger and Gadamer, both of whom would agree with Taylor on these points. See Heidegger, *Being and Time*, trans. John Macquarrie and Edward Robinson (New York: Harper, 1962), Div. I.3.; and Gadamer, *Truth and Method*, 2nd revised ed., trans. Joel Weinsheimer and Donald G. Marshall (New York: Crossroad, 1992): "To have a world means to have an orientation (*Verhalten*) toward it" (443).

11. On the idea of "dwelling," see Heidegger, "Building, Dwelling, Thinking," in *Poetry, Language, Thought*, trans. Albert Hofstadter (New York: Harper, 1971). See also Edward Casey, *Getting Back into Place: Toward a Renewed Understanding of the Place-World* (Bloomington: Indiana University Press, 1993), 109ff.

12. Taylor, *Sources of the Self,* 36. Wittgenstein speaks similarly of language games as an "original home" (*Philosophical Investigations,* 116).

13. Ibid., 38–39.

14. Ibid., 35. As Gadamer suggests, speaking does not belong to the "I," but to the sphere of the "we" from which the "I" emerges (see "Man and Language," in *Philosophical Hermenuetics,* trans. David E. Linge [Los Angeles: University of California Press, 1976], see 65–66).

15. Gadamer, *Truth and Method,* 458.

16. Taylor, *Sources of the Self,* 36. This idea of the social origination and character of the self has been made by George Herbert Mead, *Mind, Self, and Society* (Chicago: University of Chicago Press, 1962).

17. See Taylor, "The Politics of Recognition," in *Multiculturalism,* ed. Amy Gutmann (Princeton: Princeton University Press, 1994), 25–73, esp. 32ff.

18. Gabriel Marcel, *The Mystery of Being,* Vol. 1, trans. Rene Hague (London: Harvill Press, 1950), 182–83. See also Vol. 2, 7–17; and "The Ego and Its Relation to Others," in *Homo Viator: Introduction to a Metaphysics of Hope,* trans. Emma Crauford (Gloucester, MA: Peter Smith, 1978), 13–28.

19. I follow Edward Farley's lead here in describing the intersubjective or interhuman sphere as a primary sphere of relation connecting the social and the personal. See his *Good and Evil: Interpreting a Human Situation* (Minneapolis: Fortress Press, 1990), ch. 1.

20. "Mitsein" is Heidegger's way of describing the ontological status of Dasein's being-with-others. See *Being in Time,* Div. I.4. However, I stress here the priority of relation, unlike Heidegger, who tends to stress Dasein's individual project. "Coesse" is Gabriel Marcel's term. See "On the Ontological Mystery," in *The Philosophy of Existentialism,* trans. Manya Harari (New York: Carol Publishing Group, 1956), 39. In a poststructuralist vein, Jean-Luc Nancy adopts similar terminology; see his *Being Singular Plural,* trans. Robert D. Richardson and Anne E. O'Brian (Stanford: Stanford University Press, 2000), 28–47.

21. Paul Ricoeur, *Oneself as Another,* trans. Kathleen Blamey (Chicago: University of Chicago Press, 1992), 3. See also 29ff.

22. Ibid.

23. See Ricoeur, "The Task of Hermeneutics," in *Hermeneutics and the Humans Sciences,* ed. and trans. John B. Thompson (Cambridge: Cambridge University Press, 1981), 50–51.

24. I use the word *power* intentionally to invoke Foucault's insight that societal structures are inherently involved in the production of knowledge. This will become important in chapter 4. See the interview with Foucault in "Truth and Power," in *The Foucault Reader,* ed. Paul Rabinow (New York: Pantheon, 1984), 51–75.

25. See the important essay by Steven Crites, "The Narrative Quality of Experience," *Journal of the American Academy of Religion* (1971): 290–307.

26. Ricoeur, *Oneself as Another,* 143.

27. Taylor, *Sources of the Self,* 47ff. Taylor here is in agreement with Alasdar MacIntyre's influential study, *After Virtue: A Study in Moral Theory* (Notre Dame, IN: Notre Dame University Press, 1984), and draws from his idea that human beings require narrative direction to their lives, projecting life forward in the form of a "quest" (see MacIntyre, 203–4). The notion that self-understanding has a temporal depth is an insight

stemming from Heidegger's discussion of anticipatory "ecstasis" (see *Being and Time*, Div. II.3–4). See also Ricoeur's discussion of selfhood in the context of narrative frameworks, in *Oneself as Another*, chs. 5 and 6, and in the three-volume study, *Time and Narrative*, Vols. 1 and 2, trans. by K. McLaughlin and D. Pellauer, and Vol. 3 by K. Blamey and D. Pellauer (Chicago: University of Chicago Press, 1984, 1985, 1988). In an interview, Ricoeur puts it simply: "It is in telling our own stories that we give ourselves an identity. We recognize ourselves in the stories we tell about ourselves. It makes little difference whether these stories are true or false, fiction as well as verifiable history provides us with an identity" ("History as Narrative and Practice," an interview by Peter Kemp, *Philosophy Today* [Fall 1985]: 214).

28. MacIntyre, *After Virtue*, 209ff.

29. On this point, see Wilfred Sellars's criticism of what he calls "the myth of the given," in *Science, Perception, and Reality* (New York: Humanities Press, 1963); and Willard Van Orman Quine, *Theories and Things* (Cambridge: Harvard University Press, 1981). Both thinkers note how what counts for "truth" is a function of the theory that enframes it.

30. Gadamer suggests something similar in stating: "Reason exists for us only in concrete, historical terms—i.e., it is not its own master but remains constantly dependent on the given circumstances in which it operates" (*Truth and Method*, 276). For an excellent and balanced discussion of this point, see also Taylor, "Rationality," in *Philosophy and the Human Sciences. Philosophical Papers*, Vol. 2 (Cambridge: Cambridge University Press, 1985), 134–51.

31. Wittgenstein, *Tractatus Logico-Philosophicus*, trans. D. Pears and P. McGuinness (London: Routledge & Kegan Paul, 1961) 5.6. See also Gadamer, "Man and Language," 62. Elsewhere, Gadamer states that the world "is verbal in nature. . . . Not only is the world world only insofar as it comes into language, but language, too, has its real being only in the fact that the world is presented in it" (*Truth and Method*, 443).

32. Taylor, *Sources of the Self*, 45.

33. Ibid., 27–30.

34. The notion of "hybridity" comes from postcolonial studies. See Mike Featherstone, *Undoing Modernity: Globalization, Postmodernism, and Identity* (London: Sage, 1995), 86–101; Nesor Garcia Canclini, *Hybrid Cultures: Strategies for Entering and Leaving Modernity* (Minneapolis: University of Minnesota Press, 1995); James Clifford, "Travelling Cultures," in *Cultural Studies*, eds. Lawrence Grossberg, Cary Nelson, and Pamela Treichler (New York: Routledge, 1992), 96–112; Frantz Fanon, *A Dying Colonialism*, trans. Haakon Chevaliar (New York: Grove, 1965); and Robert C. Young, *Colonial Desire: Hybridity in Theory, Culture and Race* (New York: Routledge, 1995).

35. Jacques Derrida, *The Other Heading: Reflections on Today's Europe*, trans. Pascale-Anne Brault and Michael Naas (Bloomington: Indiana University Press, 1992), 9–11. References to this theme are scattered throughout Derrida's corpus. For examples, see *On the Name*, ed. Thomas Dutroit, trans. David Wood, John P. Leavy Jr., and Ian McLeod (Stanford: Stanford University Press, 1995), 71; and *Specters of Marx*, trans. Peggy Kamuf (New York: Routledge, 1994), 16.

36. See Wittgenstein, *Philosophical Investigations*, 66, 130.

37. Ibid., 68.

38. Wittgenstein at one point even calls "lying" its own language game (ibid., 249).

39. Ibid., 18.

40. Ibid.

41. Ibid., 71, see also 5. Derrida builds upon this constant and unrestricted deferral of meanings, each signifier interwoven with other signifiers in an indeterminable and in principle limitless chain of signifiers. See *Positions*, trans. Alan Bass (Chicago: University of Chicago Press, 1981), esp. 26–29; and "Structure, Sign and Play in the Discourse of the Human Sciences," in *Writing and Difference*, trans. Alan Boss (Chicago: University of Chicago Press, 1978), 278–93.

42. The philosopher of science, Karl Popper, argues in this way against what he calls "the myth of the framework," which falsely maintains that "we are prisoners caught in the framework of our theories; our expectations; our past experiences; our language"—such that we cannot communicate with anyone outside our framework ("Normal Science and its Dangers," in *Criticism and the Growth of Knowledge*, eds. Imre Lakatos and Alan Musgrave [Cambridge: Cambridge University Press, 1970], 56). For an excellent survey of this and other problems surrounding the paradigm-bound nature of rational knowledge, see Richard J. Bernstein, *Beyond Objectivism and Relativism* (Philadelphia: University of Pennsylvania Press, 1983), ch. 2.

43. Here, I am dependent upon David Krieger, *The New Universalism* (Maryknoll, NY: Orbis Books, 1991); see 110ff. Krieger goes on, then, to argue that this opens up "universal horizon" of community (114–18). Yet I am suspicious that this move is too hasty, doing an injustice to Wittgenstein. Wittgenstein places language squarely in the context of forms of life, which are themselves practices, customs, and conventions relative to a particular time and place. While these contexts may not be monadic, it is an unwarranted leap to say that "a principally unlimited *community of discourse*" is presupposed (118). Other reasons must be given for this. Indeed, Wittgenstein himself is unclear whether such a discourse is possible. For we would have to share an unlimited universal form of life, which is impossible. Recall his statement: "If a lion could talk, we could not understand him" (*Philosophical Investigations*, 223). Krieger's point that there is no speaking and thinking that is not open to intersubjective influence is well taken. It is another story, however, when we note that intersubjective influence itself is always localized by a peculiar language (see ibid., 241).

44. Wittgenstein strangely appeals to the "common behavior" of humankind as "the system of references by means of which we interpret an unknown language" (*Philosophical Investigations*, 206). He clearly is not saying that this comprises some universal language accessible to all, but hints that there must be some (behavioral?) link between languages in order to translate between their differences. While Wittgenstein does not articulate what this link may be, there is potential here to move beyond Wittgenstein (as Krieger hints). In chapter 4, I shall outline the contours of a *possible* "universality" anticipated in all local languages.

45. The term sharing (*partage*) is adopted from Jean-Luc Nancy, with modifications. See *The Inoperative Community*, ed. Peter Conner, trans. Peter Conner et al. (Minneapolis: University of Minnesota Press, 1991); and "Sharing Voices," in *Transforming the Hermeneutic Context: From Nietzsche to Nancy*, eds. Gayle Ormiston and Alan Schrift (Albany: State University of New York Press, 1990), 211–59.

46. See Nancy, "Sharing Voices," 244.

47. Gadamer, *Truth and Method*, 306–7.

48. While many contemporary authors have dismissed Gadamer's thought in light of the more radical hermeneutics of postmodern writers, his way of portraying the problem of understanding still merits a measure of consideration, especially given the issue of pluralism. Fred Dallmayr makes an excellent case for this in *Beyond Orientalism: Essays on*

Cross-Cultural Encounter (Albany: State University of New York Press, 1996), ch 2; see also Richard J. Bernstein, *Beyond Objectivism and Relativism*, part 3. Another interesting monograph that seeks to defend Gadamer in postmodern contexts is G. B. Madison's *Hermeneutics of Postmodernity* (Bloomington: Indiana University Press, 1988), ch. 7. For a good example of Gadamer's engagement with postmodern thought, see his essays in *Dialogue and Deconstruction*. Recently even John Caputo has softened his criticisms of Gadamer. See *More Radical Hermeneutics: On Not Knowing Who We Are* (Bloomington: Indiana University Press, 2000), ch. 2.

49. Gadamer, *Truth and Method*, 265ff. This recapitulates one of Heidegger's basics insights: understanding (Verstehen) is a mode of Dasein's being-in-the-world. See *Being and Time*, Div. I.5.32, 182ff.

50. Ibid., 277–85, 360.

51. Ibid., 308, 324; see also, "The Problem of Historical Consciousness," in *Interpretive Social Science: A Reader*, eds. Paul Rabinow and William A. Sullivan (Berkeley: University of California Press, 1979), 145f. Gadamer is interested primarily in the diachronic historical relation between past and present, seeking to rehabilitate the notion of tradition. I am employing Gadamer in broader terms, seeking to show how his thought throws light on the problem of pluralistic dwelling together.

52. Gadamer claims: "In reality, to be open to 'other people's opinions,' to a text, and so forth, implies right off that they are *situated* in my system of opinions, or better, that I situate myself in relation to them" ("The Problem of Historical Consciousness," 151).

53. See Gadamer, *Philosophical Hermeneutics*, trans. David E. Linge (Los Angeles: University of California Press, 1976) 15.

54. Ibid., 9.

55. Ibid., 15–16.

56. Gadamer, *Truth and Method*, 302.

57. Ibid., 299.

58. Ibid., 295.

59. Gadamer, "The Problem of Historical Consciousness," 157.

60. For example, Gadamer states: "Questions always bring out the undetermined possibilities of a thing. . . . *To understand the questionableness of something is already to be questioning*" (*Truth and Method*, 375).

61. Gadamer, "The Problem of Historical Consciousness," 155.

62. Gadamer, *Truth and Method*, 295.

63. Ibid., 294; also "The Problem of Historical Consciousness," 154–55.

64. "This implies that the text . . . must be understood at every moment, in every concrete situation, in a new and different way. Understanding here is always application" (*Truth and Method*, 309). Also, on p. 297: "It is enough to say that we understand in a *different* way, *if we understand at all*." Understanding is not an absorbing dynamism, but one that lets-be differences.

65. Gadamer, "The Problem of Historical Consciousness," 147.

66. George Steiner, *Real Presences* (Chicago: University of Chicago Press, 1989), 188.

67. This taking account of our own situation is what Gadamer calls the historically effected consciousness (*wirkungsgeschichtliches Bewusstsein*) (see *Truth and Method*, 341ff.). The task of the historically effected consciousness is self-knowledge achieved in dialectical interplay with an other. And any "[r]eal historical thinking must take account of its own historicity" (299).

68. Gadamer, *Truth and Method*, 302. Gadamer is careful to point out that there is no final self-knowledge; contra the Hegelian scheme, the cycle goes ever onward and outward, for history circumscribes and renders finite all understanding. But despite his criticisms, Gadamer relies heavily upon Hegel's dialectic of knowledge (presented in *The Phenomenology of Spirit*, trans. A. V. Miller [New York: Oxford University Press, 1977]). Every new achievement is a mediation point of reconciled contradictions, of old and new, self and other, in an expanding and self-transcending developmental process. For Hegel, this process is an unfolding teleology in which the goal of Absolute Knowledge is present all along, guiding it at each momentary development (see *The Phenomenology of Spirit*, 51).

69. Gadamer, "The Problem of Historical Consciousness," 107. Again, Gadamer echoes Hegel's idea that self-consciousness emerges in a process of growing mutual recognition between subjects, as portrayed in the discussion of "Lordship and Bondage." Hegel states: "Self-consciousness exists in and for itself when, and by the fact that, it so exists for another; that is, it exists only in being acknowledged" (*The Phenomenology of Spirit*, 111). The goal, for Hegel, is mutual and free recognition in a state of reciprocity and symmetry. On this point, see Gadamer, *Truth and Method*, 341ff. and 355. In deference to Hegel, Gadamer asserts: "The life of the mind consists precisely in recognizing oneself in other being" (346). For a telling commentary on Hegel's dialectic, see Gadamer's *Hegel's Dialectic: Five Hermeneutical Studies*, trans. P. Christopher Smith (New Haven: Yale University Press, 1976).

70. Gadamer, *Truth and Method*, 304.

71. As Gadamer suggests, speaking does not belong to the "I," but to the sphere of the "we" from which the "I" emerges (see "Man and Language," 65–66).

72. This idea of the "between" comes from Martin Buber, *Between Man and Man*, trans. Ronald Gregor Smith (London: Collins-Fontana Books, 1961), 244–47.

73. Gadamer, *Truth and Method*, 307.

74. Ibid., 305. Again, Hegel looms large in the background. We might say that Gadamer's "fusion of horizons" is something akin to Hegel's Aufhebung in which partial forms of life are both annulled and preserved, affirmed and superseded, reconciled momentarily in a more comprehensive whole. But in thinking with Hegel, Gadamer is also thinking against Hegel by underscoring the inevitable finitude and provisionality that accompanies all "fusions." Gadamer eschews teleology even as he promotes understanding as an ideal.

75. Ibid., 442.

76. Ibid., 358–59. Gadamer here speaks both of the Thou of tradition that calls to us, and the other as a person who calls to us. Though there are similarities, perhaps an indebtedness, a distinction should be drawn here between Gadamer and Martin Buber regarding the Thou. Buber's Thou is an inscrutable personal presence preceding linguisticality, not an object (an "it") that can (ever) be interpreted; Gadamer's Thou is thoroughly embedded in the interpretive event—it may be a person, a community, a tradition. A further distinction should be made between the Thou of Gadamer and the idea of the other (the "face") in Emmanuel Levinas, whose Thou-ness is not only inscrutable but demands an asymmetrical act of submissive obligation. For Levinas, the notion of reciprocity is problematic, as we shall explore in chapter 4.

77. Ibid., 361–62.

78. Ibid., 362ff.

79. "Drawing near" and "interest" are not Gadamer's terms, but adequately portray

his idea that questions draw us out toward a knowledge that we do not know but desire to know (see ibid., 366).

80. Gadamer asserts: "Knowledge always means, precisely, considering opposites. Its superiority over preconceived opinion consists in the fact that it is able to conceive of possibilities as possibilities. Knowledge is dialectical from the ground up" (ibid., 365).

81. Marcel, "On the Ontological Mystery," in *The Philosophy of Existentialism*, 39ff. In "The Ego and its Relation to Others" in (Homo Viator), Marcel gives a brief definition: availability (*disponibilité*) is "an aptitude to give oneself to anything which offers, and to bind oneself by the gift" (23).

82. Gadamer, *Truth and Method*, 367.

83. Ibid., 378–79.

84. Ibid., 303, 378f., 442.

85. Thus, Richard J. Bernstein argues that Gadamer's approach can help bear fruit in cross-cultural dialogue. See "The Hermeneutics of Cross-Cultural Understanding," in *Cross-Cultural Conversation*, ed. Anindita Niyogi Balslev (Atlanta: Scholars Press, 1996), 29-41.

86. Gadamer states: "All human speaking is finite in such a way that there is laid up within it an infinity of meaning to be explicated and laid out" (*Truth and Method*, 458). Meaning is "inexhaustible," a term that is Gadamer's more positive way of reading what Derrida calls "deferral" and "supplementation" (see ibid, 336). See Caputo, *More Radical Hermeneutics*, 46ff.

87. Lingis, *The Community of Those who Have Nothing in Common* (Bloomington: Indiana University Press, 1994), 87.

88. Ricoeur, *Interpretation Theory: Discourse and the Surplus of Meaning* (Fort Worth: Texas Christian University Press, 1976), 87f.; and *Hermeneutics and the Human Sciences*, 142ff.

89. Gadamer, *Truth and Method*, 379, italics added.

90. Gadamer, "*Destruktion* and Deconstruction," in *Dialogue and Deconstruction*, 110.

91. See Raimon Panikkar's essay, "The Myth of Pluralism: The Tower of Babel," in *Invisible Harmony: Essays on Contemplation and Responsibility*, ed. Harry James Cargas (Minneapolis: Fortress Press, 1995), 52–91. Panikkar claims that pluralism is not the single collective uniformity of differences, a Tower of Babel, but a dialogical tension between differences. I think that Gadamer's thought leads us to a similar conclusion.

92. For example, see Craig Calhoun, *Critical Social Theory* (Cambridge, MA: Blackwell, 1995), 50–51; Kathryn Tanner, *Theories of Culture: A New Agenda for Theology* (Minneapolis: Fortress, 1997), 45–47; Leela Gandhi, *Postcolonial Theory* (New York: Columbia University Press, 1998), ch. 7; Homi Bhabha, *The Location of Culture* (London: Routledge, 1994); and Clifford James, *The Predicament of Culture* (Cambridge: Harvard University Press, 1988).

93. In *Culture and Imperialism* (New York: Vintage Books, 1994), Edward Said states that "all culture is hybrid . . . and encumbered, or entangled with what used to be regarded as extraneous elements" (317).

94. See Dallmayr, *Beyond Orientalism: Essays on Cross-Cultural Encounter*, ch. 9.

95. Gadamer, "The Diversity of Europe," in *Hans-Georg Gadamer on Education, Poetry, and History: Applied Hermeneutics*, eds. Dieter Misgeld and Graeme Nicholson, trans. Lawrence Schmidt and Monica Reuss (Albany: State University of New York Press, 1992), 235–36.

96. On this idea of coordination versus agreement, see Nicholas Rescher, *Pluralism: Against the Demand for Consensus* (Oxford: Clarendon Press, 1993), 138.

97. See Gadamer, *Truth and Method*, 383ff.

98. This point is forcefully made by Foucault. See "Polemics, Politics, and Problemizations: An Interview with Michel Foucault," in *The Foucault Reader*, ed. Paul Rabinow (New York: Pantheon, 1984), 381–83. See also Jean-Francois Lyotard, *The Postmodern Condition: A Report on Knowledge*, trans. Geoff Bennington and Brian Massumi (Minneapolis: University of Minnesota Press, 1984), 66, who argues that consensus is totalizing.

99. Gadamer, *Truth and Method*, 312ff. Gadamer here retrieves the idea of *phronesis* from Aristotle's "Nichomachean Ethics" in showing how application is always a practical affair, one in which an interpreter applies something to herself or himself in her or his lived situation. See Bernstein, *Beyond Objectivism and Relativism*, 144–50, for a good discussion of Gadamer's approach to *phronesis*.

100. David Tracy, *Plurality and Ambiguity: Hermeneutics, Religion, Hope* (San Francisco: Harper, 1987), 19.

101. Nicholas Rescher makes a similar point. See *Pluralism: Against the Demand for Consensus*, 149ff.

102. Theodor W. Adorno, "Subject and Object," in *The Essential Frankfurt School Reader*, eds. Andrew Arato and Eike Gebhardt (New York: Continuum, 1995), 499.

103. See Nancy, "Sharing Voices," 244. Admittedly, I am pushing Gadamer here in the direction of Nancy's vision.

104. See Nancy, "Finite History," in *The Birth to Presence*, trans. Brian Holmes et al. (Stanford: Stanford University Press, 1993), 155.

105. Gadamer draws this out in the essay, "The Diversity of Europe," in *Hans-Georg Gadamer on Education, Poetry, and History*, 221–38. I follow here Sharon D. Welch's suggestion (which Gadamer would support) that the intention of solidarity is more inclusive and transformative than that of consensus. See her *Feminist Ethic of Risk* (Minneapolis: Fortress Press, 1990), 132.

106. Gadamer, "Letter to Dallmayr," in *Dialogue and Deconstruction*, 97.

107. See Nancy, *Being Singular Plural*, trans. Robert D. Richardson and Anne E. O'Brian (Stanford: Stanford University Press, 2000), 5, 65ff.

108. Ibid., 5.

109. Gadamer states something similar: "The very idea of a situation means that we are not standing outside it and hence are unable to have any objective knowledge of it. We always find ourselves within a situation, and throwing light on it is a task that is never entirely finished" (*Truth and Method*, 301).

110. On the dangers of communal reification, see Nancy, *The Inoperative Community*, ch. 1.

CHAPTER FOUR. DIALECTICAL PLURALISM: TRUTH, THE OTHER, AND THE PRAXIS OF SOLIDARITY

1. Hans-Georg Gadamer, "The Diversity of Europe," in *Hans-Georg Gadamer: On Education, Poetry, and History*, eds. Dieter Misgeld and Graeme Nicholson, trans. Lawrence Schmidt and Monica Reuss (Albany: State University of New York Press, 1992), 234.

2. See Craig Calhoun, *Critical Social Theory* (Cambridge: Blackwell Publishers, 1995), 93; and Charles Taylor, *The Ethics of Authenticity* (Cambridge: Harvard University Press, 1991), 52.

3. Aristotle, *Metaphysics*, III, 4, 1000b, in *The Basic Works of Aristotle*, ed. Richard McKeon (New York: Random, 1941), 726.

4. Anselm Kyongsuk Min, "Dialectical Pluralism and Solidarity of Others: Towards a New Paradigm," *Journal of the American Academy of Religion* 65/3 (Fall 1997): 587–604. See also his recently published *The Solidarity of Others in a Divided World: A Postmodern Theology after Postmodernism* (New York: T & T Clark International, 2004), which contains a revised version of this essay (173–97). It is regrettable that Min's book was published subsequent to the writing of this book. For there is much in Min's analysis that warrants consideration and, indeed, dovetails with themes I am addressing in this book.

5. See Gabriel Marcel, "On the Ontological Mystery," in *The Philosophy of Existentialism*, trans. Manya Harari (New York: Carol Publishing Group, 1956), 39ff.; and "The Ego and its Relation to Others," in *Homo Viator*, trans. Emma Craufurd (Gloucester, MA: Peter Smith, 1978), 23.

6. See Min, "Dialectical Pluralism and Solidarity of Others," 588–90. "Neither elimination of all difference nor affirmation of sheer particularity is possible or desirable in an increasingly interdependent world; the former would lead to totalitarianism, the latter to the conflict of particularisms" (589–90).

7. The term "hermeneutic of suspicion" originates with Paul Ricoeur in *Freud and Philosophy* (New Haven: Yale University Press, 1970), 32–36.

8. In a different vein but with a similar intent, Richard Kearney makes this point in his *Strangers, Gods and Monsters* (London: Routledge, 2003), 67–82.

9. For, as Max Horkheimer claims, "truth is an impetus to correct practice" ("On the Problem of Truth," in *The Essential Frankfurt School Reader*, eds. Andrew Arato and Eike Gebhardt [New York: Continuum, 1995], 429).

10. See Charles Taylor, *Sources of the Self: The Making of Modern Identity* (Cambridge: Harvard University Press, 1989), 47.

11. Simone Weil, "Truth," in *The Need for Roots: Prelude to a Declaration of Duties towards Mankind* (London: Routledge & Kegan Paul, 1952), 35.

12. David Tracy also makes this point in *Plurality and Ambiguity: Hermeneutics, Religion, Hope* (San Francisco: Harper, 1987), 48.

13. This kind of quasi-realism is Gadamer's view in *Truth and Method*, 2nd revised ed., trans. Joel Weinsheimer and Donald G. Marshall (New York: Crossroad, 1992), see 438–56.

14. For Marcel's treatment, see "On the Ontological Mystery," 12–15; and *The Mystery of Being*, Vol. 2, trans. Rene Hague (London: Harvill Press, 1950), 1–67, esp. 33ff.

15. Peter Berger, *A Rumor of Angels: Modern Society and the Rediscovery of the Supernatural* (New York: Anchor Books, 1969), 52–53, 59. See also *The Sacred Canopy* (New York: Anchor Books, 1969), 184–85.

16. Ibid., 52.

17. Ibid., 62. George Steiner makes a similar case in *Real Presences* (Chicago: University of Chicago Press, 1989), see esp. 198ff.

18. Paul Ricoeur, "Hope and the Structure of Philosophical Systems," in *Figuring the Sacred*, trans. David Pellauer, ed. Mark I. Wallace (Minneapolis: Fortress Press, 1995),

203–16; and *Interpretation Theory: Discourse and the Surplus of Meaning* (Forth Worth: Texas Christian University Press, 1976).

19. "Presence" is a term I am drawing from Marcel. See, for example, "On the Ontological Mystery," 36–40; *Presence and Immortality*, trans. Michael A. Machado (Pittsburgh: Duquesne University Press, 1967), 236–38; and *The Mystery of Being*, Vol. 1, 204ff. For other accounts of presence similar to what I have in mind here, see George Steiner, *Real Presences*, and Ralph Harper, *On Presence: Variations and Reflections* (Philadelphia: Trinity Press International, 1991). In a different way, the term has been associated with Jacques Derrida's way of extending Heidegger's criticisms of logocentrism or the "metaphysics of presence," which assumes that there is at the foundation of language an essence, the closure of "presence"—a transcendental signified—that humans can represent via language (see *Of Grammatology*, trans. Gayatri Chakravorty Spivak [Baltimore: John Hopkins University Press, 1976]). As is obvious, I am employing the term in a different sense than Derrida, but one that shows a certain affinity with his program by stressing the nonadequation of presence.

20. See Steiner, *Real Presences*, 175–76.

21. Jean-Luc Marion suggests something similar in his reading of Husserl, employing the term as a way of signifying an intuition that remains unfulfilled, not because of a "lack" but because it is "exceeded," overwhelmed by the excessiveness of the given. See *Reduction and Givenness: Investigations of Husserl, Heidegger, and Phenomenology*, trans. Thomas A. Carlson (Evanston, IL: Northwestern University Press, 1998), 34–35. For reasons that shall become evident, I do not, however, follow his way of describing presence as a given that is undecidable and thus anonymous.

22. On the notion of astonishment, see Emmanuel Levinas, *Totality and Infinity*, trans. Alphonso Lingus (Pittsburgh: Duquesne University Press, 1969), 73; and Marcel, *Creative Fidelity*, trans. Robert Rosthal (New York: Farrar, 1964), 47ff., 63–64, 70–71, 146.

23. Levinas's *Totality and Infinity* articulates such a position. And this is even further radicalized in *Otherwise than Being or Beyond Essence*, trans. Alphonso Lingis (Pittsburgh: Duquesne University Press, 1998), see esp. 112, 118. A very helpful introduction to Levinas's thought can be found in a monograph compiling conversations with Philippe Nemo, *Ethics and Infinity*, trans. Richard A. Cohen (Pittsburgh: Duquesne University Press, 1985). I have employed Levinas's language at points, but seek—contra Levinas—to preserve the integrity of the reciprocity in being-with, keeping more in line with visions of Martin Buber and Gabriel Marcel.

24. See Levinas, *Otherwise than Being or Beyond Essence*, 111, 116.

25. See the criticism of Levinas in Richard Kearney, *Strangers, Gods and Monsters*, 71.

26. Levinas, "Dialogue: Self-Consciousness and Proximity of the Neighbor," in *Of God who Comes to Mind*, trans. Bettin Bergo (Stanford: Stanford University Press, 1998), 145, 147. See also "Martin Buber and the Theory of Knowledge," in *The Levinas Reader*, ed. Seán Hand (Oxford: Blackwell, 1989), 59–74; and "Dialogue with Emmanuel Levinas," in *Face to Face with Levinas*, ed. Richard A. Cohen (Albany: State University of New York Press, 1986), 31: "I must always demand more of myself than of the other; and this is why I disagree with Buber's description of the I-Thou ethical relationship as a symmetrical copresence."

27. See Levinas, *Otherwise than Being or Beyond Essence*, 83, 87, 100.

28. Ibid., 101.

29. Jacques Derrida, *The Gift of Death*, trans. David Wills (Chicago: University of Chicago Press, 1996), 68ff.

30. See Levinas, *Totality and Infinity*, 291.

31. See Marcel, *Creative Fidelity*, 47ff., 52f.

32. See Levinas, *Totality and Infinity*,194–201; and *Ethics and Infinity*, 85–92. Edward Farley makes a similar point in his *Good and Evil: Interpreting a Human Condition* (Minneapolis: Augsburg Fortress, 1990), 39–40, 191.

33. The notion of "sympathy" as a way of feeling-along-with-another (Miteinanderfuhlung) is developed in Max Sheler, *The Nature of Sympathy* (London: Routledge & Kegel Paul, 1954), Part 1.

34. My employment of the term "wonderment"—in an interhuman sense—draws from Jürgen Moltmann's essay, "The Knowing of the Other and the Community of the Different," in *God for a Secular Age: The Public Relevance of Theology*, trans. Margaret Kohl (Minneapolis: Fortress Press, 1999), 135–152; and also from Jerome A. Miller, *In the Throe of Wonder: Intimations of the Sacred in a Post-Modern World* (Albany: State University of New York Press, 1992), see 110–115. See also Sam Keen, *Apology for Wonder* (New York: Harper, 1969).

35. This is one of Franz Rosenzweig's key points in his famous *Star of Redemption*, trans. William W. Hallo (Notre Dame, IN: University of Notre Dame Press, 1985), for example, see 177. Paul Ricoeur picks up the theme in "Love and Justice," in *Figuring the Sacred*, trans. David Pellauer, ed. Mark I. Wallace (Minneapolis: Fortress Press, 1995), 315–29.

36. On the idea of love in this sense, see the insightful study by Robert Johann, S.J., *The Meaning of Love: An Essay Toward a Metaphysics of Intersubjectivity* (Glen Rock, NJ: Paulist Press, 1966).

37. For example, see "The Trinity," in *Augustine: Later Works*, ed. and trans. John Burnaby (Philadelphia: Westminster Press, 1955), 43ff. and 166ff.; *The Confessions*, trans. Maria Boulding (New York: Vintage Books, 1998), 310; and "The Soliloquies," in *Augustine: Earlier Writings*, ed. and trans. J. H. S. Burleigh (Philadelphia: Westminster Press, 1953), 31–32.

38. Ricoeur makes this point in "Love and Justice," 325.

39. See Farley, *Good and Evil*, 190–93.

40. I am using "mystery" in Marcel's sense here. See *The Mystery of Being*, Vol. 1, ch. 10, and Vol. 2, ch. 1. Marcel states: there is "an organic connection between presence and mystery. For, in the first place, every presence *is* mysterious and, in the second place, it is very doubtful whether the word 'mystery' can really be properly used in the case where a presence is not, at the very least, making itself somehow felt" (Vol. 1, 216).

41. The phrase, "distance and relation," is from Buber, though I am modifying his program here to account for Levinas's position. See Buber, "Distance and Relation," in *The Knowledge of Man: Selected Essays*, ed. Maurice Friedman, trans. Maurice Friedman and Ronald Gregor Smith (Atlantic Highlands, NJ: Humanities Press International, 1988), 49–61.

42. This echoes Jürgen Habermas's famous criticism of Gadamer's more tradition-bound hermeneutic. See his "Review of Gadamer's 'Truth and Method,'" in *Understanding and Social Inquiry*, eds. Fred R. Dallmayr and Thomas A. McCarthy (Notre Dame, IN: University of Notre Dame Press, 1977), 357–58. For an excellent commen-

tary on the well-known debate between Gadamer and Habermas, see Paul Ricoeur, "Hermeneutics and the Critique of Ideology," in *Hermeneutics and the Human Sciences*, ed. and trans. John B. Thompson (Cambridge: Cambridge University Press, 1981), 64–100. Consult also Richard J. Bernstein's balanced criticism of Gadamer in *Beyond Objectivism and Relativism* (Philadelphia: University of Pennsylvania Press, 1983), 155ff.

43. Gadamer states that "conversation should seek its partner everywhere, just because this partner is other, and especially if the other is completely different . . . for difference stands at the beginning of a conversation. . . ." ("*Destruktion* and Deconstruction," in *Dialogue and Deconstruction: The Gadamer-Derrida Encounter*, eds. Diane P. Michelfelder and Richard E. Palmer [Albany: State University of New York Press, 1989], 113).

44. Marcel, "On the Ontological Mystery," 36. See also, *Creative Fidelity*, 147–74.

45. At this point I am, with reservation, employing the soft transcendental logic of Habermas's argument that communicative action implicitly affirms an "ideal speech situation," that is, insofar as it is action oriented toward unconstrained mutual agreement between interlocutors. For Habermas, the ideal speech situation is a universal condition presupposed by all speech acts that are not purposive and manipulative but seek genuine consensus among equal and free subjects. In such a situation, the force of the better argument determines what counts for truth. See "Toward a Theory of Communicative Competence" *Inquiry* 13 (1970): 360–75; *The Theory of Communicative Action,* Vol. 1, trans. Thomas McCarthy (Boston: Beacon, 1984), 273ff.; and *The Philosophical Discourse of Modernity*, trans. Frederick G. Lawrence (Cambridge: Massachusetts Institute of Technology Press, 1987), 322ff. But whereas Habermas tends to focus on intersubjective agreement and consensus regarding competing validity claims as the telos of communicative action, I have underscored the difference-bearing nature of Gadamer's notion of understanding as a fusion of horizons. The ideal of consensus regarding the better argument, despite Habermas's intentions to the contrary, strikes me as dangerously close to the polemical attitude, for argument assumes in advance the rightness of one's position over and against others. While validity claims of a sort are inevitable, prioritizing the argumentative thrust toward agreement leads to problems. See Nicholas Rescher, *Pluralis: Against the Demand for Consensus* (Oxford: Clarendon Press, 1993), ch. 8. David Tracy seems to me to represent a more balanced retrieval of argument *within* the interpretive dialectic of understanding (see *Plurality and Ambiguity: Hermeneutics, Religion, Hope* [San Francisco: Harper, 1987], 23ff.).

46. Interestingly enough, Derrida make a similar point in "Violence and Metaphysics," in *Writing and Difference*, trans. Alan Bass (Chicago: University of Chicago Press, 1978), 78–153, see esp. 138.

47. Taylor makes this point convincingly in "The Politics of Recognition," in *Multiculturalism*, ed. Amy Gutmann (Princeton: Princeton University Press, 1994), 66ff.; and in "Comparison, History, Truth," in *Philosophical Arguments* (Cambridge: Harvard University Press, 1995), 156.

48. See Taylor, "Comparison, History, Truth," 152–53. While Taylor does not invoke the kind of transcendental claims Habermas does, he drives home a similar point.

49. Taylor, "The Politics of Recognition," 70.

50. See Calhoun, *Critical Social Theory*, 75–76; Hannah Arendt, *The Human Condition* (Chicago: University of Chicago Press, 1958); and Bernstein, *Beyond Objectivism and Relativism*, 207ff.

51. See Gadamer's retrieval of phronesis found in Aristotle's "Nichomachean Ethics" in *Truth and Method*, 312ff.

52. Taylor states it in the following way: "In the end, the presumption of worth imagines a universe in which different cultures *complement* each other with quite different kinds of contributions" ("The Politics of Recognition," 71, note 41, italics added). This is also one of the major motifs of Tracy's book, *Plurality and Ambiguity*, esp. ch. 1 and pp. 113–14; and it also looms large in William Schweiker's *Mimetic Reflections: A Study in Hermeneutics, Theology, and Ethics* (New York: Fordham University Press, 1990), e.g., see 136, 182, 240.

53. See Taylor, "Comparison, History, Truth," 151, who argues essentially the same point. I employ his use of the term "omega point." See also Bernstein, *The New Constellation: The Ethical-Political Horizons of Modernity/Postmodernity* (Cambridge: Massachusetts Institute of Technology Press, 1991), 313ff.

54. Gadamer, *Truth and Method*, 294; "The Problem of Historical Consciousness," in *Interpretive Social Science: A Reader*, eds. Paul Rabinow and William A. Sullivan (Berkeley: University of California Press, 1979), 154–55.

55. See Paul Ricoeur, "Hope and the Structure of Philosophical Systems," in *Figuring the Sacred*, trans. David Pellauer, ed. Mark I. Wallace (Minneapolis: Fortress Press, 1995), 203–16.

56. This is how the localized universal is different from Hegel's notion of the "concrete universal," a logical deep structure implicitly working itself out in finite configurations. The affirmation of the universal is a finite human anticipation of solidarity, not, as in Hegel, the self-identical universal (Absolute Idea) mediated in particular forms in a teleological scheme of development. On Hegel's notion of the Concept as the ground and source of all finite determinateness and multiplicity, see Taylor's chapter in *Hegel* (Cambridge: Cambridge University Press, 1975), ch. 7.

57. See Habermas, *The Philosophical Discourse of Modernity*, 322; see also Gadamer, "The Universality of the Hermeneutic Problem," in *Philosophical Hermeneutics*, trans. David E. Linge (Los Angeles: University of California Press, 1976), 16. Tracy makes a similar point in *Plurality and Ambiguity*, 22ff.

58. Habermas, *The Phiosophical Discourse of Modernity*, 322–23; see also "The Unity of Reason in the Diversity of its Voices," in *Postmetaphysical Thinking*, trans. William Mark Hohengarten (Cambridge: Massachusetts Institute of Technology Press, 1992), 138–39. While trying to remain true to the form of his argument, I am modifying Habermas's language in a more hermeneutical and less overtly "transcendental" direction.

59. Gadamer, "The Universality of the Hermeneutic Problem," 16. See also *Truth and Method*, 401ff.

60. This is my way of taking up yet moving beyond the kind of deconstructive "ethic of dissemination" advocated by Caputo (see *Radical Hermeneutics: Repition, Deconstruction, and the Hermeneutic Project* (Bloomington, Indiana University Press, 1987), ch. 9).

61. Habermas, *The Philosophical Discourse of Modernity*, 324.

62. See Habermas, *The Theory of Communicative Action*, Vol. 1, 285ff.

63. Taylor makes this point in *Sources of the Self*, 160.

64. See Max Horkheimer and Theodor W. Adorno, *Dialectic of the Enlightenment*, trans. John Cumming (New York: Herder and Herder, 1972).

65. I am influenced here by Valerie Saiving's important essay, "The Human Situation: A Feminine View," in *Womanspirit Rising: A Feminist Reader in Religion*, eds. Carol Christ and Judith Plaskow (San Francisco: Harper, 1979), 25–42.

66. See Frantz Fanon, *The Wretched of the Earth*, trans. Constance Farrington (New York: Grove Weidenfeld, 1963); Robert C. Young, *Colonial Desire: Hybridity in Theory, Culture, and Race*; and Edward Said, *Orientalism: Western Conceptions of the Orient* (New York: Vintage, 1979). On gender relations, see Luce Irigaray, *This Sex Which Is Not One* (Ithaca: Cornell University Press, 1977); and the essays in *A Mind of One's Own: Feminist Essays on Reason and Objectivity*, eds. Louise M. Antony and Charlotte Witt (Boulder: Westview, 1993).

67. Theodor Adorno, *Minima Moralia: Reflections from Damaged Life*, trans. E. F. N. Jephcott (New York: Verso, 1974), 71.

68. See Tzvetan Todorov's *Conquest of America*, trans. Richard Howard (New York: Harper Perennial, 1992), for an excellent account of how both logics of assimilation and exclusion were operative in the Spanish colonization of America.

69. Sharon Welch addresses this point, suggesting that conversation is not simply semantic play but a critical praxis that transforms material and power conditions that perpetuate domination (see *A Feminist Ethic of Risk* [Minneapolis: Fortress Press, 1990], 133ff.).

70. Habermas, *Communication and the Evolution of Society*, trans. Thomas McCarthy (Boston: Beacon, 1979), 97. See also Bernstein, *Beyond Objectivism and Relativism*, 190–92.

71. Habermas, "A Reply to My Critics," in *Habermas: Critical Debates*, trans. John B. Thompson and David Held (Cambridge: Massachusetts Institute of Technology Press, 1982), 221.

72. See Bernstein, *Beyond Objectivism and Relativism*, 195. Bernstein seeks to appropriate Habermas's transcendental move in a more pragmatic modality, granting its plausibility in terms of its interpretive power instead of its transcendental universality (see 192ff.). I follow Bernstein's interpretation. Indeed, the viability of a dialectical pluralism of solidarity is granted only in the conversational solidarity it seeks to promote and preserve.

73. See Martin Jay, *Adorno* (Cambridge: Harvard University Press, 1984), 66.

74. For an excellent treatment of the moral imperative of hospitality, see Thomas W. Ogletree, *Hospitality toward the Stranger: Dimensions of Moral Understanding* (Philadelphia: Fortress Press, 1985). Jacques Derrida has recently taken to writing on this theme, drawing inspiration from Levinas. See *Of Hospitality*, trans. Rachel Bowlby (Stanford, CA: Stanford University Press, 2000); "Hostipitality," in *Acts of Religion*, ed. Gil Anidjar (New York: Rutledge, 2002), 358–420; and *On Cosmopolitanism and Forgiveness*, trans. Mark Dooley and Richard Kearney (New York: Routledge, 2002). Derrida, however, so radicalizes the openness of hospitality that the other is welcomed regardless of status. An enemy or terrorist or monster is equally invited. For Derrida, the other, to be truly other, must not be expected or anticipated, but must be anonymous, unnamed, and in the end, unrecognizable. This, in my judgment, surrenders all categorical leverage not only to name evil, but also to welcome the other as unique and different. It renders hospitality moot. See Kearney, *Strangers, Gods and Monsters*, 68–72.

75. Ogletree, *Hospitality toward the Stranger*, 8.

76. Todorov make this point in *The Conquest of America*, 251.

CHAPTER FIVE. THE TRANSCENDENT GRAMMAR OF PRESENCE AND THE RELIGIOUS SENSIBILITY

1. Martin Heidegger, "The Origin of the Work of Art," in *Poetry, Language, Thought*, trans. Albert Hofstadter (New York: Harper, 1971), 54.

2. See Friedrich Schleiermacher, *On Religion: Speeches to its Cultured Despisers*, trans. and ed. Richard Crouter (Cambridge: Cambridge University Press, 1988), ch. 2; and the Introduction to *The Christian Faith*, 2nd. ed., trans. and ed. H. R. Mackintoshand and J. S. Stewart (Edinburgh: T. & T. Clark, 1928), esp. §§4 and 7. See also the essay by Ernst Troeltsch, written later in his life, "The Place of Christianity among the World Religions," in *Christian Thought: Its History and Application*, ed. Baron von Hügel (New York: Meridian Books, 1957), 35–63. While refusing to reject outright other religious faiths as false, seeing all faiths on a common or generic playing field, Schleiermacher still wishes to retain the provisional superiority of Christianity. Troeltsch rejects this latter point in order to underscore the historicity of all faith. For him, the most we can say is that Christianity (for example) is normative "for us," for the "we" of our own context and tradition (55). This key point sets the stage for the whole problem of religious pluralism.

3. While it has asserted itself throughout the history of religions, and in Christian history in particular, two prominent twentieth-century examples of this approach are Karl Barth, *Church Dogmatics*, Vols. 1–2, ed. and trans. G.W. Bromiley (Edinburgh: T & T Clark, 1961), 280–361; and Hendrick Kraemer, *Religion and the Christian Faith* (Philadelphia: Westminster, 1956), 340–65. See also Harold A. Netland, *Dissonant Voices: Religious Pluralism and the Question of Truth* (Grand Rapids: William B. Eerdmans Publishing Co., 1991), for a more recent Evangelical defense of this position.

4. Schubert Ogden notes this binary logic of true-to-false in *Is there Only One True Religion or Are there Many?* (Dallas: Southern Methodist University Press, 1992).

5. For example, Schleiermacher states that Christianity is "the most perfect of the most highly developed forms of religion" (*The Christian Faith*, §9.4, 38). For more recent examples, see Wolfhart Pannenberg, "Toward a Theology of the History of Religions," in *Basic Questions in Theology*, Vol. 2 (Philadelphia: Westminster, 1971), 65–118; and Paul Tillich's *Systematic Theology*, Vols. 1–3 (Chicago: University of Chicago Press, 1951–1963)—though Tillich later softened his view dramatically in the essay, "The Significance of the History of Religions for the Systematic Theologian," in *Christianity and the Encounter of World Religions* (Minneapolis: Fortress Press), 63–79.

6. See, for example, Karl Rahner, "Christianity and the Non-Christian Religions," in *Theological Investigations*, Vol. 5 (Baltimore: Helicon, 1966), 115–34; and *Foundations of Christian Faith* (New York: Seabury, 1978), 311–21.

7. David J. Krieger, *The New Universalism: Foundations for a Global Theology* (Maryknoll, NY: Orbis Books, 1991), 18–28.

8. Paul J. Griffiths argues this point in "The Properly Christian Response to Religious Pluralism," *The Anglican Theological Review* 79 (1997): 19.

9. For excellent accounts and criticisms of some of the key issues, see the essays in *The Myth of Christian Uniqueness: Toward a Pluralistic Theology of Religions*, eds. John Hick and Paul F. Knitter (Maryknoll, NY: Orbis Books, 1989); and Paul F. Knitter's *Theologies of Religions* (Maryknoll, NY: Orbis Books, 2002).

10. I stress here the point that there are many *possibilities*, not that there actuality *are* many true religions, for the second position would entail making claims that far exceed

the knowledge of any historically embedded inquirer. On this, see Ogden, *Is there Only One True Religion or Are there Many?* esp. chs. 3–4.

11. Some well-known examples of this line of thinking include Aldous Huxley, *The Perennial Philosophy* (New York: Harper, 1945); Huston Smith, *Forgotten Truth: The Primordial Tradition* (New York: Harper, 1976); and Frithjof Schuon, *The Transcendental Unity of Religions* (New York: Harper, 1975).

12. This point is made by George A. Lindbeck, in his now classic *Nature of Doctrine: Religion and Theology in a Postliberal Age* (Philadelphia: Westminster Press, 1984), see esp. ch. 2. Lindbeck argues against an "experiential-expressive" approach, which holds that religious language derives its power from a prior form of experience that is the same for all and guides but cannot be fully brought into the language that expresses it. He proposes thinking about religions by reversing the movement, to the degree that experience itself is shaped by the language of a community. This "cultural-linguistic" approach, so he suggests, better accounts for religious diversity.

13. A long list of scholars have been critical of the term "religion" for its potential to mask totalizing agendas that obfuscate real historical difference. See, for example, Wilfred Cantwell Smith, *The Meaning and End of Religion* (New York: Macmillan, 1964); John B. Cobb Jr., "The Religions," in *Transforming Christianity and the World*, ed. Paul F. Knitter (Maryknoll, NY: Orbis Books, 1999), 15–33; Jonathan Z. Smith, *Imagining Religion: From Babylon to Jonestown* (Chicago: University of Chicago Press, 1982); Talal Asad, *Genealogies of Religion: Discipline and Reasons of Power in Christianity and Islam* (Baltimore: John Hopkins, 1993); and Russel T. McCutcheon, *Manufacturing Religion: The Discourse of Sui Generis Religion and the Politics of Nostalgia* (New York: Oxford University Press, 1997).

14. For instance, Stanley Hauerwas argues that the "very language of 'religion' denotes an Enlightenment mentality that suggest that the various historical faiths are but manifestations of a common phenomenon called 'religion'" (*After Christendom?* [Nashville: Abingdon Press, 1991], 84).

15. Indeed, those who lobby against the term often trade upon its very meaning, assuming its signifying status as an operative term. This irony is played out graphically in Talal Asad's *Genealogies of Religion*.

16. A superb example of the historicist approach can be found in Jonathan Z. Smith, *Imagining Religion*. For further analyses and criticisms, see the review essay by Catherine Bell, "Modernism and Postmodernism in the Study of Religion," *Religious Studies Review* 22/3 (July 1996): 179–90; and Ivan Strenski's 'Religion, Power, and Final Foucault,' *Journal of the American Academy of Religion* 66/2 (1998): 345–67.

17. This effect was clearly not what Troeltsch intended when he stated that the most one could claim about one's own religious faith (i.e., Christianity) is that it is valid "for us" ("The Place of Christianity among the World Religions," 55), for he goes on to talk about the "Divine Life" as it may be encountered by other traditions, advocating a common religious telos for humankind (see esp. 60f.). Indeed, Troeltsch saw the problem with historicism.

18. While I have stated it here somewhat simplistically, such seems to be the basic approach underlying John Milbank's ambitious work, *Theology and Social Theory: Beyond Secular Reason* (Oxford: Blackwell, 1990). Milbank in fact shows a dangerous proximity to the polemical approach in his declaration of the superiority of the Christian metanarrative over others (see ch. 12).

19. An example is S. Mark Heim's book, *Salvations: Truth and Difference in Religion* (Maryknoll, NY: Orbis Books, 1995). Though Heim at least acknowledges the "possibility" of other salvations, each of which is for them the "only way," the danger in this view is that it promulgates in each the praxis of communal closure, while suggesting, much like Rorty does, that such closure is only inevitable and benign. Others still, like Lindbeck in *The Nature of Doctrine*, join ranks here in emphasizing that it is impossible to speak of a continuity among faith traditions, for each operates according to maxims that grow out of its own unique interpretive context. Religious pluralism then means a variety of "cultural-linguistic" horizons of faith references.

20. In this regard, I heartily concur with James M. Gustafson's criticisms of this approach. See his recent *Examined Faith: The Grace of Self-Doubt* (Minneapolis: Fortress Press, 2004), 37–44, 84–95. See also his earlier essay, "The Sectarian Temptation: Reflections on Theology, the Church and the University," *CTSA Proceedings* 40 (1985): 83–94.

21. Taylor, "Comparison, History, Truth," in *Philosophical Arguments* (Cambridge: Harvard University Press, 1995), 152–53. See also "Understanding and Ethnocentricity," in *Philosophy and the Human Sciences, Philosophical Papers*, Vol. 2 (Cambridge: Cambridge University Press, 1985), 125f.

22. Ibid.

23. The argument of the preceding paragraphs is presented in more detail in my "Religion within the Limits of History: Schleiermacher and the Study of Religion—A Reappraisal," in *Religion* 32 (January 2002): 51–70.

24. Thus, I find it ironic that someone like John Cobb refuses to grant the term "religion" any cognitive status in light of his own Whiteheadian metaphysics. Given that process thought functions so prominently as a theoretical framework shaping Cobb's vision of plurality, why is a vision like that of W.C. Smith's or John Hick's so criticized for being a "quest for what is common" and accordingly not being pluralist enough (see *Transforming Christianity and the World*, 44)? Does not Cobb's Whiteheadian "common ground" become itself an essentialism guiding his interpretation of religious traditions—that is, Buddhism? Despite his claims to the contrary, Cobb in the end does employ a universalizing interpretive grid to understand other non-Christian traditions as "religious" and on a similar semantic playing field. This becomes especially apparent in his essay, "Order out of Chaos: A Philosophical Model of Interreligious Dialogue," ibid., 113–27.

25. I am employing Emmanuel Levinas's depiction of the infinite, with slight modifications. See *Totality and Infinity*, trans. Alphonso Lingis (Pittsburgh: Duquesne University Press, 1969), 48–52; "Philosophy and the Idea of the Infinite," trans. Alphonso Lingis, in Adriaan Peperzak, *To the Other: An Introduction to the Philosophy of Emmanuel Levinas* (West Lafayette, IN: Purdue University Press, 1993), 88–119; and "God and Philosophy," in *Of God who Comes to Mind*, trans. Bettina Bergo (Stanford: Stanford University Press, 1998), 58–78.

26. Levinas, *Totality and Infinity*, 33–35.

27. See John D. Caputo, *The Prayers and Tears of Jacques Derrida: Religion without Religion* (Bloomington: Indiana University Press, 1997), 154–59. See also Jacques Derrida, *On the Name*, ed. Thomas Dutoit, trans. David Wood, John P. Leavey Jr., and Ian McLeod (Stanford: Stanford University Press, 1995); and "Faith and Knowledge," in *Acts of Religion*, ed. Gil Anidjar (New York: Routledge, 2002), 42–101.

28. See Levinas, *Totality and Infinity*, 34.

29. In this regard George Steiner suggests against Derrida that the chain of signifiers is infinite not because of the utter deferral of meaning, but because the meaning of presence is incapable of being exhausted, a fact that "makes us close neighbors to the transcendent" (*Real Presences*, [Chicago: University of Chicago Press, 1989], 215, see also 59).

30. For example, see Derrida, *The Politics of Friendship*, trans. George Collins (London: Verso, 1997). See also Caputo, *On Religion* (London: Routledge, 2001), 7–17.

31. I am dependent here on Richard Kearney's way of unpacking the logic of possibility in eschatological terms. See his excellent book, *The God who May Be* (Bloomington: Indiana University Press, 2001), esp. chs. 5–6.

32. This is my own take on a point made by Paul Ricoeur in the essay, "Hope and the Structure of Philosophical Systems," in *Figuring the Sacred*, trans. David Pellauer, ed. Mark I. Wallace (Minneapolis: Fortress Press, 1995), 230–16. For Ricoeur, hope is that which pushes discourse forward by affirming an excess of sense over nonsense, the promise of meaning over meaninglessness, an excess objective and actual in reality but which is "not yet" fully disclosed. This "not yet" is why he sides with Kant's "nonconclusive dialectic" of finitude over the closure of Hegel's absolute knowledge.

33. I am relying again upon the logic of Peter L. Berger's argument in *A Rumor of Angels: Modern Society and the Rediscovery of the Supernatural* (New York: Anchor Books, 1969), 52–53, 59. See also *The Sacred Canopy* (New York: Anchor Books, 1969), 184–85.

34. See Schleiermacher, *The Christian Faith*, §4, 16. My approach here bears an affinity with the way in which Schleiermacher relates a generic anthropological disposition with specifically determinate religious contents.

35. See Levinas, "God and Philosophy," in *Of God who Comes to Mind*, 69.

36. For Derrida's treatment of Levinas, see his *Adieu to Emmanuel Levinas*, trans. Pascale-Anne Brault and Nichael Naas (Stanford: Stanford University Press, 1999). See also the insightful study of Levinas by Jeffrey L. Kosky, *Levinas and the Philosophy of Religion* (Bloomington: Indiana University Press, 2001).

37. Here I follow one of the basic themes of Edward Farley's book, *Good and Evil: Interpreting a Human Condition* (Minneapolis: Fortress Press, 1990), 109–11, 121–24.

38. For detailed and influential descriptions of anxiety, see Søren Kierkegaard, *The Concept of Anxiety*, trans. R. Thomte and A. B. Anderson (Princeton, NJ: Princeton University Press, 1980); Martin Heidegger, *Being and Time*, trans. John Macquarrie and Edward Robinson (New York: Harper, 1962), sec. 40, 228–41; Reinhold Niebuhr, *The Nature and Destiny of Man: A Christian Interpretation* (London: Nisbet and Co., 1941), Vol 1, 195–206; and Paul Tillich, *The Courage to Be* (New Haven: Yale University Press, 1952), 40–63.

39. Maurice Blondel makes an interesting statement that draws the point out: "It is because I have the ambition of being infinitely that I feel my powerlessness. . . . Man, by himself, cannot be what he already is in spite of himself, what he claims to become voluntarily" (*Action* [1893] trans. Oliva Blanchette [Notre Dame, IN: University of Notre Dame Press, 1984], 327). Though Blondel's analysis focuses on the "willing will" versus the "willed will," his depiction of the anticipatory incompleteness of human desire fits well with the emphasis of this discussion. Indeed, Blondel's influence looms in the background of my conception of the passion of trust.

40. H. Richard Niebuhr, *Faith on Earth: An Inquiry into the Structure of Human Faith* (New Haven: Yale University Press, 1989), 78.

41. On the idea of such a fundamental affirmation, see Paul Ricoeur, *Oneself as Another*, trans. Kathleen Blamey (Chicago: University of Chicago Press, 1992), 315–16; *The Conflict of Interpretations*, ed. Don Ihde (Evanston, IL: Northwestern University Press, 1974), 341, 452; and *History and Truth*, trans. Charles A. Kelbley (Evanston, IL: Northwestern University Press, 1965), ch. 6.

42. Berger suggests that there is a core trust at the root of everyday experiences of order, play, hope and humor. These four "prototypical gestures" are only possible, he claims, because of a more basic conviction that reality is trustworthy. See *A Rumor of Angels*, 55–85. For an extended discussion of the implications of hope in this regard, see Gabriel Marcel, "Sketch of a Phenomenology and a Metaphysic of Hope," in *Homo Viator*, trans. Emma Crauford (Gloucester, MA: Peter Smith, 1978), 29–67.

43. On the notion of limit-questions, see Steven Toulmin, *An Examination of the Place of Reason in Ethics* (Cambridge: Cambridge University Press, 1970), 202–21. I am here following Shubert Ogden's appropriation of Toulmin in *The Reality of God and Other Essays* (Dallas: Southern Methodist University Press, 1977), 30f. See also David Tracy, *Blessed Rage for Order* (San Francisco: Harper, 1988), ch. 5. Tracy, following Ogden, makes the idea of limit-questions fundamental to his theological approach.

44. The term "limit-expression" is drawn from Ricoeur's essay, "Naming God," in *Figuring the Sacred*, 228ff. See also Tracy's appropriation of Ricoeur in *Blessed Rage for Order*, 123ff.; and in *The Analogical Imagination* (New York: Crossroad, 1991), 160ff.

45. I am borrowing the term "theodicy" from Berger's depiction in *The Sacred Canopy*, ch. 3. See also Clifford Geertz's discussion of suffering and evil in *The Interpretation of Cultures* (New York: Basic, 1973), 98–108.

46. An excellent example of theodicy is found in African-American spirituals, whose invoking of a better world resisted the degradation of slavery and segregation. Some key texts are found in Erik Routley, ed., *Rejoice in the Lord: A Hymn Companion to the Scriptures* (Grand Rapids: Eardmans, 1985). For good commentaries, see the classic by Howard Thurman, *The Negro Spiritual Speaks of Life and Death* (New York: Harper, 1947); and James H. Cone's *Spirituals and the Blues* (New York: Seabury Press, 1972).

47. Theodicies do not have to be explicitly religious. Any concrete value that resists negation and promulgates trust can function as a theodicy. This includes the communal focus of political ideologies (i.e., Marxism) and nationalisms as well as the individualism of new-age therapies and commodity driven materialisms.

48. For an example, see Schleiermacher, *On Religion*, 23; and *The Christian Faith*, §§6–7. Here I am following the logic of Schleiermacher's *On Religion*, which—contrary to most readings that place undue weight on his definition of religion in the second chapter—seeks to show how religion, far from being an ahistorical and "mystical" kind of experience, is bound ineluctably to the finite forms of historical life. For Schleiermacher, religion only becomes what it is, formally speaking, as it is actualized and embodied in the play of history. Readers should focus especially on the fifth and final chapter in order to better understand the overall argument of the book, *On Religion*. His dogmatic work, *The Christian Faith*, follows a similar flow. See Brian Gerrish, "Friedrich Schleiermacher on the Task of Theology," in *Tradition and the Modern World: Reformed Theology in the Nineteenth Century* (Chicago: University of Chicago Press, 1978), esp. 35–39; and Edward Farley, "Is Friedrich Schleiermacher Passe," in *Christian Faith Seeking Historical Understanding: Essays in Honor of H. Jack Forstman*, eds. James O. Duke and Anthony L. Dunnavant (Macon, GA: Mercer University Press, 1997), 9–27.

49. On the idea of "founding" trust, see Edward Farley's discussion of "being founded" in *Good and Evil*, 144ff.

50. See H. Richard Niebuhr, *Radical Monotheism and Western Culture* (Louisville: Westminster/John Knox Press, 1960), 119. See also Brian A. Gerrish, *Saving and Secular Faith* (Minneapolis: Fortress Press, 1999), ch. 2.

51. Of course there are those acosmic religious traditions that devalue our present finite existence as illusion (*maya*, in Shankara's tradition of Advaita Vedanta), as the product of some primal fall (as in forms of gnosticism), or as caught up in a hopeless state of structural oppression and sin (as in some of the more radically apocalyptic, sectarian, and/or eschatologically focused forms of Christianity). Yet even here worth is placed on the possibility of attunement to what is truly real and worthwhile (i.e., Brahman, the One, or God). There is still an operative trust in the trustworthiness of things, though this trust has become one step removed from the present state of this world.

52. In this way, the religious sensibility functions as a kind of "depth dimension" of human culture itself, looming large as the impetus to all formulations that invoke the meaningful vitality of things. On this idea, see Paul Tillich, *Theology of Culture* (Oxford: Oxford University Press, 1959), 5ff. I am therefore in essential agreement with his statement: "religion is the substance of culture, culture is the form of religion" (42). The only qualification I would hasten to add—and Tillich would likely agree—is that the religious sensibility operates as an implicit dynamism, while specific "religious faith" must be explicit as an overt appeal to transcendence. For example, Marxist atheism is not a religion as such, though it functions ideologically as a concretization of trust and so arises out of the potency of the religious sensibility. It has a "religious" dimension to it without making an overtly "religious" appeal. This undercuts the finality of secularity without denying the force of its iconoclasm.

53. This is one of the key themes of Blondel's *Action*, which seeks to show how all finite goods, as stopping points, are inadequate to the nature of action and thereby relativized. "All attempts to bring human action to completion fail; and it is impossible for human action not to seek to complete itself and to be self-sufficient. . . . The need man has for an infinite fulfillment remains incurable" (299). Substitute the word *trust* for "action" here and the quote describes the very impulse behind the religious sensibility. The founding of trust by a transcendent value is required by forces inherent to the act of trust. Blondel designates such a terminus *God*, the "one thing necessary" to human action (314ff.). But in a pluralistic vision we must be more circumspect in the application of the word *God*. Hence my choice of the term, "transcendence."

54. On this point, see Paul Ricoeur, *Fallible Man*, trans. Charles A. Kelbley (New York: Fordham Press, 1986), ch. 2. For example: "The complete discourse on finitude is a discourse on the finitude and the infinitude of man" (25).

55. See Ogden, *The Reality of God*, 33ff.

56. See Tillich, *Theology of Culture*, 47 and 53ff.

57. See Ogden, *The Reality of God*, 33.

58. Ibid., 34. For a good summary statement of Ogden's position, see John Haught, *What Is Religion?* (New York: Paulist Press, 1990), 145–57.

59. See Tillich, *Dynamics of Faith* (New York: Harper, 1957), 10f. Tillich's notion of faith as "ultimate concern" is another way of bringing together the subjective and objective poles of the religious sensibility. "Ultimate" qualifies both the content and the character of the "concern." Yet another way of stating this is to say, as traditional

theology has done, that faith refers to the faith which is believed (*fides quae creditur*) as well as to the faith through which it is believed (*fides qua creditur*). See Ogden, *Is there Only One True Religion or Are there Many?* 10.

60. See Tracy, *The Analogical Imagination*, 163.

61. "Seeing as" is a way of construing the character of faith that hearkens back to Ludwig Wittgenstein's duck-rabbit example of how we do not simply "see" the world but interpret and construe it according to a pattern that remains underdetermined (*Philosophical Investigations*, 3rd ed., trans. G. E. M. Anscombe [New York: MacMillan, 1958], 194e). John Hick develops this idea into the notion of "experience-as." According to Hick, we experience something in light of our interpretation of it, as having this or that character of meaning. There is no uninterpreted experience, and this includes that of faith. See *An Interpretation of Religion*, 140–42; and *God Has Many Names* (Philadelphia: Westminster Press, 1982), 81.

62. Clifford Geertz, *The Interpretation of Cultures*, 90. His well-known definition of a religion reads as follows: "a system of symbols which acts to establish powerful, pervasive, and long-lasting moods and motivations in men by formulating conceptions of a general order of existence and clothing these conceptions with such an aura of factuality that the moods and motivations seem uniquely realistic."

63. In this way, in agreement with Ricoeur, I see an inherent dialectical connection between "manifestations" of transcendent power and their interpretive testimonial capacity in the "proclamatory" character of limit-expressive language. Through limit-expressions, the metaphoric nature of the word itself is infused with disclosive power, arising out of and modifying the more symbolic nature of manifestation. Metaphor and symbol are dialectically interwoven (this is expressed in Christianity as a dialectic between preaching and sacraments). See Ricoeur, "Manifestation and Proclamation," in *Figuring the Sacred*, 48–67, esp. 61–68. See also *Interpretation Theory: Discourse and the Surplus of Meaning* (Fort Worth: Texas Christian University Press, 1976), ch. 3. We shall explore this further in chapter 6.

64. See H. Richard Niebuhr, *Faith on Earth: An Inquiry into the Structure of Human Faith*, ed. Richard R. Niebuhr (New Haven: Yale University Press, 1989), 47f. See also Wilfred Cantwell Smith, *Faith and Belief* (Princeton: Princeton University Press, 1979). Smith describes such faith as "an orientation of the personality, to oneself, to one's neighbor, to the universe; a total response; a way of seeing whatever one sees and of handling whatever one handles; a capacity to live at a more than mundane level; to see, to feel, to act in terms of, a transcendent dimension" (12).

65. This is the advantage of Niebuhr's and Smith's efforts to widen the meaning of "faith" to include much more than "belief" (cognitive assent) or "beliefs" (items of such assent). Bernard Lonergan suggests a similar point: "beliefs result from judgments of value, and judgments of value relevant to religion come from faith." Lonergan, like Smith, also sees interreligious value in distinguishing belief and faith, for in it "we have secured a basis both for ecumenical encounter and for an encounter between all religions with a basis in religious experience." See *Method in Theology* (New York: Seabury, 1972), 118–19, 122–24.

66. Even in radical apocalyptic schemes or gnostic dualisms it is *this* world that is rendered endurable at this moment, its negativity resisted in the act of hope's stretch into something more. In this manner, conceptions of an afterlife make sense, as the antici-

pated envisionment of a reality which reconciles us with all that is worthwhile and yet not fully realized in this life. The afterlife gives *this* life ontological weight, making fidelity an imperative and hope an assurance.

67. Thus, I come to conclusions similar to those of John Hick, though I have employed a different interpretive strategy than he does in order to eschew a monist pluralism. See his *Interpretation of Religion*, esp. chs. 2–3. Hick uses the term "salvation" to connote the process of moving from self-centeredness to reality-centeredness.

68. This amounts to a rethinking of Schleiermacher's basic point that the "feeling of absolute dependence" frames religious assertions, not God of Godself. See *The Christian Faith*, §4, 12ff. Religious faith thematizes the shape of trust, not the Whence of trust.

69. But I have, in the main, avoided this Tillichian turn of language (which hearkens back to the Xenophanes and to the early Greek philosophical criticisms of Homeric anthropomorphisms) to preclude confusions, confusions that prompted Hick to shift his approach from talk of the "God" with many names (in *God Has Many Names*) to talk of the "Real" that is interpreted variously (in *An Interpretation of Religion*). Talk of "the God behind God" still can too closely traverse the theistic framework. For a good example of this, see Paul Tillich's *Biblical Religion and the Search for Ultimate Reality* (Chicago: University of Chicago Press, 1955).

70. Wilfred Cantwell Smith, *Toward a World Theology: Faith and the Comparative History of Religion* (Maryknoll, NY: Orbis Books, 1981), 168.

71. See Alfred North Whitehead, *Religion in the Making* (1926) (New York: New American Library, 1974), 137f.

72. Whitehead, *Science and the Modern World* (New York: Free Press, 1925), 191–92.

73. By "creativity" I am referring most specifically to Whitehead's cosmology. See his *Adventures of Ideas* (New York: Macmillan Company, 1955), 181, 237–38; *Process and Reality: An Essay in Cosmology*, eds. David Ray Griffin and Donald Sherburne (New York: Free Press, 1978); and *Religion in the Making*. On the use of the metaphor of creativity to speak of ultimate Reality, see Gordan Kaufman's *In the Face of Mystery* (Cambridge: Harvard University Press, 1993), esp. chs. 19–20; and Edward Farley's *Divine Empathy: A Theology of God* (Minneapolis: Fortress Press, 1996), 134–41.

74. Kaufman, "On Thinking of God as Serendipitous Creativity," *Journal of the American Academy of Religion* 69/2 (June 2001): 416.

75. See Whitehead, *Religion in the Making*; and John B. Cobb's essay, "Order Out of Chaos," in *Transforming Christianity and the World*, 113–27.

CHAPTER SIX. MAKING THE DIFFERENCE: RETHINKING RELIGIOUS PLURALISM IN LOCAL AND UNIVERSAL HORIZONS

1. Thales. The quote is found in Aristotle's "De anima," A5, 411a7, from G. S. Kirk et al., *The Presocratic Philosophers*, 2nd ed. (New York: Cambridge University Press, 1983), 95.

2. David Tracy, *On Naming the Present* (Maryknoll, NY: Orbis Books, 1994), 137.

3. See Peter C. Hodgson, *Winds of the Spirit: A Constructive Christian Theology* (Louisville: Westminster/John Knox Press, 1994), 106f., 309.

4. This is an adaptation of H. Richard Niebuhr's depiction of faith in *Faith on Earth: An Inquiry into the Structure of Human Faith*, ed. Richard R. Niebuhr (New Haven: Yale University Press, 1989), 47.

5. Anthony Giddens, *The Consequences of Modernity* (Stanford: Stanford University Press, 1990), 105.

6. Brian A. Gerrish, *Saving and Secular Faith* (Minneapolis: Fortress Press, 1999), 56. See also Edward Farley's discussion of tradition in *Deep Symbols: Their Postmodern Effacement and Reclamation* (Valley Forge, PA: Trinity Press International, 1996), ch. 3.

7. John F. Haught, *Mystery and Promise: A Theology of Revelation* (Collegeville, MN: Liturgical Press, 1993), 63.

8. This point echoes a major "functionalist" theme in the tradition of the sociology of religion inaugurated by Emile Durkheim's work, *The Elementary Forms of the Religious Life* [1912], trans. Joseph W. Swain (New York: Free Press, 1965). It is a key point made by Andrew Greeley in *The Denominational Society* (Glenview, IL: Scott, Foresman, 1972), 9. For an excellent statement of the social world-shaping capacity of religion, see William E. Paden, *Religious Worlds: The Comparative Study of Religion* (Boston: Beacon, 1988), ch. 3.

9. Thus, in the Jewish tradition, God reveals Godself, establishes a covenant with the people and institutes the law, thus calling into being a distinct nation, all in one founding event at Sinai. For Christians, it is the Christ event in Jesus of Nazareth that discloses a distinct way of dwelling together, calling into being a new kind of sociality. One could apply this equally to the Hindu notion of dharma, the Buddhist conception of the sangha and its precepts, and so on. I draw the term, "ecclesia," from Edward Farley, *Ecclesial Man: A Social Phenomenology of Faith and Reality* (Philadelphia: Fortress Press, 1975), 114ff.

10. The discussion here echoes George Lindbeck's "cultural-linguistic" model of communal intratextuality: language frameworks shape the subjectivities of individuals. See *The Nature of Doctrine: Religion and Theology in a Postliberal Age* (Philadelphia: Westminster Press, 1984), 32ff.

11. See Peter L. Berger and Thomas Luckmann, *The Social Construction of Reality* (New York: Anchor Press, 1967), 158. See also Gerrish, *Saving and Secular Faith*, 54f.

12. See Lindbeck, *The Nature of Doctrine*, 40. See also William C. Placher, *Unapologetic Theology: A Christian Voice in a Pluralistic Conversation* (Louisville, KY: Westminster/John Knox Press, 1989).

13. For examples, see the essays in Jerald D. Gort, Hendrik M. Vroom, Rein Fernhout, and Anton Wessels, eds., *Dialogue and Syncretism: An Interdisciplinary Approach* (Grand Rapids: Williams Eerdmans, 1989). See also Robert Schreiter's discussion in *The New Catholicity: Theology between the Global and the Local* (Maryknoll, NY: Orbis Books, 1997), ch. 4.

14. See Aylward Shorter, *Toward a Theology of Inculturation* (Maryknoll, NY: Orbis Books, 1988); Peter Schineller, *A Handbook on Inculturation* (New York: Paulist Press, 1990); and Steven Bevans, *Models of Contextual Theology* (Maryknoll, NY: Orbis Books, 1992).

15. For a brilliant theological use of *mestizaje*, see Virgilio Elizondo, *The Future Is Mestizo: Life Where Cultures Meet* (New York: Meyer-Stone Books, 1988). See also the excellent essay by Fenando F. Segovia, "Two Places and No Place on which to Stand," in *Mesizo Christianity: Theology from a Latino Perspective*, ed. Arturo J. Banuelas (Mary-

knoll, NY: Orbis Books, 1995), 29–42. From an Asian-American perspective, Jung Young Lee speaks similarly of "marginality." See *Marginality: The Key to Multicultural Theology* (Minneapolis: Fortress Press, 1995).

16. See Edward Said, *Culture and Imperialism* (New York: Vintage Books, 1994), 317.

17. I am building here upon the discussions of chapters 3 and 4 (especially in light of postcolonial theory) as a way of preserving yet turning inside-out the "cultural-linguistic" model of postliberalism. Kathryn Tanner's book, *Theories of Culture* (Minneapolis: Fortress Press, 1997), is instructive in this regard, but does not go far enough toward providing criteria for an interreligious plurality.

18. See Robert J. C. Young, *Colonial Desire: Hybridity in Theory, Culture and Race* (London: Routledge, 1995), 4.

19. The reader might perceive a relation between succumbing and what Christians have called "sin." Such a perception would not be altogether untrue. But neither would it capture the point being made. I am intentionally avoiding the term "sin" here not simply because it is a Christian way of conceiving the problem, but because of its forensic connotations as such. Succumbing is not a transgressive rebellion against an established juridical order—whether divine or human—that deserves condemnation; results in guilt; and requires punishment, satisfaction, and/or forgiveness. Seen only in the context of sin, the appeal to transcendence serves merely to bolster the finality of a designate social order, proffering homogeneity rather than opening up a relational fecundity. Yet it would be true to say that succumbing (like "sin") has definite moral implications. For it breeds an intersubjective violence.

20. With modifications, I am again drawing from Reinhold Niebuhr's discussion of anxiety. See *The Nature and Destiny of Man*, Vol. 1 (London: Nisbet and Co., 1941), 182ff.

21. This is not to suggest that human beings are therefore "fallen." It simply means that the possibility of succumbing is inherent in the constitution of dwelling together. See Paul Ricoeur, *Fallible Man*, trans. Charles A. Kelbley (New York: Fordham Press, 1986), 133–46. Finitude is not itself an imperfection or fallen condition that makes temptation in this regard inescapable. Given this, I am puzzled by Paul Tillich's claim that creation and fall coincide, that mortal existence (as a suspension between the finite and the infinite) necessarily entails estrangement and alienation. This seems a retreat into gnosticism. See his *Systematic Theology*, Vol. 2 (Chicago: University of Chicago Press, 1957), 44–78.

22. On the inevitable yet not necessary character of succumbing, see Reinhold Niebuhr, *The Nature and Destiny of Man*, Vol. 1, 150, 242. Here, I refer to the unnecessary nature of succumbing because trust is elemental; succumbing is inevitable because the tragic conditions of finitude seem weighed toward its possibility as already there, as somehow inherent in things.

23. On the posture of insistence, see Edward Farley, *Good and Evil: Interpreting a Human Condition* (Minneapolis: Augsburg Fortress, 1990), 133f.

24. See ibid., ch. 6. See also the fascinating study by Jean-Luc Marion, *God without Being*, trans. T. A. Carlson (Chicago: University of Chicago Press, 1991), ch. 1.

25. Marion states the point thusly: "The idol depends on the gaze that it satisfies, since if the gaze did not desire to satisfy itself in the idol, the idol would have no dignity for it" (*God without Being*, 10).

26. I bracket "sin" again for its forensic connotations. For broad discussions of sin, see Farley, *Good and Evil*, esp. 120–21, 139–40; and Hodgson, *Winds of the Spirit*, 208–30.

27. Despite the astuteness of Marion's monograph (*God without Being*), it relies too heavily on a theory of revelation to offer a workable criterion here for us. For Marion, as in Karl Barth, all talk of God must be related to God's own iconic revealing if it is to resist becoming idolatrous. The question then is: how do we know it is God's presence being revealed? I do not think Marion adequately answers this question; indeed, on his own terms, he cannot without falling into a metaphysics of presence that denies ontological difference. How does the icon (e.g., the Eucharist) open up the invisible? The final answer is "because it does" ("to give itself to be seen, the icon needs only itself," 24), and this seems to get us nowhere beyond the communal enclosure of one tradition (i.e., Christianity). It is not enough to say that the icon "does not result from a vision but provokes one" (17).

28. The potential interreligious fruits of taking such an anthropological turn toward soteriological criterion are numerous. For one such possibility, played in terms of Buddhist-Christian dialogue, see my essay, "Toward the Other: Christianity and Buddhism on Desire," *Journal of Ecumenical Studies* 39/3–4 (Summer–Fall 2002): 325–39.

29. Availability, as self-transcendence, is comparable to John Hick's way of articulating the soteriological dynamic of religious faith as a move from egocentricity to Reality-centeredness. See his *Interpretation of Religion: Human Responses to the Transcendent* (New Haven: Yale University Press, 1989), chs. 3, 17–18. Availability is an openness to the other that signifies a larger openness to Presence. But whereas Hick's idea of "Reality-centeredness" tends to be a bit vague and abstract, the notion of availability provides us with a rich array of substantive features—what I shall call a "justice-making love."

30. See Wilfred Cantwell Smith, "Idolatry in Comparative Perspective," in *The Myth of Christian Uniqueness*, eds. John Hick and Paul F. Knitter (Maryknoll, NY: Orbis Books, 1985), 53–69; see esp. 58–61.

31. Thomas Altizer, in *Radical Theology and the Death of God* (Indianapolis: Bobbs-Merrill, 1966), sums up the radicality of such iconoclasm nicely: "To exist in our time is to exist in a chaos freed of every semblance of cosmological meaning and order" (102). The death of God, of anything sacred, opens up the horizon for human finitude to be what it is. This is one powerful way of conceptualizing the qualitative difference between the finite and infinite, but it is not the one I advocate here. As sheer centerlessness, it leads to value dispersion and thus lacks the productive power to resist idolatry. There is also the ironic danger that, by erasing the infinite, the finite will simply replace the infinite as such, an act tantamount to idolatry. This is why deconstruction cannot itself be a positive position, for it would then simply be a new metaphysic, undercutting is own prioritizing of deferral. It would be a totalizing polemic against closure. Such a tendency is found in Altizer and in the deconstructive a-theology of Mark C. Taylor; see *Erring: A Postmodern A/theology* (Chicago: University of Chicago Press, 1984).

32. See, for example, Jacques Derrida, "Faith and Knowledge," in *Acts of Religion*, ed. Gil Anidjar (New York: Routledge, 2002), 42–101.

33. Again, I draw from Richard Kearney, *The God Who May Be: A Hermeneutics of Religion* (Bloomington: Indiana University Press, 2001), see esp. 101–11.

34. This is a way of thinking through Paul Tillich's idea of the "sacramental basis of all religions," modified by a second element, "a critical movement against the demo-

nization of the sacramental, that is, making it into an object that can be handled." See his "Significance of the History of Religions for the Systematic Theologian," in *Christianity and the Encounter of World Religions* (Minneapolis: Fortress Press, 1994), 71. Tillich then goes on to name a third element, an "ought to be" or "the ethical or prophetic." This is also key. The idea of availability is my own extrapolation of this third element. As we shall see, the sacramental, iconoclastic, and ethical are all inner moments of one another.

35. Paul Avis, *God and the Creative Imagination: Metaphor, Symbol and Myth in Religion and Theology* (New York: Routledge, 1999), 81.

36. George Steiner, *Real Presences* (Chicago: University of Chicago Press, 1989), 82f.

37. This is why, while appreciative of Linbeck's postliberal line of thinking, I do not grant it full sway. Though the narrative sway of a community informs the intentions by which actions occur as meaningful, the linguistic capacity of the projective imagination always surpasses that sway. Human beings are not the passive recipients of a world; human beings are authors of that world, bearing forth its meaning and vitality in ongoing acts of appropriation and revision. The danger of idolatry looms large in a strictly intratextual approach. For it invokes a logic of conformity rather than creativity. For excellent defenses of postliberalism, see John E. Thiel, *Nonfoundationalism* (Minneapolis: Fortress Press, 1994); and Emmanuel Katongole, *Beyond Universal Reason: The Relation between Religion and Ethics in the Work of Stanley Hauerwas* (Notre Dame, IN: University of Notre Dame Press, 2000).

38. See Paul Ricoeur, "Pastoral Praxeology, Hermeneutics, and Identity," in *Figuring the Sacred*, ed. Mark Wallace, trans. David Pellauer (Minneapolis: Fortress Press, 1995), 311.

39. The following analysis depends on the work of Ricoeur. See his *Interpretation Theory: Discourse and the Surplus of Meaning* (Fort Worth: Texas Christian University Press, 1976), esp. 46ff.; *The Rule of the Metaphor*, trans. Robert Czerny, with Kathleen McLaughlin and John Costello, SJ (Toronto: University of Toronto Press, 1977); and "The Metaphorical Process as Cognition, Imagination, and Feeling" (1978), in *Critical Theory Since 1965*, eds. Hazard Adams and Leroy Searle (Tallahasse: University of Florida Press, 1986), 424–34.

40. See Ricoeur, *The Rule of the Metaphor*, 80.

41. Ibid., 231f.; and "The Metaphorical Process as Cognition, Imagination, and Feeling," 427, 429.

42. See Ricoeur, *The Rule of the Metaphor*, 225; and "The Metaphorical Process as Cognition, Imagination, and Feeling," 433.

43. Ricoeur, "The Metaphorical Process as Cognition, Imagination, and Feeling," 426.

44. Ibid., 431ff.; and *The Rule of the Metaphor*, 245.

45. Ricoeur, "Naming God," in *Figuring the Sacred*, 222–23. On Marcel's idea of fundamental feeling, see *Metaphysical Journal*, trans. Bernard Wall (London: Rockliff Publishing Corporation Ltd., 1952), 247, 309–10.

46. Ricoeur, *The Rule of the Metaphor*, 247ff.; and "The Metaphorical Process as Cognition, Imagination, and Feeling," 427.

47. Ricoeur, "The Metaphorical Process as Cognition, Imagination, and Feeeling," 427.

48. Ricoeur, "Toward a Narrative Theology," in *Figuring the Sacred*, 240. In this way, to read Ricoeur as a postliberal thinker in the line of Lindbeck is to misread him.

Though he is slippery on this point, Ricoeur's sense of narrative is not "intratextual," for meaning happens "in front of" texts, in their reception, between the world of text and the world of its readers. True, narratives provide the means for action to have character, but they are metaphoric constructions that make identity an unstable adventure rather than a self-secured point of departure.

49. On the idea of revising a narrative, see Ricoeur's essay, "Pastoral Praxeology, Hermeneutics, and Identity," in *Figuring the Sacred*, 303–14, esp. 308–10.

50. Thus I use the word *icon* here in Ricoeur's sense, which produces a different emphasis than Marion's way of employing the term in *God Without Being*. While, in Marion's words, it is true that the icon "summons sight in letting the visible be saturated . . . with the invisible" (17), it is also the case that it is produced by the projective imagination, not simply "given." Indeed, its production is induced by the anticipation of the invisible: Presence.

51. Examples of this *via negativa* can be found cross-culturally. In Jewish and Christian traditions, it the theme of the "hidden" God, the *deus absconditus*. Blaise Pascal captures its impulse famously: "Every religion which does not affirm the God is hidden, is not true" (*Pensées*, trans. A. J. Krailsheiner [New York: Penguin, 1966], 584). God remains hidden even as God is disclosed. Such an affirmation is found in the Hebrew scriptures (e.g., Exod. 3 and Isa. 55: 8–9, 45: 15), and indeed functions to prohibit idolatry. Stated more philosophically, it arises in Philo of Alexandria, Origin, Augustine, Pseudo-Dionysius, Eriugena, and Eckhart, among others, as a radical neutralizing of any and all positive attributive language about the divine. Luther makes the theme key to his "theology of the cross" in the "Heidelburg Disputation" (see Thesis 19–20). In non-Western traditions, it surfaces as the eternal Tao that cannot be expressed, Brahman without attributes (*nirguna* Brahman) versus Brahman with attributes (*sirguna* Brahman), the Emptiness of things (as in the Buddhist concept of *sunyata*), and so forth. An exhaustive survey of such epistemological agnosticism is not within the scope of this study. For excellent treatments of this theme as it is borne out variously, see Hick, *God Has Many Names* (Philadelphia: Westminster Press, 1982), ch. 3; and *An Interpretation of Religion*, esp. 236–40; Raimundo Panikkar, *The Silence of God: The Answer of the Buddha* (Maryknoll, NY: Orbis Books, 1989); and Masao Abe, *Buddhism and Interfaith Dialogue*, ed. Steven Heine (Honolulu: University of Hawaii Press, 1995), chs. 7–8.

52. Ruether, "Feminism and Jewish-Christian Dialogue," in *The Myth of Christian Uniqueness*, 142. Italics added.

53. See Gabriel Marcel, "On the Ontological Mystery," in *The Philosophy of Existentialism*, trans. Manya Harari (New York: Carol Publishing Group, 1991), 39f.

54. See "Astasahasrika Prajnaparamita," 22:402–3, in *The Buddhist Tradition in India, China and Japan* (New York: Vintage Books, 1972), 81–82.

55. See Walter Lowe, *Theology and Difference: The Wound of Reason* (Bloomington: Indiana University Press, 1993), 89–90. Lowe makes a similar point by drawing from an early essay by Immanuel Kant, which is found in *Kant's Cosmogony, as in His Essay on the Retardation of the Rotation of the Earth and His Natural History and Theory of the Heavens*, trans. W. Hastie (New York: Johnson Reprint Corporation, 1900). Kant writes: "all that is finite, whatever has limits . . . is equally far removed from the infinite" (139; cited in Lowe, *Theology and Difference*, 89).

56. Tracy, *Plurality and Ambiguity: Hermeneutics, Religion, Hope* (San Francisco: Harper, 1987), 83–84. See also *On Naming the Present: God, Hermeneutics, and the Church* (Maryknoll, NY: Orbis Books, 1994), 16f.

57. On the drama of embrace, see Miroslav Volf, *Exclusion and Embrace: A Theological Exploration of Identity, Otherness, and Reconciliation* (Nashville: Abingdon Press, 1996), esp. 140ff.

58. For Volf, waiting and reciprocity are two elements in embrace, see ibid., 142f. I distinguish them from embrace to emphasize the dialectical nature of embrace.

59. On the idea of recognition, see G. W. F. Hegel, *The Phenomenology of Spirit*, trans. A. V. Miller (Oxford: Oxford University Press, 1977), ch. 4; Charles Taylor, "The Politics of Recognition," in *Multiculturalism*, ed. Amy Gutmann (Princeton: Princeton University Press, 1994), 25–73; and Craig Calhoun, *Critical Social Theory* (Cambridge, MA: Blackwell Publishers, 1995), ch. 7.

60. See Ricoeur, "Love and Justice," in *Figuring the Sacred*, 315–29.

61. In this regard, I am in agreement with Carter Heyward's description of justice as the "shape of mutuality in our life together, in our societies and relationships—friendships, families, local and larger communities, the world itself" (*Touching Our Strength: The Erotic as Power and the Love of God* [San Francisco: Harper, 1989], 190).

62. The idea of justice as a "logic of equivalence" comes from Paul Ricoeur, "Love and Justice," see esp. 325–26.

63. Niebuhr, "Christian Faith and Natural Law," in *Love and Justice: Selections from the Shorter Writings of Reinhold Niebuhr*, ed. D. B. Robertson (Cleveland: World Publishing Company, 1967), 49.

64. On this idea of justice, see Derrida, "Force of Law: The Mystical Foundations of Authority," trans. Mary Quaintance, in *Acts of Religion*, 230–98.

65. Paul Ricoeur makes this point, in "Love and Justice," in *Figuring the Sacred*, 328. See also Volf, *Exclusion and Embrace*, esp. 220–25. Volf states: "Without the will to embrace, justice is likely to be unjust" (224).

66. As Niebuhr puts it, "Anything short of love cannot be perfect justice" ("Christian Faith and Natural Law," 50).

67. See Gordan D. Kaufman, *God, Mystery, Diversity* (Minneapolis: Fortress Press, 1996), 200–01. See also Hodgson, *Winds of the Spirit*, 306–7.

68. See Alfred North Whitehead, *Adventure of Ideas* (New York: The New American Library, 1955). For Whitehead's notion of "adventure," see 272–82; and for his concept of "beauty," see 251–64.

69. This is precisely why I am in agreement with Paul Knitter's liberative approach to interreligious dialogue, which emphasizes the ethical grounds for shared concerns across religious boundaries. See his essay, "Toward a Liberation Theology of Religions," in *The Myth of Christian Uniqueness*, 178–200; and *One Earth, Many Religions: Multifaith Dialogue & Global Responsibility* (Maryknoll, NY: Orbis Books, 1995).

70. "Dangerous memory" is Johann Baptist Metz's term. See his *Faith in History and Society: Toward a Practical Fundamental Theology*, trans. David Smith (New York: Seabury Press, 1980).

71. Hodgson makes a similar point in *Winds of the Spirit*, see 99–114, 304–11.

72. Anselm Kyongsuk Min, "Dialectical Pluralism and Solidarity of Others: Towards a New Paradigm," *Journal of the American Academy of Religion* 65/3 (Fall 1997): 590.

73. Theodor W. Adorno, "Subject and Object," in *The Essential Frankfurt School Reader*, eds. Andrew Arato and Eike Gebhardt (New York: Continuum, 1995), 500.

Name Index

Subject Index